# LOVE AND WAR

JAMES HEWITT

BLAKE

Published by Blake Publishing Ltd,
3 Bramber Court, 2 Bramber Road,
London W14 9PB, England

First published in hardback in 1999

ISBN 1 85782 3184

British Library Cataloguing-in-Publication Data:
A catalogue record for this book is available
from the British Library.

Typeset by BCP

Printed in Great Britain


1 3 5 7 9 10 8 6 4 2

# Acknowledgements

I have kept a journal for much of my life. But I have never written a book before and I could not have written this one without the help of colleagues — especially Rupert Mackenzie-Hill and Francis Showering; the dedicated work of two lawyer friends who were of immense help in compiling this; and the insight of my family — my father John, my mother Shirley, my sisters Syra and Caroline for their love and support, and especially Caroline's husband Peter Bayley for his help.

The past years have not been an easy time for my family. To see their name besmirched in print has been harmful to them and caused pain and heartache. My family has been a tower of strength in the face of this and nobody has been stronger or more loyal or more supportive than my mother. I owe her more than I can say. As a poet once said:

> *When most of life*
> *Is froth and bubble*
> *Two things stand alone*
> *Friendship in another's trouble*
> *And courage in one's own.*

# FOREWORD

J ames Hewitt's story is, amongst other things, one of
contrasts. A fairly consistent description by those who
knew him during any part of his fifteen years in
the Army is of a capable, charismatic leader, respected and
universally liked. In addition, many talk of James's huge
sense of loyalty and duty to all things army, as well as to his
friends, his family, his country and, in this case, to a very
particular person.

I've known James before, during and after the much-
publicised affair. I've seen a man at the top of his career —
picked amongst fellow officers to lead what was to be the
only unit from our regiment to see front-line action during
the Gulf Conflict. I was with him during that conflict when
he was nicknamed 'Ice Man' for the extraordinary coolness
and quiet, capable manner with which he led us into Iraq to
take part in over 60 separate contacts with the then enemy,
for which he was Mentioned in Despatches for his courage
in action.

I spent time with James over 15 years: on holiday,
socialising and pursuing sporting interests, unaware of an
affair that was a secret as tightly guarded as the Crown
Jewels themselves — kept from nearly everyone for almost
five years.

During the storm of publicity surrounding the release of
Anna Pasternak's *Princess in Love*, I, like many others,
wondered what on earth had led James to become involved

in this book — and it certainly appeared from a distance that there must be some involvement. Why would he go public about something he had manged to keep such a secret for so long? If he was involved, how and why? Whilst I have never found it my place to ask as a friend, I have found the answers in this book.

And the price of this alleged involvement? I've watched James's ranking as public enemy rise to the number one slot — right up there with Saddam himself. I've watched his life being destroyed by the effects of bad publicity, by the back-turning of people who believed what they read in the papers — the public, some friends and a few influential senior officers in his regiment, a regiment to which he was and still is devoted. I know a little about the isolation and of the level of despair to which James sank and the effect this had on his family. I've read the hate mail and I've watched the newspapers manipulate the facts and ruthlessly hound a sensitive, courageous and honourable man like the pack of cackling hyenas they can at times be.

And the resulting book? Not what I expected. Hardly a gripe or complaint. But a charming book, reserved at times, humorous and passionate at others — a good deal about Diana, a person with whom James was evidently captivated. And his delightful observations are not the normal 'royal watcher's' combination of second or third-hand research combined with hypothesis, guesswork or plain fiction. It's the real thing and all the more interesting.

I'm with James on his decision to publish this book. Not everyone will be. But I see this as an ultimate triumph of good over evil. If you read between the lines, I hope you will see evidence of the goodness in the man and the inherent evil of the 'gutter' press. A press that thrives on sensationalism for its own commercial ends and that seems capable of talking about people only as either extremely nice, or as extremely nasty. And if you talk to any of the many people who know James well, you will find they will side with the decent guy description.

*Captain Rupert Mackenzie-Hill, The Life Guards*
*21 July 1999*

# INTRODUCTION

This is not an autobiography in the conventional sense, it is an account of certain aspects of the first 40 years of my life, some of which has already received a great deal of publicity.

Every time I open a British tabloid newspaper and read about myself, the words 'cad' or 'rat' are attached to my name. Sometimes it seems that serial killers get a better press. Most of what is written about me is not true. Some journalists feel free to fabricate at will, even inventing long quotations from me that inevitably conclude with the words 'Hewitt confided to a friend' — seemingly a licence to print whatever they choose to think up.

What should I do? Go to the High Court and bring a string of character witnesses to testify that I did some worthwhile things for my country? Or just do nothing and go to my grave with these curses inscribed on my tombstone?

It became apparent that there was only one path open to me and that is finally to tell my story as clearly and honestly as I can. Hence this book.

I have never before written about my relationship with Diana, Princess of Wales. I feel that a sufficient interval has elapsed since her cruel death to try to make sure that our time together is not at the mercy of a cuttings library where it is impossible to distinguish fact from fiction. However, my story is not about Diana — much more, it is about the effect she had on my life.

In 1986, her marriage to Prince Charles was over in all but name. That autumn I spent a lot of time with Diana giving her riding lessons. We fell in love and contrived to see as much of each other as possible. To have a private affair with a public person is not the easiest of operations but Diana could have been an SAS commander, such was her skill and ingenuity at managing it.

Our relationship reached its most impassioned when I was sent to fight in the Gulf War five years later in 1991. I was the commander of a tank squadron. Diana wrote to me — nearly every day. She wanted to come out to see me on the pretext of a 'royal visit' to the troops, but her plans were thwarted. Instead, she went to visit my mother and sisters in Devon — and the wives and families of my men in Germany.

But before I came home from the Gulf, a newspaper made our affair public. I knew it had rarely been private. Almost from its inception, the Palace, the police, the Prime Minister and the Prince of Wales (I later learned) had been aware of what was happening. When Diana came to stay with me in Devon, not only would she be accompanied by two detectives (and sometimes her sons) but the police forces of the four counties she drove through would be alerted of her presence.

But those that knew kept their counsel. I have learnt much in retrospect but I wonder if they knew how serious it had been. Diana was still married but she was convinced Prince Charles would die in an accident. She would make plans for our future together; she gave me brochures of houses in the West Country where she thought we might live. But from the moment the world got to know about our relationship it proved impossible to continue.

All three of us talked to writers about the breakdown of the marriage: Diana in tapes for Andrew Morton, Prince Charles to Jonathan Dimbleby and me to Anna Pasternak. The incredible pressure of those times, the speculation and the wild rumours were so strong it was natural to want to set the record straight. I will go through the painful details later in the book but let me declare now: I made a big mistake in speaking. Subsequently, Anna published a romance, *Princess in Love*, which I have never read but which has been a cross I have had to bear for the past five years.

I loved Diana. I love her still. I feel blessed that she loved me and we were able to enjoy a few short years which reached heights of happiness I have never known before or since. But part of me wishes it had never happened; that she and Prince Charles had had a successful marriage. I know for certain that if Diana, Princess of Wales, had gone on to become Queen of England, we would have had in Buckingham Palace a woman whose compassion and thoughtfulness and understanding of the problems of ordinary people would have made her a Queen who would have changed the face of British society like no other before.

# 1

I had started a new life. My army career was over after seventeen years and I was now running The Eversfield Manor Equitation Centre in North Devon.

1995 had been a good year with visitors from all over Britain as well as France, Switzerland and Norway. I wanted the centre to be more than a riding school but a place where people could come and stay for a few days in some degree of luxury — good food and wine — and experience the countryside. But horses were our main attraction. We had quiet mounts for novices, and hunters and eventers for those with more experience. They would ride out with me over the moors — fast, open countryside. And there was the added bonus that experienced clients were able to hunt with one of the local packs of fox hounds.

We also had some memorable shooting weekends. The undulating ground of Dartmoor and Exmoor is excellent for high and fast pheasant. On several occasions our shooting party would manage more than 200 birds. The landowner's gamekeeper would sell most to the local butcher but would gift a brace of pheasant to each gun, so clients went home with something to hang in their larders. On the warm summer evenings I would take people along the Tay Valley to fish for salmon and trout. I knew of a little pool in the River Tamar where invariably the fish would lay up at the end of the day. And if anybody drew a blank there, they had the consolation of coming back and catching a rainbow trout in the pool at Eversfield.

I was happy or, at least, content. At the age of 38 I was doing the two things that fulfilled me most — running a business and teaching people to ride — and I expected to continue like this for the rest of my life.

I was brought up in Devon. It was there that I learnt to ride and to love the countryside. My mother had a riding school which I intended to come and run after I left the army. But the area was unfortunately being built up with new roads cutting our stables off from good country. So I decided we should apply for planning permission for residential houses to be built on the land. I was in luck: no sooner had I obtained it than a property developer came along with an offer I couldn't refuse.

Indeed I'm glad I didn't refuse it — it was just before the bottom fell out of the property market. These two pieces of good fortune enabled me to look for a place in need of complete renovation to start a centre of my own.

Eversfield Manor, by the village of Bratton Clavelly, fitted the bill perfectly. The eight-bedroom house sat proudly on the brow of a hill surrounded by forty acres of paddocks and woods and gardens, with the limitless wilds of Dartmoor beyond. A stream ran along the valley on the west side of the property. I dug out four carp ponds and restocked them, and dug and stocked another pond with trout. There was stabling for a dozen horses and dining and living rooms that could easily accommodate as many guests.

I was aware as I renovated the house that I was

attempting to rebuild my own life. The last four years had been a continuous hell. I felt battered by the press, I had little strength with which to fight back and I just wanted to get on with my work undisturbed. In the winter of 1991 the exhilaration of commanding a tank squadron in the Gulf had turned to desperation when a newspaper revealed my affair with Princess Diana. My days as an army officer had been numbered from that moment on.

The following year the book, *Diana: Her True Story*, based — it was later revealed — on taped interviews with the Princess herself, chronicled the disintegration of her marriage. The air was full of rumours, a few touching on the truth, others wildly wrong. One of them even had me and Diana living together in a house in Fulham. You can only keep silent for so long in the face of daily accusations in the press. I did an interview with Anna Pasternak for the *Daily Express*, acknowledging my friendship with Diana — but lying about the true nature of it. It did no good — in fact, it made things worse. The media knew most of the facts and ridiculed it. I became more of a target.

Prince Charles had gone on the record about the breakdown of his marriage, his adultery and the part Camilla Parker Bowles had played in his life.

Many unauthorised books were in the works, so Anna Pasternak suggested to me the time was right to put the record straight with a factual book. This seemed sensible enough, but when the publishers saw some of her early work they demanded more sensation. I had no desire to go along with this and I asked to get out of it. I was told I couldn't. My mind was in turmoil. I was badly advised. The result was a messy compromise: *Princess in Love*, a book for which both Anna and I were damned.

There were only three of us in the house on Monday, November 20th 1995 — my mother Shirley, Terrence Rowland the estate manager, and me. The weather had turned foul and the mists from the moor shrouded the day in darkness by the middle of the afternoon. I had put the riding courses on hold and taken the opportunity to do some work on the stables and refurbish parts of the house.

We ate an early dinner in the kitchen that night. Like everybody else in the land we intended to watch the special edition of *Panorama* on BBC1. It had been announced that the programme would be devoted to an interview with Princess Diana — her first since she had become engaged to Prince Charles in 1981. Now she had been separated from him for nearly three years.

Nobody, it seemed, had any idea what she was going to say, least of all me, although we had kept in touch. I still had her private number but we hadn't spoken recently. However, Prince Charles had admitted his adultery with Camilla Parker Bowles in a television interview with Jonathan Dimbleby — it's the only thing that anybody remembers from that programme — and I very much doubted if Diana was going to let that go by without comment.

I wanted to watch the interview on my own and decided to combine it with an early night. I had to be up at dawn to exercise the horses. The programme was already under way by the time I got to my room and switched on the television. Diana was telling her interviewer about her eating disorders and depressions and her fears about enemies within the Palace. These were subjects I knew only too well. Then it came to the matter of Camilla. 'There were three of us in the marriage,' she said, 'so it was a bit crowded.'

The phrase was familiar — I had heard her use it before. But the person sitting there on the screen wasn't so familiar. It was almost as if the BBC had engaged some actress to play the part. Instead of the confident, flirtatious, wickedly humorous Diana who could win the Nobel prize for charm, there was the former Lady Di — shy, bashful, rarely meeting the eye of the interviewer. When she did look up through dark eye-liner (which she never usually wore) she spoke like a witness giving evidence, choosing her words with care.

I sympathised with what she was doing — telling her side of the story directly to the world without having to use a friendly journalist as an intermediary. But then along came the thunderbolt. 'Were you unfaithful with Captain James Hewitt?'

Diana bowed her head and lowered her voice. 'Yes, I adored him. Yes, I was in love with him.' She paused. 'But I was very let down.'

My pulse rate quickened. The interviewer didn't ask *how* she was let down, but moved on to other subjects, none of which I can recall as my mind was racing. The music played, credits rolled, the programme was over. I flicked off the television and lay back on the bed, immediately hit by the enormity of the situation, trying to work out in my own mind the consequences of what she had said.

But I was not left alone with my thoughts for long. Without warning the bedroom was flooded with a blinding white light, dazzling in its intensity. It was as if daylight had prematurely arrived, only this was much brighter than daylight.

I wondered what to do. Should I call the police? Not long after my friendship with the Princess began to be written about, the security services had kindly informed me that I was a potential terrorist target. There was an Operation Order on my house. It meant that if I dialled 999 and gave the code word — Jurassic — there would be a tried and tested police and ambulance reponse. This involved not just police but the fire brigade, helicopters and road blocks if necessary. They guaranteed to be here in 20 minutes maximum.

I thought it better to find out what it was first. Conscious of the fact that I didn't want to silhouette myself, I got off my bed and made my way across the room below the line of the window. I surreptitiously pulled back the temporary white blind and looked out. There were images flashing in the dark and in their midst an enormous searchlight, the kind anti-aircraft gunners used in the Second World War only at a much closer range. It was set up on the hillside directly in line with my bedroom window, about a hundred feet up from the stream and on the edge of the road that bordered my property.

Some television news company had decided to illuminate Eversfield Manor. I made my way to another window more oblique to the light, and could make out a dozen or more television cameras trained on the house like snipers. There had been a trickle of vehicles gathering at the gate during the day. This used to be the normal course of events whenever Diana's private life hit the headlines. But I never made any statements and I thought — erroneously — that maybe the law of diminishing returns or no return at all would make me a less interesting target.

When I got down to the kitchen my mother and Terrence were already there. There was no need to tell them what all the fuss was about. We could hear the intimidating sound of people wandering around the outside of the house and then a bold hammering on the front door.

Terrence was adept at dealing with the press. A bridle path ran across the highest point of the property which the public had access to. Reporters used to pretend to walk their dogs along it and he was very good at telling them that they were obliged to keep moving. If we heard noises at night he would sometimes go out on the parapet with a powerful torch and check out the grounds to see if anyone was snooping about. They frequently were — press or paparazzi hoping to sneak some sort of compromising photograph. Tonight the light was coming in the opposite direction. Terrence went to the door — several camera crews were clustered there — and told them as politely as he could that whatever they wanted I had nothing to say and could they turn off the spotlight as the village needed to get some sleep.

They did — eventually. But the next morning the press and television presence was even greater: about thirty cars on the road by the main entrance and another fifteen at the end of the back drive. Columbus, my mother's Norfolk terrier, was the world's worst guard dog and when he sauntered up to the back gate to inspect them, fearless reporters tucked notes into his collar asking me for my reaction to Diana's statement or just a quote.

But I truly had nothing to say, except to ask them to leave.

The local police arrived and drank cups of coffee in the kitchen and did what they could to keep people away. The following day when we ran out of food, they provided a valuable escort for Terrence when he drove to the local shops.

But I stayed inside. I felt under siege in my own house. It was more than a week before I went out, so I had plenty of time to digest Diana's broadcast. The more I thought about it, the more rehearsed it seemed. When Martin Bashir asked her if she had been unfaithful with me, she skilfully deflected the answer from the physical to the emotional. 'Yes, I adored him. Yes, I was in love with him.' Then immediately, having made this admission, she was able to regain the sympathy of the public by saying I had let her down. But despite that, and however rehearsed her words might have been, they meant a great deal to me. She had never made such an unequivocal public declaration of love about any man in her life before — and, tragically, she was never to do so again. The truth was that for five years I had adored her, too, and however much I tried to suppress it, I knew I was still in love with her.

I can vividly recall the day I first saw Diana — young and shy and blushing. It was in the summer of 1981 — I think it was the weekend before she got married. She was watching polo at Tidworth. I was playing for the Army and Prince Charles was playing for the Navy in the Rundle Cup. There were a lot of press around and she was uncomfortably trapped in a small stand that had been erected for the game. She was obviously having difficulty coping with her new-found stardom. There were hordes of photographers and they wouldn't stop snapping away at her. She started to cry and then ran away and got into a car. She couldn't cope with it. I remember feeling angry and sorry for her.

Five years later, I saw her again in Buckingham Palace. I didn't realise it at the time but it was a day that would alter both our lives.

I suppose there was a certain amount of irony in the

fact that at the time I was responsible for guarding the sovereign. I was Staff Captain of the Household Division and my job was to implement ceremonial policy and rota the guard not only at Buckingham Palace, but also at Whitehall, St James's Palace, Windsor Castle, and the Tower of London.

My regiment, The Life Guards, was part of the Household Division, 'the sovereign's own troops'. Tradition has it that there is a mounted guard at Horse Guards in Whitehall which is still used on official occasions as the entrance to Buckingham Palace. The regiment used to be billeted at Horse Guards and whenever the sovereign was seen to be about to leave the sanctuary of the Palace, they would get a whistle, mount up and escort him or her wherever he or she wanted to go.

Nowadays the police have overall responsibility for the security of the royal palaces but I liaised closely with them. At night, for example, the ceremonial guard change into combat gear and patrol the grounds of Buckingham Palace in a much stealthier manner.

I was a career soldier and, like most soldiers, was unconditionally prepared to lay down my life for Queen and country (although little realising that such an opportunity later might await me at the hands of Saddam Hussein). But in 1986 my role was to organise military ceremonial. I was based in Horse Guards but I would quite often go to Buckingham Palace to discuss arrangements for State Visits or events such as Trooping the Colour.

I have always enjoyed organising things so I liked the work and the prospect of writing much of the ceremonial procedure for the Household Division for Prince Andrew's wedding was something I relished. He was to marry Sarah Ferguson (the daughter of a former Life Guards officer) in Westminster Abbey on 23rd July 1986.

It was early in May when I came out of a wedding meeting at Buckingham Palace with the Queen's equerry, Lieutenant-Commander Tim Lawrence (later to become the Queen's son-in-law when he married Princess Anne). It was a sultry afternoon and I felt the heat, wearing what was known as 'dismounted review order' — a heavily quilted red tunic with its high collar, overalls, boots and spurs. There was some official business going on in the quadrangle and I felt obliged to wait at the East Door until it finished.

I heard a voice behind me. It was Princess Diana. I was surprised to see her there. It wasn't uncommon to pass Prince Philip or Prince Edward in the palace corridors because they lived there. You couldn't pretend you were invisible so you always said a respectful 'Good morning, sir' and they would acknowledge you. But she didn't live in Buckingham Palace — she lived at Kensington Palace.

But there she was, at the bottom of the stairs, in a long summer skirt with bare feet, her shoes in her hand. I muttered a 'Good afternoon, ma'am,' and she giggled and said: 'Like the outfit.' We fell into a brief conversation. She asked me what I was doing there and I tried to explain some of the ceremonial plans for the wedding. I wish I could remember the exact words we spoke but I do remember exactly what I was feeling: just completely bowled over by someone so feminine and friendly and captivatingly beautiful.

We had spoken for less than five minutes when I could see the quadrangle had cleared. So I said goodbye and returned to Whitehall and my charts and rosters. Unusually in the succeeding weeks in the lead-up to the wedding I encountered the Princess several times in the palace corridors, but never again alone. However, her greeting always had a warmth to it which remained with me for the rest of the day.

About once a month I would go over to Clarence House to have a glass of sherry with Sir Martin Gilliatt, Private Secretary to the Queen Mother for thirty years. This had nothing to do with my job. During the war my father's cousin, Eardly Hewitt, had saved Sir Martin's life when his plane crashed in Borneo. So when I took up my post in the Household Division, Eardly — long retired, a wonderful eccentric who looked like Van Dyke's portrait of Charles I — wrote to Sir Martin asking him to 'keep an eye on the boy'.

Occasionally I would attend small parties in Sir Martin's rooms, so when an invitation to drinks came from Hazel West, wife of Lieutenant-Colonel George West, the Assistant-Comptroller in the Lord Chamberlain's Office, I assumed it was as a result of meeting them at Sir Martin's. In the normal run of things our circles were very different — they were senior courtiers and I was an army officer aged 28.

In fact, I very nearly didn't go. I had been invited to a dinner party that evening — there was never any shortage of invitations for single officers in London — and it certainly held out the prospect of more fun. But it would have been discourteous to accept and not turn up so I decided to combine them both.

The party was held in two rooms in the Wests' spacious apartment in St James's Palace. There were no more than twenty people there. I accepted a glass of champagne at the door and went to look for Hazel West whom I found in the drawing room. As soon as I entered I caught sight of Princess Diana. She wasn't being chaperoned in any way, but was seemingly on her own just wandering about. Hazel greeted me in her usual graceful fashion and almost immediately introduced me to the Princess. She asked if we knew each other. I reminded her we had bumped into each other at Buckingham Palace. Diana said: 'You look a lot better in uniform.'

It set the tone for the rest of the evening. Hazel went off to greet other guests and Diana and I continued to talk. She mentioned she'd seen me playing polo and the conversation got on to the subject of horses. She seemed to know that I had given lessons to Princess Michael of Kent the previous summer. 'Surely she's such a good rider she doesn't need lessons?' Diana suggested a little pointedly. I explained that Princess Michael had wanted to learn all about dressage — the ultimate relationship between horse and rider. She used to come to the indoor riding school at Knightsbridge and ride my charger, Foxhunter, which I taught to do counter-canters, extended trots, half-passes and other dressage movements. Foxhunter looked like a 'black' but was, in fact, very dark brown. He used to go a bit light in the summer and I was worried that it might not be appropriate to ride him during the Birthday Parade where all the officers' mounts must be black. So Princess Michael had thoughtfully sent me a bottle of dye from her hair-dressers.

'Did you use it?' asked Diana.

'No, I didn't. I think it was a bit of a joke,' I replied, 'but you can borrow it if you like.'

She made a face. Then I asked her: 'Are you keen on riding?'

Her smile disappeared and she shuddered. 'I'm terrified of horses. I fell off a pony and broke my arm when I was a child and I've been a bag of nerves ever since. I'm not sure I ever want to ride again.'

I said that that would be a shame. That sort of thing happened to quite a lot of people and it was nearly always possible to give them their confidence back. I could try — if she wanted.

Her response was immediate: 'That would be wonderful. I'd love you to teach me. Could we go riding together?'

I was a little taken aback: 'If you'd like to do that I'm sure I can arrange it.'

She said she wanted it to be a low-key thing, nothing formal. I assured her there would be no problem with that.

And that was it. Diana left. I looked at my watch — we had been talking for the best part of an hour. I realised I was going to be too late for dinner. But as I left the Wests' apartment I was aware that I had no desire to go to any dinner party. So I walked up St James's and went into the Suntory Japanese restaurant where I had a meal on my own. I was happy to be alone with my thoughts.

The next day Hazel West, who was also one of Diana's ladies-in-waiting, telephoned me and confirmed that the Princess wanted to take some riding lessons and asked me to sort it out. I cleared it with the commanding officer at Knightsbridge Barracks — he was delighted — and we arranged that it would indeed be low key so that instead of the whole guard turning out every time she came to the barracks it would just be like a normal visitor, rather than a royal guest. Her initial arrival was a bit more formal, but it soon became normal.

I decided that we would begin in the indoor riding school so that I could assess what sort of a rider she was. She had said she was dreadful but I was later to discover it was her habit to say she was 'dreadful' at everything — except swimming and dancing. She had clearly ridden before so we didn't have to start from basics. But she hadn't been on a horse for many years and was more than a little nervous.

My main concern was to make sure that she didn't fall and injure herself again. The secret of teaching anybody to ride is to choose the right horse. You want it to be forward going and free enough to be an enjoyable ride, but you don't want it to be too strong or to run the risk of its taking off. In fact, most of the horses at Knightsbridge were pretty shock-proof and reliable due to the nature of their work in the middle of a busy city. But there was one in particular that was extremely steady, Gary, a trumpeter's grey horse that I selected for Diana. I knew that Gary would not take off with her even if somebody fired a shotgun immediately behind him. Such animals are few and far between.

To begin with, Diana looked somewhat tentative and awkward but it wasn't long before she started to relax a little and developed a good seat. After a few days' instruction we ventured out into Hyde Park. Invariably we took the same route: left out of the gates of the barracks towards Kensington Palace along Rotten Row, through the avenue of sycamores and chestnut trees. Hazel West, a fine horsewoman who is now a Jockey Club Steward, rode with us and Sir Christopher Airey, the Major-General commanding the Household Division, would sometimes come along. He and Diana got on like a house on fire.

Initially there was a lot of security about. White police cars patrolled the outside roads of the park and those detectives in close protection followed on the inside in plain cars. The police already knew me well from my official security duties. They gave me a small radio and told me that if there was any problem or I spotted anything or anyone abnormal or I needed any back-up I should contact them immediately.

But as we settled into a routine the police presence diminished or, at least, became less conspicuous. And nothing did go wrong. Everything went right. We rode once a week at varying times when Diana could fit it in to her busy schedule, but usually around ten in the morning. Most of the time it was walking with a little trotting and very occasionally we cantered. Rotten Row is a long straight and it's the sort of sight that can encourage a horse to go a little quicker than his rider intends. But Gary proved totally trustworthy. Despite this I was aware that Diana, although she put on a brave face, never really lost her fear.

There were times, when we rode on alone, when she would ask me whether I wasn't ever scared myself. I would take out different horses from the stables to see how they were going and some of them were a bit fresh to start with. I told her I knew how she felt. At one stage in my life I had lost my confidence when I was required to exercise point-to-pointers as a young schoolboy. But I had overcome this and, in truth, after that never felt more at home than when I was on a horse.

I could hardly remember a time in my life when I wasn't on horseback. I told her how my parents had bought me Bobby Shafto, a skewbald from a gypsy encampment, when I was eighteen months old. All my childhood my sisters and I would ride for hours on end over the commons of East Devon. We would play cowboys and Indians and I was always forced to be the Indian — the one who was shot — so I had to learn how to keep falling off. As I grew up I would emulate the cowboys that I saw in movies, riding under a low branch and catching it, lifting myself out of the saddle. Or — and this was harder — I would jump from a tree on to a moving horse, with my sisters' encouragement.

I explained to her how everybody needed to build

their confidence with horses. The best way to do it is just to go out and enjoy yourself, learn in your own time and your own way. Then, when you acquire a natural ability, you can refine your technique. Too many instructors make riding too technical from the start and this inevitably tends to put some people off.

After a few sessions I got the feeling that Diana was not just trying to get back her confidence as a rider; in some deep-seated sense she also needed to rebuild her confidence as a person. She said that there had been nobody to encourage her after that childhood fall so she found it much easier to stick with swimming and some tennis. As a child she would go to Sandringham for holidays and everybody there seemed to be very good at riding.

It's surprising how inconspicuous we were. I didn't wear uniform — just a hacking jacket, tie, breeches and boots. I used to wear a trilby — somewhat illegal, although I insisted that Diana wear a hard hat which had the effect of making her less noticeable. But not *completely* unnoticed. One morning we passed the Duke of Luxembourg who's the Colonel of the Irish Guards and he gave a pretty astonished salute!

On another occasion we crossed the grass to the place where four members of the Blues and Royals were blown up by an IRA bomb in July of 1982. Seven horses were killed, too. Diana asked if I knew the men and I did. I told her how Lieutenant Anthony Daly, who died, had only just married. He wasn't due to be Captain of The Queen's Life Guard on the day of the bomb but had stood in for a friend who was going to a wedding. She digested this information in silence and rode back to barracks lost in her own thoughts.

There were some drunks who used to gather at the end of Rotten Row nearest to Park Lane and Diana sometimes liked to stop and talk to them. At the time I always wondered if they knew who she was. Then I actually got my answer some years later when one of them wrote to me saying that he'd cleaned up his act and now owned a shop in London and how much he had enjoyed our chats.

From time to time we met socially. On one occasion the Wests had the riding party to dinner round their kitchen table. On another, Diana invited me and Sir Christopher Airey to lunch at Kensington Palace. Her mother, Frances Shand Kydd, was there. Diana would later insist: 'Don't you think my mother's beautiful?' She was quite fixated with that.

As the weeks went by, it became more and more apparent that she didn't just want to learn to ride, she wanted to get away. And to talk. She would phone me frequently on the pretext of fixing up our next session but the calls would go on for an hour or more. There was nothing sensational in them: just gossip. Diana had a need to take the formality of her daily duties as a princess and bring it down to earth with chatty asides and observations.

I also realised, when we were together, that she saw herself as if she were trapped in some tower, unable to lead a normal life. She was always questioning me about what dinners or parties I had been to, what my week had been like, who I'd been with. It was obvious she was missing that kind of life and, to some extent, wanted to live it vicariously through me.

She was very keen to know about my girlfriends, past and present, and why I hadn't settled down. I pointed out that it was part of the ethos of the regiment. They preferred bachelor officers who would get out and do sports and not have family ties when it came to postings abroad or war. It was still frowned upon to get married below the rank of captain, and you still had to ask the commanding officer's permission.

'I married when I was just twenty,' she said.

'I know,' I replied.

I also knew now that her marriage was going through a bad patch. I was genuinely sorry for her, for both of them. I had always thought they made a good couple and I didn't really want to hear otherwise. But sometimes she could hardly bring herself to refer to her husband by name. It was just 'him' — this was the sad side of a girl who flowed with fun and charm and flirtatiousness. She could make the sullen waters of the Serpentine sparkle just by riding past them.

My own life was going through a strange phase. I was a bachelor officer in a vibrant city. I went out at night to parties and dinners and balls. I felt part of these events but at the same time not part of them. At some of the dinners I attended people knew we were riding together but if there were behind-the-hand whispers, I was the last to hear about them. I never spoke about Diana — and I never stopped thinking about her.

I realised I was becoming obsessed with her. I lived from week to week. I couldn't wait to see her again. It was just a complete joy. It was like stepping through a little window into another time and space where those couple of hours together were something very special. And then it would all disappear until the following week. And from her phone calls and her conversation she gave every indication of just wanting to be with me.

Sooner or later I knew things were going to come to some sort of head. My father, a retired captain in the Royal Marines who was separated from my mother, came up to London. We had dinner together in Jakes, a quiet restaurant just off the Fulham Road that was a favourite of his. He knew that I was teaching Diana to ride and asked me how it was going.

'It's developing into something more,' I confessed. 'What should I do?'

Somehow you always expect parents to have instant solutions to any problem, just as they did when you were a child.

'I'd be very careful,' he said. Then he asked: 'Do you love her?'

I was stunned into silence. We had never reached such an intimate or personal moment in our lives before. I couldn't answer his question directly because I simply didn't know the answer.

'I need to be there for her,' I replied. I knew that.

In the late autumn I came to the end of my time at Horse Guards and was promoted to acting major, taking over Headquarters Squadron at Combermere Barracks in Windsor. The Squadron dealt with the administration of the Regiment which was part of 5 Airborne Brigade. In time of war, our main responsibility would be the protection of the mainland but our continuing role was to prepare for 'out-of-areas' operations — we could evacuate British nationals from trouble spots anywhere in the world.

When I told Diana I was moving to Windsor she was, at first, disappointed. But she was anxious to continue riding and saw the half-hour journey down the M4 as little hindrance to this. She drove herself in her dark green Jaguar with her detective by her side. We would continue to ride most weeks, save when I was away from barracks on training exercises — not least learning to become a paratrooper. She gave me a mobile phone so that we could keep in touch when I was away.

I had Gary moved to Combermere Barracks and our rides now were in Windsor Great Park. We had the keys to go where we liked. It was wonderful — like a secret garden on a vast scale. We could even ride down the Long Walk, an area not normally ridden on by others, which the Queen's carriage goes along to Ascot.

Diana began to unburden herself more intimately. She told me about her bulimia. I had never heard the word before and could barely believe her descriptions of what it truly meant.

I asked her what caused it. 'Unhappiness,' she said.

I pointed out, maybe a little insensitively, that she didn't seem that unhappy. She replied that she wasn't when she was riding Gary. The significance of the remark was not lost on me.

Sometimes we would go for lunch at the Officers' Mess afterwards. There you wouldn't have thought she had a care in the world. She was the most popular guest imaginable, putting everyone at their ease, laughing at people's jokes, holding court, having fun. She felt secure because it was behind closed doors. Everyone was very friendly. No word of anything ever reached the newspapers.

Invariably we were left alone afterwards. If it was known that we were in the mess and the doors were shut, that meant that we were having a private conversation and people respected this. Sometimes a steward would knock on the door with more coffee or the Commanding Officer, Lieutenant-Colonel James Ellery, would let it be known that he was in the mess and he would come and join us. But, looking back, it was a surprisingly private place to be.

Diana sensed this, too. We were sitting there alone one winter's afternoon on a large leather Chesterfield sofa. At least, I was sitting on the sofa and she was sitting on the back of it with her boots on a cushion. She had been her usual jolly self at lunch but I could now see that she was feeling miserable. She didn't want to go home to a lonely palace. More than ever she needed a sympathetic ear.

I asked her what was wrong. She told me how her relationship with her husband had deteriorated really badly. She spelled out her situation with brutal simplicity: they were not in love and their marriage was on the rocks.

My immediate reaction — I remember it clearly — was 'this doesn't bode well for the stability of the monarchy'. That's how I felt, sad for them both and dreadful for her. I was concerned with her happiness

She said that one of her problems was that there was absolutely no one to help her. The Palace was against her and she found it hard to know who would be for her.

I said that she could rely on me. She turned to me and, without warning, grabbed my hand. And suddenly it all came out, all in a rush. Her eyes were tearful and she spoke with a passion far removed from her usual teasing flirtatiousness.

'I need you,' she said. 'You give me strength. I can't stand it when I'm away from you. I want to be with you. I've come to love you.'

Then she leant forward, and kissed me.

# 2

And so we embarked on an affair which was to continue for most of the next five years. It was wonderful — exhilarating, passionate and intensely loving. We were young — in our twenties — and when we were together life was carefree and full of fun. We seemed to leave reality behind. I think probably all lovers live in a fantasy world that belongs just to them, and we were no different.

Diana initiated it. There was no way that I would have dared to make the first move. In truth, for most of our time spent riding together, I just assumed her relationship with Prince Charles was going through a bad patch. But she was adamant it was over in all but name. She told me how hard she had tried to make it work but since the birth of Prince Harry her husband had taken little interest in her. On one occasion she decided to take the bull by the horns and demanded to know why she was being physically rejected.

He joked that he thought he might be gay. But she knew that the reverse was true and that he had resumed his relationship with Camilla Parker Bowles. Diana was very bitter about this and always put the blame for the break-up of her marriage on Camilla.

So she sought a relationship elsewhere — with me. There were, of course, immense problems. I was single and unattached but she was a married woman. I didn't need to remind myself that she was the wife of the next King of England and the mother of a future King of England. So when she telephoned me on the evening of the day we kissed in Combermere Barracks, I faced the dilemma of whether I should take the inevitable step towards becoming involved or point out to her the impossibility of our being able to conduct a relationship.

Strange as it may seem, I had no real option. Diana was emotionally very fragile. The bulimia had taken its toll on her: she was painfully thin and her skin hung almost lifelessly on her bones. She was a woman deeply damaged by rejection. Whether it was true or not, she saw herself as being wholly alone in a hostile world, with no one to turn to to share her problems with or give her guidance.

I was her friend. I knew I was the first person she would telephone about anything — we had spent countless hours on the phone. Having gone along with our flirtations for the past months, to draw back now and suggest we just remain as friends would have had a devastating effect on her. I also knew I was captivated by her.

I had been aware for some time that we would reach this situation. One day at a friend's house in Ascot I had looked up the word 'treason' in the *Encyclopaedia Britannica* and found the definition — 'It is treason to violate the king's consort or his eldest unmarried daughter as well as the wife of his eldest son and heir.' That certainly included Diana. It didn't say whether it still carried the death penalty but I knew that if word ever got out the punishment would probably be worse than death, and I wasn't far wrong.

In retrospect it is amazing that we were able to conduct our affair for many years and, despite the fact that Diana was the most written-about woman in the world, nothing of substance appeared about it in the papers. During that time we would meet at Kensington Palace, sometimes at a friend's house, at Highgrove and at my family home in Devon.

I pretty well put myself in Diana's hands. It was she who had a busy schedule so it was natural that she should work out when we might see each other. As I drove down the M4 from Windsor for our first dinner alone together at Kensington Palace, I nervously played out in my mind the dangers of bumping into Prince Charles, or anyone else come to that.

But Diana had the situation completely under control. I turned left off Kensington High Street towards Kensington Palace. You drive up the private road between the Royal Garden Hotel and Kensington Gardens. Halfway up there is a police barrier. I rolled down the car window and said that I was Major Hewitt come to see the Princess of Wales and a very friendly policeman said: 'That's fine, sir. You know where to go.'

I did. I continued a hundred yards up to the Palace and then turned right into the centre square with a large flowerbed in the middle and drove three-quarters of the way round to the big black door which was the Wales's apartment. Diana instructed me to park right outside. Hide in plain sight, as the Americans might say.

I knocked at the door and waited. This was a strange situation to be in. I felt no real apprehension, just excitement. I didn't have long to wait. A footman opened the door and escorted me along a corridor, through a hall and up a substantial set of steps. Diana was waiting at the top. She was tall and willowy and strikingly beautiful. She had dressed simply in a pale blue silk shirt — she liked pale colours — and a calf-length, pleated skirt. I reached the top of the stairs and kissed her on the cheek — the footman was behind me. I couldn't help noticing she was wearing low shoes — she was 5 feet 11 and I was 6 feet and when she wore heels I often found myself looking up at her. I could smell the fresh and very English aroma of Lily of the Valley — her favourite scent. She wore simple gold earrings but no necklace and looked utterly adorable. I had brought her a box of Benedicks Bitter Mints which I had bought in the mess. She expressed her delight at this and gave me a warm embrace.

She led me into her drawing room, which was distinctly feminine and almost childlike with lots of soft toys. The room was very much hers, with her own desk with her telephone on it. The footman had disappeared leaving some drinks by the side of the room. Diana said I should serve myself. I went across and poured us each a glass of champagne from a newly opened bottle. We made small talk about the traffic on the M4 and suchlike — the sort of things you discuss when you're avoiding anything too relevant. I mentioned that I recognised the opera that she was playing — *The Pearl Fishers*. She said that it wasn't an opera but a CD with duets from famous operas but that particular one between the tenor and the baritone was her favourite. I confessed I had never seen *The Pearl Fishers* but they'd used the duet in the Mel Gibson film, *Gallipoli*, on the night before they went into battle. Diana said that was where she first heard it, too.

The footman knocked on the door and announced that dinner was ready. Possibly he was the butler — he was quite a young man who wore Kensington Palace buttons on his dark blue blazer. He took our drinks and we passed through a more formal drawing room with a grand piano covered with family photographs. Beyond lay the dining room with a highly polished oval mahogany table that could seat more than twelve people. I had been there before for lunch but on this occasion it was laid for just two people with places set pretty well at right angles at one end.

Diana thanked the butler and he said goodnight. There were plates of smoked salmon already at our places. Diana drank only still mineral water but encouraged me to help myself to some Chablis. The room was dominated by two large and really striking paintings of nineteenth century battles with soldiers in red uniforms — one was certainly Waterloo. We went across to the silver hot plates and served ourselves the main course. It was chicken in a lemon and cream sauce with mashed potatoes and mange tout and French beans. Diana insisted I had some claret to accompany this.

The wine relaxed me and I asked if she was expecting Prince Charles to return that evening. She laughed and shook her head, saying there was no risk of him appearing. She told me that they had a diary conference every week so she knew where he was and he knew where she was.

After we had finished the main course, Diana suddenly got up and ran into the next room, saying that we must have one of the chocolates that I had brought. She came back with both the Benedicks box and a book that was also in a box, a small dark blue oblong box.

'Smell it,' she said. I obliged. It smelt just like a rose. Indeed there was a rose on the cover with the words 'Penhaligon's scented treasury of verse and prose' beneath and above it just one word — 'Love'. I opened it and began to read out one of the extracts. It was from Christopher Marlowe:

> *Come live with me and be my love,*
> *And we will all the pleasures prove*
> *That hills and valleys, dales and fields.*
> *Or woods or steepy mountain yields.*

'Do you like it?' Diana asked.
I said that I did.
'Well, look at the front,' she said.
I turned the pages back to the inside of the front cover. There was a painting of a little window box full of flowers with the words: 'Flowers may fade but true love never' written on it. Beneath she had written 'To James' and, below that, four little crosses for kisses.

That evening our affair began.

Life fell into a pattern. Diana still came to ride with me

in Windsor Great Park on a regular basis, but about twice a week I would come to Kensington Palace in the evening and make my way back to Windsor at about three or four the next morning. Although the Palace housed Princess Margaret, Prince and Princess Michael of Kent, the Duke and Duchess of Gloucester, their mother Alice and Diana's sister Jane and her husband, Sir Robert Fellowes, the Queen's private secretary, I rarely encountered anybody. The place was always quiet. There were usually quite a lot of cars about but not much life. One evening I bumped into Prince Michael of Kent. I knew him because he had occasionally ridden with us when I had tutored Princess Michael. He said a convivial 'Good evening' and we both went on our separate ways.

Occasionally Diana would invite somebody over for drinks in the early evening. She was very friendly with Harry Herbert, the son of the Earl of Carnarvon — the Queen's racing manager. On other occasions it would be Carolyn Bartholomew who had been at school with her and then shared her flat in Coleherne Court when they were both single, or Kate Menzies whose family owned the chain of newsagents.

But they would rarely stay for long. One thing was absolutely fixed in Diana's life and that was *EastEnders* on BBC television. She was absolutely fixated with the soap and if she was unable to see it she would tape it and watch it later in the evening. If she was away on an engagement she made sure Paul Burrell would tape it for her. (Paul — a footman turned butler — used to work for both her and Charles but later became very much Diana's man.) She tried to get me hooked on *EastEnders* — and failed miserably. I asked what was so involving about it. She said she loved the intrigue and the way they finished each episode on a cliff-hanger so you just had to watch the next one. She maintained it kept her 'in touch'. On more than one occasion she mentioned how she envied the freedom of the regulars at the Queen Vic to live their lives.

When the television wasn't on, music usually filled the apartment. She loved Verdi and Mozart and had a host of classical compilation CDs like *The Essential Pavarotti* or *The Best of Bach*. Her other passion was clothes. She would take me up to the long wardrobe that ran along the length of her bedroom and bathroom. It overflowed with hundreds of outfits. She was always very anxious to know which ones I liked and which ones she should wear on certain occasions. I wasn't completely ignorant of designer names — I had grown up with two sisters — and I had reasonably firm ideas of what I liked and what I didn't like. She welcomed my opinions.

Over the years her clothes were to become a barometer of the change in Diana. When we were first together she was more cautious and conservative in what she wore. But then, as she regained her confidence, the bulimia receded and she worked out to get into much better shape, and her tastes developed. She wanted to show herself off as a woman. Without being too overt she opted for sexier clothes. It was very important to her to be appreciated and even desired.

Normally before we had dinner the boys, Prince William and Prince Harry, would come down from the nursery. They were always terribly excited to see her, bursting with tales of what they had been doing that day. Diana encouraged me to read them stories. My preference was *The Wind in the Willows*, which communicated the romance of the countryside, but William's favourite was always *Winnie the Pooh*.

They would play with their toys — William was very keen on soldiers and Harry tended to follow whatever William did. I would tell them a bit about what it was like to be in the army. They both seemed fascinated so I suggested to Diana that maybe they would like to visit Combermere Barracks and she readily agreed.

It was arranged that they would come down after her riding lesson the following week. I asked the regimental tailor to run up two little uniforms for them and they seemed thrilled by them, asking me to make sure that their berets were worn like proper soldiers. They climbed all over the tanks and other armoured vehicles and played with the guns and appeared to have the time of their lives. They wrote me a lovely letter afterwards which I treasure to this day. Diana loved it, too. The day seemed to mean a lot to her. It was a sort of ideal situation. I said to her that it would be nice for them to join the regiment. She replied: 'Yes, I'd like that, too. But sadly this family goes into the navy.'

It was fine for us to be seen together in public in this context. It was known, at least in court and army circles, that she was having riding lessons with me. Nothing could be more natural than for the boys to come and visit her and take a look round regimental HQ.

Being seen together in London, however, posed a trickier problem and not one that we ever really resolved. Diana was unable to go anywhere without security. It was particularly strong in the late eighties as she was seen to be a very real target for the IRA. This usually meant that there would always be a detective with her in her car and they would be followed by a back-up car with two further police officers. When I had been at Knightsbridge Barracks my job had involved attending security briefings, especially if there was a big state occasion coming up like the Queen's Birthday Parade. The IRA was, in fact, very well penetrated in terms of intelligence at that time and if any of the 'moles' supplied hard intelligence there would be an alert. This would not necessarily lead to an increase in the police presence — it was always a fine line balancing the potential danger with the risk that your informant might be compromised — but it did signal maximum vigilance.

So Diana not only lived like the proverbial bird in a gilded cage, when she was allowed her flights out of it she was never really free.

Diana still suffered from bulimia. The fact that she had started a relationship with me did not provide her with an instant cure for her illness. She told me that when she was alone — and very lonely — in Kensington Palace she would go to the kitchen and 'pig' her way through whatever comfort food she could find. She would then make her way to the bathroom to make herself sick. She said she had tried to explain this to Prince Charles but he had been largely repulsed by it. He seemed unable to understand her illness or truly to sympathise with her. And that in itself was a symptom of it, along with his rejection of her physically and as a companion. She felt utterly helpless and in a loveless marriage that she could never get out of since divorce was completely out of the question.

I asked her if there wasn't someone within the Palace system who could give her some help and advice. She said there wasn't. The only person who could really help her was the Queen. She would see her sometimes when she swam in the morning at Buckingham Palace. But then they would only exchange pleasantries about the children. Things were so bad at one stage that she did summon up the courage to make an appointment with the Queen to explain the whole situation to her. Diana said she met with a very concerned response. The Queen promised she would do what she could to take some pressure off her and later newspaper editors were asked not to subject her to too much scrutiny. But when it came to the issue of her marriage to Charles, the Queen said there was nothing she could do. It would be wrong for her to intervene. Diana knew she was in a very difficult position and was grateful to her for her sympathy.

So Kensington Palace remained a prison for her with me as a frequent visitor. She said she never suffered from bulimia when she was with me and as the months went on she became less despairing and bouts of the illness became less frequent.

We would occasionally eat meals out, usually at San Lorenzo near Harrods in Knightsbridge, but we would always arrive separately and make sure that someone else joined us at the table, very often Carolyn and William Bartholomew who were in on our secret. I would get there first and Diana would arrive with a detective in one of the black Ford Sapphires from the Palace. It and the back-up car would wait round the corner while we were having our meal and whichever detective was accompanying Diana would eat at the next door table.

San Lorenzo has had a steady stream of celebrities since people like Mick Jagger, Peter Sellers, Princess Margaret and Lord Snowdon frequented it in the sixties. I had gone there before either with a group of people or a girlfriend and it was always a trendy, buzzy sort of place. But as I waited for Diana I didn't need to be told when she had entered the restaurant. The level of conversation dropped noticeably as those at tables who could see the entrance leaned forward and told their companions who had just arrived.

Little did they know that the most inveterate people-watcher in the place was Diana herself. She would indicate any good-looking women in the restaurant and ask me in a whisper whether I found them sexy and fancied them. She was always intrigued to know what sort of women I liked. Then she would speculate on what sort of lives they lived. She felt envious of them; she knew she was missing out on so much.

Much as we lived for the evenings that we spent together at Kensington Palace, we both would have loved to be able to go out and just do the things that normal couples do — movies, pizzas, parties. Diana would question me endlessly about the rest of my social life, even asking me if I had any other girlfriends. I didn't. But I did go to dinners and parties either locally in Ascot or, more often, in London. I'd been in Knightsbridge Barracks for some time so I knew quite a few people. I was happy to go along to these social occasions but they always seemed very empty without her.

She had a full diary of official appointments. She was truly punctilious about doing what she saw as her duty but she preferred to do so on her own, finding joint appearances with Prince Charles an increasing strain. It wasn't easy for her — putting on a front — and I doubt if it was very enjoyable for him, either.

One night she sprang a surprise on me. She asked me to turn up at Kensington Palace much earlier than usual and in black tie. It transpired she had arranged an evening at the opera. She knew I particularly loved Mozart and had got a box for *Cosi Fan Tutte*.

'It's just right for you,' she said, 'it's about two badly behaved army officers.' I pointed out to her that the two fiancées of the officers were just as badly behaved (in the story the men assume disguises and successfully seduce each other's fiancée.)

Inspector Ken Wharfe, Diana's favourite bodyguard, was a great music lover — if prompted and permitted he would on occasion burst into song — and he made up the party along with Kate Menzies and Catherine Soames, ex-wife of Nicholas Soames MP, one of Prince Charles's best friends. We travelled together in a Palace car — I think it was the only time I travelled in the same car as Diana in London. Although it was not an official occasion, obviously people recognised her but, as ever, there was safety in numbers and no press comment about my presence there. I suppose I could have been escorting either of the other two girls.

Even though we were not alone it was one of the most romantic evenings we ever spent together. Diana had devised a secret signal. Not long after our affair began she informed me that whenever she touched her nose that would show she was thinking about me. It was something she did frequently at lunch in the mess at Combermere. That evening at the opera whenever our eyes met she would always touch her nose. With that and the champagne and the Mozart it was a night that I wished would go on for ever.

One spring evening when we were together at Kensington Palace she seemed out of sorts. When I asked her what was the matter. She said, 'Oh, nothing,' in the way people do when there is something wrong. So I asked again and she confessed she was dreading another weekend on her own at Highgrove.

'I wish we could spend the weekends together,' she said. Without stopping to think it through I replied: 'Why not?'

Her eyes lit up. 'Would you really come down to

Highgrove?'

This time I did pause for thought. 'Would that be possible?' I asked.

She looked at me with wicked determination in her eyes. 'I'll make it possible.'

What she did was to invite some other people — among them Hazel West and William and Carolyn Bartholomew — so that it seemed just a normal weekend house party with a few friends. She gave me detailed directions how to get there. From Tetbury in Gloucestershire you follow a winding road to the west. The main entrance to the house is almost hidden, recessed on a sharp corner, but everyone uses the back entrance.

The security at Highgrove is quite intense. There is a little police box shrouded in Cotswold stone. Inside were five police watching the constantly switching television monitors which covered all the gardens. The inner part of the estate — there is a large seven or eight hundred acre farm beyond — is also ring-fenced by electric security devices. Although there was no overt military presence there, it seemed to me that it was as secure, if not more so, as any of the royal palaces that I had been involved with when I was at Knightsbridge. I calculated they probably needed a team of at least fifteen police to provide the rotating security.

I arrived in my Renault Savanna late on a Friday afternoon. They were expecting me. A policeman welcomed me cordially and told me to go and park in front of the house. They must have telephoned Diana because she came out of the front door as soon as I got out of the car and greeted me with a warm embrace.

As we went through the front door I couldn't help noticing on the right-hand side of the porch a pair of Wellington boots, some secateurs, a pair of gardening gloves and a little flower basket — all of which clearly belonged to Prince Charles.

Diana showed me to my room as my bags were taken from the car. There was time to freshen up and have a shower before joining the others in the snug little drawing room to the left of the front door. People were already in there having pre-dinner drinks. There was a well-stocked bar with champagne on ice but the house speciality seemed to be a particularly appealing orange vodka. Diana was drinking a mineral water. I once asked her why she didn't drink alcohol, apart from the occasional sip of champagne. At first she said that she didn't like the taste of it. Then she confessed that if she started to drink she would never know when to stop. She was afraid she would become an alcoholic. She said it with a laugh and I was never quite sure whether she was joking or not, although I suspected her experiences with bulimia had made her wary of any other form of addiction.

In fact, she was able to control her bulimia more than she acknowledged, even to herself. That evening she ate if not a hearty dinner at least a sensibly portioned one and she told me later that night she had not been sick. The meal was served in an elegant dining room by staff in uniform. Diana had a hidden bell under the table so that she could summon them and they would appear, seemingly miraculously, just as the last person had finished his or her course.

It was at Highgrove that I realised just what a good friend Carolyn Bartholomew was to Diana. It seemed at times that her only concern was for Diana's well-being and happiness. Carolyn knew the immense inner burden she carried and told me she was worried about her mental stability and physical health. I asked quite genuinely whether my relationship with Diana was putting more of a strain on this. Carolyn was adamant that the reverse was the case. She urged me to keep it going. She told me she could see that I gave Diana support and the result was that she seemed happier and healthier than she had in a long while. I also remember her saying something about me being the one light in her life.

That first weekend at Highgrove worked marvellously. We didn't do much: went for walks, read the papers, ate and gossiped. I was aware that the cooks and various people who looked after the house worked jointly for

Charles and Diana so we behaved very properly. Diana even came into my room one morning to make sure I'd ruffled my bed sufficiently so that it looked slept in. She was careful and even calculating in the ways of deception.

But one thing, above all, nagged at her. It was the fact that Camilla Parker Bowles would come and be the lady of the house when she wasn't there. However much dislike she felt for Charles, this rankled much more. As I've said she constantly put the blame on Camilla for the failure of their marriage. She felt doubly betrayed. Before they were married she and Charles had stayed with the Parker Bowles (who lived not far away). Camilla had made overtures of friendship but now Diana considered her to have been cruelly deceitful. Charles had bought Highgrove around that time and the house and especially the gardens very much had his stamp on them. Diana always said it had never really been her home and she was much more attached to Althorp, her father Lord Spencer's house, where she had spent her teenage years.

But she, too, had loved our weekend at Highgrove and she reasoned that since Charles went there openly — to the staff and security at least — with Camilla there was no reason why I should not come on my own without the cover of other guests or the front of riding lessons. She used to ring and let me choose the menu. The cooks made an excellent cottage pie or we'd have pheasant in season or duck or steak. When it was just the two of us dinner would more often than not be eaten off trays in the small drawing room and we would watch videos during supper like millions of couples all over the country.

While I was writing this book, I went to see the Jim Carey film, *The Truman Show* and, halfway through, I realised why it stirred such a sense of *déjà vu* in me. Truman, without knowing it, was living in a soap opera — growing up with cameras recording his every move. It was just like the gardens at Highgrove. You'd be walking along and you'd hear an imperceptible 'whirr'. Looking up you'd see a tiny remote-control camera in a tree adjusting its position to follow you along a path.

It was only the security police doing their job. Diana had warned me about this and when we strolled together at first I had to stop myself from taking her hand or putting my arm round her shoulder. After a while it became second nature. The system had its benefits. William and Harry used to play in a beautifully constructed tree house which Diana always insisted was too high and too dangerous. But if either of them had fallen, somebody would have been on the spot within seconds. Even when we were romping with the boys in the swimming pool, the all-seeing eyes would be on us.

The only place that was safe from the cameras was the walled garden which Prince Charles had created pretty well from scratch. It was a marvellous place, full of fruit trees and rare organic vegetables: white Belgian carrots, green zebra tomatoes and broad beans with amazing red flowers. It was a sanctuary for him and I couldn't but admire the work and care he must have put into it.

Diana and I would sometimes link arms and walk there before dinner. One evening I told her the story of how I had actually invited Charles and her to dinner when they were on their honeymoon. I was in charge of the Guards Division Free Fall Parachute Display team and we had flown to Cyprus for a competition. And on that first weekend in August 1981 the Royal Yacht *Britannia* was taking the newlyweds close by the island. I knew Prince Charles passingly well from polo — at one stage he actually played for The Life Guards team — and he once wrote me a most thoughtful letter. It was after an inter-regimental match which are traditionally bloody affairs. I think the Queen was watching the game. I was following the line of the ball I had just hit when Captain Arthur Denaro came at me at a huge angle, yelling at me to get out of the way, wildly swinging his mallet which went nowhere near the ball but straight into my face. It was a mess — blood everywhere, the worst injury I've ever had. I was lucky to get away with a broken jaw. Diana asked me if Denaro had been punished. Well, a foul was awarded against him, I said, but he went on to become a major-general and is currently commanding Sandhurst. Prince Charles in his letter had said how sorry he was to see me injured so badly and hoped that I would make a rapid recovery.

So, since everyone in Cyprus was dying to meet his bride, I felt emboldened to send him a signal asking them to come ashore and join us for supper. 'I would have loved to have come,' said Diana, 'but Charles never mentioned any invitation.' I told her I doubted if he had even seen it. Probably the signals officer on *Britannia* just binned it. Also I was secretly relieved I didn't have to pay for a meal, since I was up to my ears in debt and it would be embarrassing to have my credit card thrown back at me.

Diana wanted to know why and I told her the sorry tale of how I had arrived at RAF Brize Norton just a few minutes after the designated check-in time of 6 a.m. I shared a flat in Ascot at the time with a chap called Charlie Graham and we were having a party the night before we were due to fly so we decided to leave early the next morning. But the fog was thick and we were a few minutes late. The flight wasn't even due to leave till nine but thanks, most probably, to inter-service rivalry the RAF people were sticking to the rule book so we watched them booking all the families who were behind us in the queue on to the plane. The trip was only costing them £20 a head so I offered to pay £20 for each of my chaps. They still wouldn't wear it. The matter was eventually referred to a superior officer, who gave orders that I should get everyone to Heathrow and pay for the fares out of my own pocket. It cost me £2,500 — a lot of money for an impoverished subaltern.

Diana was outraged at this and insisted she would use her influence to make sure I was reimbursed. It was a generous offer but it wasn't necessary. Some years later when I was a captain, Major-General Sir Christopher Airey, whom she had got to know well when we rode in Hyde Park, had had to close down the Free Fall team and, on learning of my expensive trip to Cyprus, insisted that I be paid back the money from the funds that were left.

Diana wanted to know more about parachuting. 'I could never do that,' she said. 'You must have very little fear.'

'On the contrary,' I told her, 'I'm petrified every time I jump.'

This intrigued her. 'So why do you do it?' she asked.

This was not something I had ever really thought through. 'To conquer my fear,' I found myself saying and I suppose this was true. You set yourself physical challenges in life in order to test yourself. As Clint Eastwood said: 'A man's got to know his limitations.'

Some of the days I spent with Diana blend into each other and others remain more clearly in the memory. But that evening — sultry but no sun — I can recall as if it was yesterday, maybe because I have thought about it so many times. I remember being aware at the time that the emotional situation we found ourselves caught up in was in many ways more terrifying than jumping out of a plane. There was no parachute to ensure a safe landing in our relationship.

But for the most part the time spent at Highgrove was carefree and happy and very loving. I got to know the staff and would go into the kitchen and chat and thank them for dinner. I realised how unsettling it was for them to have Charles and Camilla on some weekends and us on others. I'm sure they'd rather have been serving a happy, stable family.

But the Princes, on the whole, seemed to adapt to the system. We would play games with them during the day and at night, when their nanny Barbara Barnes was safely out of sight, Ken Wharfe and I and William and Harry would have tremendous pillow fights. I remember accidentally catching William full in the face with a swinging pillow one night and he burst into tears. But he soon recovered and told me not to worry. At least it wasn't a polo mallet.

One evening when Carolyn Bartholomew was there Diana came into the drawing room brandishing a video and announced: 'I've got something really interesting for you to see — a wonderful wildlife programme. It won't bore you, will it?'

'No, no,' we insisted stifling our yawns and wondering where Diana had acquired this sudden interest in wildlife. She carefully slotted it in and sat back and proudly pressed the remote control. Up on the screen came two women, large, very shapely and stark naked, who proceeded to wrestle in mud. Diana scanned our faces hoping that she had managed to shock us but we just roared with laughter. It was extremely funny. We demanded to know where she'd got hold of it but she wouldn't say and to this day I have no idea.

# 3

In London our affair continued with undiminished intensity. We would meet as frequently as we could, and Diana would telephone constantly. She would often want to know how she had looked in the papers or on television at public engagements. It wasn't vanity — well, maybe a bit — but it was the fact that she wasn't getting any feedback from anybody else. Now she had me she could cope better with the lack of support from her husband. She maintained she was never praised or even thanked for carrying out her public duties. The only communication from Charles was criticism.

We used to write to each other a lot, letters that lovers write. To make sure that mine were not opened by equerries or secretaries I would have to put my initials JLH in the bottom left-hand corner of the envelope. That was the Palace system for getting mail through. I would send her love poems, which I knew she adored. Not being a particularly gifted poet myself, I would copy out my favourites such as Elizabeth Barrett Browning's 'How do I love thee? Let me count the ways' or Shakespeare's sonnets — 'So you are to my thoughts as food to life/Or as sweet-seasoned showers are to the ground.' I remember once I sent her Shakespeare's most famous sonnet 'Shall I compare thee to a summer's day?' — and on the very day she received it she was at a school where someone recited the same poem to her. She insisted it was all part of fate — we were fated to be together.

However that might be, it was still difficult to go out in London. We had lunch at the home of Lady Carina Frost in Carlyle Square in Chelsea. She was a true friend to Diana. The Bartholomews remained stalwart friends as well, making their house available if we needed a private place. A fellow officer at Combermere, Simon Faulkner, was the only colleague who was aware of my relationship with Diana and he and his wife, Izzy, invited us to dinner at their home in Gratton Drive, Windsor, the army married quarters, and I have always been most grateful for their friendship.

Since my father left home it was my habit to go at least one weekend a month to visit my mother, Shirley, and sisters, Syra and Caroline (my twin) in Devon. They lived in a house called The Shieling, which means 'homestead' in Gaelic, in the small village of Ebford. It was there that my mother ran the Exeter and District Riding School. The house had extensive stables, there was a mobile home in the back yard where working pupils lived and an indoor riding school so that people could have their lessons whatever the weather.

Diana had already met my sisters. They had come up to London one night with my father and I had booked a private room in a restaurant. The girls got on like a house on fire. Diana had plied them with questions about our home life and I was soon to find out why. One evening, shortly afterwards, she was complaining that she had nowhere to go at the weekends when Highgrove was otherwise engaged so why didn't she come down to

Devon.

I could think of a hundred reasons why: Saturday was about the busiest day for people learning to ride and, although our relationship had stayed out of the papers, the presence of the Princess of Wales in Ebford was not likely to go uncommented on. Of course, I desperately wanted her to come, but I always knew in my heart-of-hearts that the moment we became the subject of press speculation would mark the beginning of the end of our relationship.

'What about the security?' I asked.

'Leave that to me,' she replied. I telephoned my mother to make sure it was all right and she took it in her stride. I was twenty-eight years old and other girlfriends had been to stay before. Quite often when I had been at home on previous weekends Diana had telephoned and my mother was aware that we had an involvement that went far beyond mere friendship.

Within days our house and the riding school were being checked out by people from the Royal Protection Squad. I went down early to help get things ready and my mother made the decision to cancel all classes on Saturday afternoon so there would be fewer people about.

Her visit was hardly a secret from the police, however. The Protection Squad was obliged to inform all the police areas that they would be going through on any royal journey. This was partly a matter of courtesy but, more importantly, any chief constable would want to know when a senior member of the Royal Family was on his patch. You have to have a set procedure for guarding a VIP — once you start digressing from that people don't know what's going on. So as Diana's dark green Jaguar XJS convertible drove west from London, the police back-up car from one boundary authority would hand over to the one from the next and so on, like passing the baton in a relay race.

For her first visit the two detectives who had been following in an unmarked car checked into the George and Dragon Hotel in Clyst St. Mary, the nearby village. They hardly left their rooms for two days and my mother learned — much later — that the hotelier had told people they might be a bit 'funny' as they say in those parts.

There was nobody around when her Jaguar swept up our drive on a windy Saturday afternoon. Inside the house my mother curtsied on meeting Diana, who immediately told her that there was no need to do that, but my mother always did, which I think Diana appreciated.

She was wearing a knitted sweater and blue jeans and travelling light. After insisting that she hump her own bag up to our room, she joined the family for a cup of tea. The ice had been broken at the meal in London and she was soon swapping reminiscences about schooldays with Syra and Caroline, laughing and giggling as if they were still schoolgirls.

I showed her round the stables and asked her if she felt like some exercise before dinner. She was game for anything so we saddled up a couple of horses — there was a hog-maned bay called Rusky who was ideal for her — and took off down the village lanes for the moors.

It was a treasured experience at last to have the woman I loved on the land I loved. I could sense her happiness, too. It was as if she was free again. Well, almost — I made sure we were never more than a hundred yards from the road where Ken Wharfe was following in the car. He and I always remained within radio contact.

In subsequent visits Ken Wharfe decided that there was no need for the additional protection officers at the hotel so it was just him or Allan Peters or Graham Smith who would accompany Diana down in the car and stay in the house. My mother always asked them to eat dinner with us and Ken endeared himself to the family by cooking it on more than one occasion, singing all the while. He had a beautiful tenor voice — I'm sure he could have sung professionally — and I can never eat spaghetti vongole without the sound of Ken singing 'Panis Angelicus' echoing in my mind.

Diana didn't cook but was always eager to help with clearing the table and washing up. As she became more familiar with the kitchen she would sometimes take control. On one occasion she opened a cupboard and found some little mini drums of spices that had been there for so long that the writing on the labels had faded.'Ugh. These are foul. You can't keep these!' she proclaimed, dumping them in the garbage bag. My mother was delighted — it was something she had been intending to do for years.

My abiding memory of the days Diana spent at home in Devon was of this family atmosphere, secure from the outside world. Time seemed to stand still and whatever fears the future held were put to one side. When I started to write about this I asked my mother and my sisters what memories they had.

My mother said she had been rather taken aback one Sunday when she had asked: 'Can I use your phone? I have to ring the Queen.' Diana's mobile phone frequently had difficulty picking up a signal in Devon.

At breakfast one morning my mother had given me a dressing down for taking the butter from the dish with my knife and spreading it straight on my toast. 'You should put it on the side of your plate, first.'

I protested that this was unnecessary but Diana chimed in: 'You're quite right, Mrs Hewitt.'

Later Diana had let out an accidental belch and I had apparently pronounced: 'What a turn off,' in order to get my own back.

Syra recalled trying to teach Diana to ride side-saddle on Rusky. She really wanted to be able to show the Royal Family that she could do it but there was never enough time for her to perfect it. Syra insists there was an evening when, for some challenge nobody can remember, I put my terrier, Nimble, on the table and let him remain there until I finished dinner. I don't recall that — too much wine, perhaps — but I do remember Diana coming across the cat's bowl with 'PUSSY' written on it, becoming helpless with laughter and daring me to eat out of it. Rarely being able to resist a challenge, I finished the entire cat's dinner.

Caroline has slightly more serious memories. She loved the evenings when it was warm enough for us to sit out on the terrace. We would have drinks there and sometimes supper, too. As she got to know us better Diana was never slow to speak her mind about her husband. They had lost the ability to communicate. 'He talks to the flowers instead,' she once said. Her doubts about her marriage went right back to her wedding day. One evening she told the whole table with total candour: 'As I was walking down the aisle of St Paul's on my father's arm I thought "What on earth am I doing here?"'

The extraordinary thing about Diana's weekends at Ebford was that nobody outside the family ever noticed her. Or, if they did, no word of it came back to us or got into the local papers. I think it was because nobody expected to see her there. A friend called John Martin kept a horse with us and I remember Diana was looking over the stable door admiring it when he arrived and stood virtually beside her. They said 'good morning' to each other but nothing registered.

The only person who did get noticed was one of the bodyguards who was traversing some farmland, following us at the usual discreet distance. A farmer had been watching him for some time and thought he was behaving rather suspiciously. He came up to him, threatening to call the police if the man didn't give a good explanation of what he was up to. The Royal Protection officer insisted that he was on a walking holiday and had lost his way — he managed to get away with a warning.

In the summer, when I was on leave, I brought Gary down to Devon so that Diana could ride him along the routes I had taken as a child. It was an extraordinarily nostalgic thing to do — romantic, too.

My sisters and my mother firmly endorsed our relationship — they heard from Diana's lips how much happier she was with us than in the cold confines of Kensington Palace. But my mother told me, much later, that she had always had a residual worry. She thought: 'How can there be any future in this?'

The same fear was never very far from the top of my mind. On winter weekends Diana and I would take the car and head for Budleigh Salterton. We would walk along the beach followed by my labrador, Jester and, fifty yards behind him, the obligatory bodyguard. It was atmospheric and bracing with the wind and even the rain. Diana usually wore a puffa jacket with the collar up and a baseball cap. She had perfected the art of angling her head to say 'hello' to people we passed without revealing her full face.

It was there, with no distractions other than the rolling waves, that we had our most serious discussions about what might happen in the future. Diana was always searching for happiness — who isn't? But she felt entirely trapped in the Palace system. Her back was against the wall and she couldn't see any way out. There was nobody in the Royal Family to turn to. Although she was grateful to Sarah Ferguson for taking some of the press flak that might be aimed at her, she didn't feel close to her. She thought Fergie was trying to compete too much. They had different personalities: Diana was fundamentally shy and Fergie much bolder and brasher. Unlike the public perception of it, Diana's relationship with the Queen Mother was not good.

She respected the Queen, and when matters with Charles became untenable, as I said, she went to see her and sought her help. She wanted the Queen to prevent her son from seeing Camilla. But the Queen told her that she thought it best if she did not interfere in their marriage.

Diana was absolutely certain that she herself would never be Queen of England. She didn't mind — she had no desire to be. But she did want William to be King one day and brought him up with that role in mind. To begin with she couldn't see how she and Charles would ever be divorced. Her astrologer had told her that Charles would die and she would be free and she clung to this prophesy as if it were her only hope. When Charles nearly died in the avalanche at Klosters which killed the Queen's equerry, Major Hugh Lindsay, she saw this as a sign that he was dicing with death.

She often urged me to consult the same astrologer but I didn't really believe in the occult and never went. And —

as events so tragically turned out, her astrologer could not have been more wrong. But Diana, thinking she would be a free woman one day, fantasised about being an army wife. She thought we could live together on Dartmoor and even went so far as to find in a brochure a thatched Devon longhouse that could be our home. It was on the market at half a million pounds, a sum well beyond my pocket. 'I'll buy it,' she insisted, 'and I'll put it in somebody else's name.' I pointed out that administratively this would never work.

Usually I was happy to go along with her plans for the future. I loved her and I fervently wished that there was some way that we could be permanently together. Looking back, I suppose we were both caught up in a world of make-believe but whatever it was it gave us happiness and hope.

Diana responded to my mother's hospitality by inviting her and Syra to come and stay at Highgrove. Against my advice, Syra decided to teach riding all day and then drive up in time for dinner. She became so hopelessly lost that Ken Wharfe got into his car and drove into Tetbury to look for her. Dinner had been cleared away by the time she reached the house. I was just a touch angry as I knew this might happen — she had even missed the motorway exit — but Diana soothed any possible family feud by making sure there was a glass of chilled champagne and tray of hot food ready for her when she eventually made it. Syra did succeed in coming down in time for breakfast the next morning and William and Harry put on a pretty impressive sword fight for her benefit.

Diana went out of her way to spoil my mother, who worked far too hard at the riding school. Shirley was impressed at how the vast bath that was run for her at Highgrove would be at exactly the right temperature. Diana succeeded in creating a warm family atmosphere in the house with the boys romping around in their dressing gowns and dinner on trays in the small drawing room.

If we couldn't live together, Diana became more and

more determined that we should spend weekends with each other, whatever the obstacles. One evening at Kensington Palace she was making plans to come to Devon the following Saturday when I pointed out to her that I had to stay in Windsor as I had promised to be a godfather at a christening.

'Whose christening?' she demanded.

I could sense the signs of dejection and rejection in her voice. 'Jack Faulkner,' I said, 'Simon and Izzy's son.'

Her eyes lit up. 'But I know them. I can come with you.'

I pointed out that for her to accompany me in public to a crowded church ceremony was bound to cause comment — and worse. But her mind had been working overtime. 'I know. I can be a godmother. Then I'll have every right to be there.' I thought it was going a bit far as she barely knew the couple but she insisted that she wanted to play a bigger part in my life and this was a perfect opportunity to do so.

I couldn't deny that it was a good ploy but it was with some embarrassment that I approached Simon in the mess the next day with the suggestion. However, he seemed surprisingly amenable to the idea, called Izzy and it was all agreed. So Diana was duly added to the godparents, came to Windsor for the christening and then to the lunch afterwards back at the mess. The real reason was so that we could spend the rest of the day together.

On another occasion in the summer she was expecting me at Highgrove for the weekend but my polo team had reached the final of the Captains and Subalterns Cup. 'Fine,' she said, 'I'll come and watch.'

For a normal person to come and watch a polo game there is no problem, but the Princess of Wales could only be there for a purpose. 'You can't just turn up,' I protested. 'What will people think?'

Diana knew this might create comment but she was a much more determined individual than anyone gave her credit for at the time. She asked me who was the other team in the final and when I said the 13/18th Royal Hussars she clapped her hands together in delight. 'That's one of my regiments,' she said. 'I'll get them to invite me.'

The following day she rang the commanding officer of the 13/18th and congratulated him on the success of his polo team and told him that, as Colonel of the Regiment, she would love to come to the final.

There was no way he could say 'no, don't come'. On the contrary he seemed exceptionally pleased about it and laid on a special lunch in the pavilion. The Life Guards team duly turned up with sandwiches and beer for picnics at Tidworth only to be told by a pretty proud adjutant from the 13/18th that there was a rather special guest coming — Her Royal Highness The Princess of Wales — and they rather hoped she would stay to present the cup. He just didn't want it to come as a shock to us and he knew that we were aware of the etiquette on such occasions — and on this occasion we were not asked to lunch.

It was a perfect summer's day. My mother and Caroline had come up from Devon to watch and we spread out a picnic with Giles Stibbe (now second-in-command of the regiment), Mitford Slade, Rupert Mackenzie-Hill and Milo Watson. Before we had reached the strawberries and cream we realised we had acquired two new guests: Diana and William.

'You're meant to be eating with the nobs in the pavilion,' we teased her.

'They've reached coffee,' she said, 'and I told them it would be very unfair if I didn't go across and offer some crumbs of encouragement to The Life Guards.' With that she dropped down on the rug and, giving my mother a concealed wink, grabbed a salmon sandwich and bit heartily into it.

The match ran very much in our favour but unfortunately I got hit on the upper arm by a hard-struck ball. The bruise came up like a lump in a Tom and Jerry cartoon, so I rode off to get some ice to bring it down. Prince William watched all this and came running across to me shouting 'James! James! What's happened! What's happened!' He was really concerned but I was more worried about the people round us who would see that he must know me quite well. So I walked hastily off in the other direction fussing about the ice.

Diana later explained to him that I had not meant to be unfriendly and the next time I was at Highgrove the first thing he did was to inspect the bruise. I'm pleased to say we beat her regiment quite easily that afternoon. The subsequent photograph of Diana presenting me with the Captains and Subalterns Cup is one that might have made its way into the regimental magazine, never to be seen again. As events turned out, it must have been reprinted more times than anyone could have imagined.

It was at Tidworth that I first saw Diana in the summer of 1981. Seven years later she was a far different person from the shy and tearful girl who had fled from the photographers. She was 'more lovely and more temperate' than that summer's day and, to a large extent, her confidence and self-esteem were back. I felt extremely proud of her.

Quite early in our relationship I had asked Diana if Prince Charles knew we were having an affair. She said that nothing had been said in so many words but the fact that he had Camilla and she had me was a sort of unacknowledged pact. He was always very nice and pleasant to me on the few occasions when we encountered each other — sometimes at St. James's Palace when I had gone there to visit Sir Martin Gilliatt.

Although I had been fed a lot of hatred about him by Diana, I couldn't help liking him. There are two sides to every story and I don't think she was entirely blameless in the events that led to their estrangement. I sometimes saw him at polo and he would inquire quite affably how Diana's riding was coming along. Once, when the three of us were together, I ventured to suggest that she had made such good progress that she would soon be able to join him hunting. This didn't go down too well — that was Camilla's territory.

Occasionally I saw Camilla, too. Andrew Parker Bowles was Colonel Commanding the Household Cavalry.

I would encounter him when I had to go back to Knightsbridge Barracks on business or just to see friends. Camilla would sometimes be in the mess and we would say hello. I think it was quite widely known among the officers there that she was having an affair with Charles.

We were all invited to his 40th birthday party at Buckingham Palace in 1988. Although by then they were living virtually separate lives in private, Charles encouraged Diana to invite some of her own friends so that she would be more at ease. I didn't terribly want to go on my own so I asked Diana if Simon Faulkner and Colonel James Ellery could come with me. She immediately said yes, without having to consult anyone.

So the three of us — dressed in black tie — were dropped off in the forecourt of Buckingham Palace on a brisk November evening. It was a vast affair — several hundred people — in the ballroom. Rather in the manner of a wedding there was a line-up consisting of the Queen, the Duke of Edinburgh and the Prince and Princess of Wales with whom one would shake hands before one could join the throng. I remember it was quite a long wait and I was dying for a drink but there was no way you could get one until you had met the Royals. As I paced about Simon Faulkner anxiously warned me that when I met Diana I 'shouldn't make it too obvious'. There was hardly any need for such a warning — I had managed not to make it obvious for the past two years.

We were graciously welcomed. 'Good to see you, again,' Prince Charles said as he greeted me. I had never met Diana on a formal occasion like this before and for the first time I experienced the incredible aura that just radiated from her, overpowering and almost eclipsing the presence of Charles and his parents. She had told me that one of her 'crimes' was that she got more attention than he did, most notably when they were on a visit to Australia. But there was nothing she could do about it. I took her hand and bowed.

There was an interesting mix of people in the ballroom, downing canapés and champagne. The very fact you had been invited gave you licence to talk to people without introduction and I had a very funny conversation with Barry Humphries — well, he was very funny. Prince Edward came up and said hello and we chatted with Elton John. I made no attempt to find Diana but eventually she found me. We made eye contact and she whispered 'I'm glad you came,' before continuing her round as the most in-demand person in the room.

I didn't bring Charles a present. Somehow it didn't seem appropriate. Later I gave Diana a very special gift. It was as the result of a bribe. She had never abandoned the childhood habit of biting her nails, perhaps understandably considering the stress she had been under. I promised I would give her a present of her choice if she managed to stop biting them. She agreed — and chose a pair of emerald earrings, her favourite stone. After one or two false starts — or stops — she kicked the habit and I judged her nails to be the right shape. It was an expensive bribe. The earrings cost a small fortune, and I had to sell my hunter, Another Grudon, to pay for them.

Diana was generous in her presents to me. She gave me a tie-pin with a fox's head in diamonds, a gold fob watch with the words 'I will love you always' inscribed on it. She had some cufflinks made in the shape of an owl with piercing blue eyes and, most precious of all, sent me a gold cross which bore the message 'I shall love you forever.' Sadly these are no longer mine to treasure. They were stolen from the boot of my car when I moved from Devon to London. They meant a great deal to me.

Whenever I would come to Kensington Palace I would always try to bring Diana some small gift — a box of chocolates or little trinket. She delighted in receiving them. As I mentioned, she had an enormous array of soft toys in her drawing room and bedroom. So one night I brought her a wide-eyed owl. She put it in pride of place on her bed, alongside a brown bear which was always there. Later that night I asked her who had given it to her and she said it was Barry Mannakee, her former bodyguard.

I said that it was a bit of a personal present to get from

a bodyguard. She replied very simply: 'He was my lover.' When Charles had resumed his affair with Camilla, Diana had turned to Barry. She said other members of the Royal Family had had affairs with their bodyguards and Barry had been her friend when she felt friendless. She also said that she loved him and that they took him away. He was moved to other duties so she no longer saw him. Several months passed and one day she and Charles were in an official car on their way to the airport when he said in a matter-of-fact way: 'Oh, I don't know if you've heard, but Sergeant Mannakee is dead.' Diana, now in tears herself, said that she just collapsed and Charles did nothing to comfort her.

She held on to me. 'They killed him. I'm certain they killed him.'

I asked her who 'they' were but she was too distressed to give a coherent answer. 'MI5, people in the Palace, somebody who wanted him out of the way.'

I had read about Sergeant Mannakee's death. It was as a passenger in a motorcycle accident — not an easy murder to stage, although not an impossible one. But on my drive back to Windsor that night my thoughts were not of any dangers that might befall me. I just felt hurt that she had had a lover before me. I thought I was special. But then I tried to rationalise this way of thinking as vain male pride.

However, in the years that have elapsed since then, one thing has become more and more worrying to me. I doubt if my friendship with Diana was just a happy accident. Perhaps I was set up and Mannakee was removed because it was unacceptable for the Princess of Wales to be conducting an affair with a sergeant in the Royal Protection Squad. But his departure had no beneficial effect on the marriage.

Charles continued to ignore her and see Camilla and Diana became more and more desperate, more bulimic, more of a nuisance, suicidal even. So somebody had to be found, not to become her lover but a male friend who would lift her spirits and help her confidence in the absence of a caring husband. She later told me that the drinks party at Hazel West's house had been held with the express intent of enabling her to meet me.

In retrospect it is impossible to say who either initiated or approved this idea. Buckingham Palace is a place of long corridors and quiet whispers; there are fawning factions and warring factions. From my knowledge of it and from what I learnt from Diana there was no straightforward pyramid of command as there is in the army. Hazel West would not have played the role that she did without the tacit approval of those above her. When my friendship with Diana turned into an affair obviously several people knew about it starting with Ken Wharfe and the Royal Protection Squad. They would have been failing in their duty if they had not reported it to their superior officers. How much higher than that did it go? My estimate would be 'very high'. If Prince Charles had wanted to stop Diana and me seeing each other, this would have been accomplished. But he didn't.

So the whole plan of providing a companion for the Princess nearly worked perfectly. She had an officer who was single and reasonably presentable, who would teach her to ride and keep her company.

Only one thing went wrong — we fell in love.

# 4

Unlike Diana, I was lucky enough to spend my childhood in a happy and close-knit family. I was born in Londonderry on April 30th 1958 — a full hour and three-quarters after my twin sister, Caroline. We had an elder sister, Syra, who was born in Devon 18 months earlier.

My father, John Hewitt, had been posted to Northern Ireland with the Royal Marines. He was, I have frequently been told, a well-respected and popular officer. There was a military tradition on his side of the family — his father was an admiral in the Royal Navy who sadly died before I was born. My father was a superb athlete. His speciality was the modern pentathlon and he represented his country in the 1952 Helsinki Olympic Games. This consisted of a steeplechase on an unfamiliar horse, a series of epée fencing matches, pistol shooting, a 300-metre freestyle swimming race and a 4,000-metre cross-country run. He didn't win a gold medal but he certainly set a standard for me to aim for. He later served in Korea.

My mother's father was a dental surgeon who practised in London but the family home was Devon. Shirley was not a traditional service wife, but happier in the hunting field with her horses. Indeed it was through horses that my parents met.

We three children grew up on ponies and the freedom which that gave us was marvellous. When the family returned to live in Devon, we would leave the house and spend hours on end riding in the countryside.

I was sent to a prep school in Exeter and then on to Millfield, a public school with a somewhat eccentric headmaster, Jack Mayer — or Boss Mayer, as he was known — who, despite my lack of academic prowess, thought I would fit in at the school. He recognised that I was dyslexic but he had a belief that if you could build your confidence in the sporting world it would help your academic work as well.

I liked the regime at Millfield and made good friends, especially Francis Showering who remains close today and John Ryan, now an American attorney. There was no uniform — you wore plain clothes. It was a mixed school which worked very well. You learnt to respect the opposite sex and possibly understand them a little better than people from all-boys schools — or maybe not!

I was keen on sport. I fenced and shot, ran cross-country and swam for the school — although not as well as Duncan Goodhew who went on to win a gold medal in the 1980 Moscow Olympics. I was in the polo team and show-jumping team. From the moment I arrived I used to hunt a lot and qualify all the point-to-pointers (they had to have hunted seven times in a season before they could race). I was quite small to begin with and these fit horses would occasionally take off with me which could, at times, be quite hair-raising and more than a little embarrassing when you found yourself overtaking the huntsman and his hounds.

I joined the army section of the Combined Cadet Force

but it seemed rather tame so I gave it up and did archaeology instead which meant that you could travel round Somerset to old churches and archaeological digs which fascinated me.

I made it to house prefect which permitted me to smoke a pipe — not a privilege that remains today. I was seventeen when I left and armed with seven indifferent O-levels but no prospect of a university education. This was a disappointment as I had set my heart on becoming a surgeon.

I took my Assistant Instructor's Examination so that I could help my parents in the riding school at home but I knew I needed a little more adventure. I went to the Army Careers Office in Exeter and the information I read there and the people I spoke to confirmed my feeling that a Short Service Commission could be stimulating. So I filled in the required papers.

When I told my father, he got in contact with General 'Monkey' Blacker with whom he used to compete in pentathlon. The General invited me to lunch at the Queen's Head Hotel at Aldershot and later kindly wrote to his old regiment — The 5th Royal Enniskillen Dragoon Guards — who offered me a place on the proviso that I passed Sandhurst.

I was posted to Catterick in Yorkshire to undergo basic recruit training along with 30 other potential officers who were all going to join one of the Cavalry Regiments. We were being prepared for the RCB (Regular Commissions Board) at Westbury in Wiltshire. Over a period of three days you take written papers, undergo various interviews, do leadership tests and psychological tests and if you're mad enough you join the army.

I didn't fail, but neither did I sail automatically into Sandhurst. I was sent to what is known as Rowallan Company. The purpose of this was further to develop my character. An adjutant who saw my file later told me that I had done well at the RCB but they thought I might be too easy on the soldiers under my command. Rowallan was to toughen you up — real 'outward bound' stuff: canoeing, abseiling, exercises, map-reading and various endurance tests. A lot of people give up the notion of the army after that but I found I truly enjoyed it and took up my place on the Standard Military Course at Sandhurst.

My company there was commanded by Major Tim Toyne Sewell, who was later to return as a major general and Commandant of the Royal Military Academy. He was a man of knowledge and vision and we benefited from his leadership. Once Sandhurst was a two-year course but now it was reduced to a compact seven months so it left one with very little time to do anything other than study. I reached the dizzy heights of Junior Under Officer and so lead my platoon at the pass-out parade when I graduated.

Among the friends I made at Sandhurst was Charlie Graham who was destined for a career in The Life Guards. The more I learnt about this regiment — the senior one in the British Army — the more I liked it. They traced their history back to the time when Oliver Cromwell had displaced the monarchy and a troop of eighty private gentlemen picked up their swords and raised a Guard for Charles II in exile.

I paid a visit to the regimental HQ at Horse Guards and realised that The Life Guards would give me a chance of soldiering in London, unlike the 5th Skins who would spend most of their time in Germany. Also I would be able to indulge my passion for horses much more fully, not just in regimental duties but with a prospect of hunting and possibly polo, as well.

So I went along to see the Household Cavalry representative in Sandhurst, then Major Andrew Parker Bowles of the Blues and Royals, and he arranged for me to be interviewed by senior officers within the Regiment.

The Colonel of The Life Guards was Admiral of the Fleet the Earl Mountbatten of Burma. I and another potential officer, Johnny Gorman, had to go and be interviewed by him in his flat at Kinnerton Street in Knightsbridge on February 8th 1978. Actually there wasn't a lot of interviewing. I mentioned that he and my father had played polo together in Malta and 'Col Dickie' (as he was known) talked for 45 minutes about polo and horses and his career in the navy. Tea and cakes were provided and at the end he offered us both a pink gin and said: 'Well, you seem to fit the bill.' Then he paused. 'But I'll have to clear it with Her Majesty.'

The Queen, indeed, was Colonel in Chief of the Regiment but I doubt if she was consulted about the suitability of Johnny or myself. I saw a bit of Col Dickie who used to come and support The Life Guards polo team. It consisted of Charlie Graham, Ian Forbes Cockell and myself under the captaincy of Peter Hunter and we had some good seasons, winning all the regimental competitions. I remember the sad day in August 1979 when some RMP motorcyclists descended on the ground at Cirencester and told us Lord Mountbatten had been assassinated. There were two minutes' silence in his memory and we played in black arm bands. He was an inspiration to all servicemen.

I spent time as an instructor at the Guards Depot at Pirbright, where I learned how to parachute and went on to run the Household Division Freefall Parachute Team. This was a different game from the 800-foot drops from a static line that was the basic military requirement. Here we had to freefall from 3,000 feet. I don't think I ever lost my fear. In fact it increased as the years went on — you became more aware of the number of things that could go wrong.

In 1981 I did my first two-year tour in Detmold in Germany. The Cold War was still a real threat and our Chieftan tanks would take part in massive NATO exercises. I found the work very fulfilling. I went as a lieutenant and left as a captain and second-in-command of a tank squadron.

Together with Charlie Graham and Dennis Darley who became close friends, I took advantage of our location to see as much as possible of Europe, not least the ski slopes in winter.

Dennis was Master of the Weser Vale blood-hounds and I whipped-in to him as his number two. Hunting live quarry is illegal in Germany so we indulged in what was known as 'clean boot' hunting. The human 'quarry' wears a sock for three days and then leaves it for the hounds so that they can immediately learn to recognise his scent. He then sets off through the country on a pre-designated line — there was some magnificent scenery in the region of the River Weser. Half an hour later the mounted field and the hounds literally hunt him. When they catch him no blood is shed. Despite their name, blood-hounds are fairly docile. The only risk the quarry ran was of being licked to death.

Dennis Darley was a good friend to me and I succeeded him as Master of the Weser Vale in a second tour in Germany. His father, Colonel Mark Darley, had commanded the Household Cavalry Regiment at Knightsbridge and had a reputation for being a fierce disciplinarian. Later on, when he retired, he actually came to work for my mother at our family riding school and they became very close. But there was a deeply unhappy side to that family. Dennis's brother hanged himself when he was at school and Dennis never really got over it, eventually taking his own life.

I had expected to return to Windsor after Germany but had the good fortune to be selected to go to the French Ecole Nationale d'Equitation in Saumur. They take one officer a year from the British Army. This was originally a wholly military establishment — in fact, it was still under the command of General Dumont Saint-Priest — but now had a broader sporting base although many of the instructors, the legendary *Cadre Noir*, were officers and those that weren't also wore an imposing black uniform. I was obliged to wear army uniform, too. They taught *Haute Ecole* — the only place in the world it was practised other than in Vienna — and dressage to the very highest standard while demanding proficiency in show-jumping, cross-country and other disciplines. You had four horses allocated to you so there wasn't much time for rest and relaxation.

I adored it. I rented a small sandstone house in Fontevrault in the garden of my landlady, Christine Cremer, who was half English and half French and became a lasting friend. My riding skills improved considerably and it turned out to be one of the most carefree years of my life. I met a French girl called Catherine. She was from Normandy and was taking a separate course from mine, learning to ride side-saddle as well as specialising in dressage. There were beautiful sand tracks that snaked for miles through the woods surrounding the academy and we would ride together there after tuition.

Catherine was 25 — the same age as me — tall, with short dark hair, a great sense of humour and a stunning smile. She had a sense of style quite unlike any girl I had met in England at that age. She was an excellent horsewoman and an even better cook. She would take over the kitchen of my house and cook wonderful dinners for our fellow students. Together we explored the chateaux of the Loire valley, and the wine caves and even the mushroom caves. She would drag me along to concerts in Tours and Angers. She adored contemporary classical music — something she never managed to convert me to. We would have picnics on the banks of the River Thouet where she would work on my French and dip in the icy water when the days were stifling. There was a strong spiritual side to her and she loved the abbey church of Fontevrault where Henry II and Queen Eleanor were buried along with their son, Richard the Lion-Heart, who has an imposing tomb effigy over his grave.

As the course drew to an end I was assigned to return to Combermere Barracks and Catherine was due to go back to her parents' home in Normandy. We talked about her coming over to get a job in Windsor but we both knew that life there would be nothing like the one we had enjoyed in Saumur that summer. 'Nobody can ever take this away from us,' she said when we parted. And that was it — I never saw her again.

I had arranged for some other students from Saumur to come over and see the Three Day Event at Badminton which is world-renowned among riders. I managed to find them accommodation in a local girls' school. That night I phoned home to Devon and my sister Caroline said she needed to come and see me the next day to discuss something.

I didn't press her any further. I sensed it couldn't be other than bad news and I wasn't wrong. My parents had split up and my father had left home. I had seen the strains in their marriage but nobody on the outside can really know what's happening on the inside.

I made arrangements to make sure the French students were well looked after and set off for Devon. On the way I stopped in Exeter and bought a box of silk spotted handkerchiefs which I distributed to my mother and sisters at dinner that night. They had exactly the right effect. The crying stopped and we laughed once more like we used to. It was hardly a cure-all, but a gesture that indicated we were still a family and would look after each other come hell or high water.

There was no question of me leaving the army to run the family business but at least I was moving back to Britain where I could give more moral support to my mother.

My army work over the next years was varied and stimulating: exercises from Combermere Barracks, Junior Division Staff College at Warminster and Staff Captain at Knightsbridge. Part of my job there involved choosing remounts (new horses) from the Veterinary Corps Depot at Melton Mowbray in Leicestershire. Before the cavalry moved on to tanks, Melton Mowbray was an important depot for the regiment. This was less the case now since the horses were used mainly for ceremonial occasions, but as Secretary of the Guards Saddle Club I had to look after the welfare of our grooms and horses there. And officers were still invited to hunt with the Quorn, the Cottesmore and the Belvoir — arguably three of the best packs in England. We would take the horses up there to give them a break from London and usually make sure that they were good chargers that could hunt well. I kept my own horse, Another Grudon, at Melton Mowbray and tried to hunt as often as I could.

Apart from my day-to-day duties rostering the guards

at the royal palaces, I would work closely with the Chief of Staff of the London District on State Visits when the army, the navy and the air force might all be involved as 'street liners' or in other capacities. I also helped to organise annually the Queen's Birthday Parade which was the preserve of the seven regiments in the Household Division.

When the Duchess of Windsor died in 1986, the Brigade Major was away so it fell to me to get out her file and see what the contingency plans were for her funeral. They had actually been agreed and drawn up during the Duke of Windsor's lifetime. It was to take place in St. George's Chapel in Windsor, but was low key with no procession. I was the staff officer responsible for the smooth running of the ceremony and liaising with the Lord Chamberlain's office. We rehearsed a coffin-bearing party at dawn with a weighted coffin. The Duchess was buried next to her husband at Frogmore within the grounds of Windsor Castle. The plans said there should be a Guard of Honour at the graveside but the Queen decided that this should not take place so rather fewer troops were needed than was at first imagined.

There was no shortage of ceremony, however, at the marriage of Prince Andrew and Sarah Ferguson in July of that year. I actually went on breakfast television to try to explain to Selina Scott the intricacies of the Household Division's role that day. I was a little intimidated by live TV and I'm not sure that she followed every detail, but she certainly smiled a lot. People often compared Selina to Diana and although they had similar blonde features and demure smiles, the broadcaster seemed to me outgoing and confident whereas the Diana I was getting to know was haunted by self-doubt and low esteem.

Three years later, on a hot English summer's day in Gloucestershire she had become an entirely changed woman. I had been staying at Highgrove and we had taken William and Harry to a local gymkhana in which they were competing. Diana didn't appear to have a care in the world. She was happy to mingle with the crowds and sit on the ground by the ring. I was slightly concerned about being seen with her in public but she had a devil-may-care attitude to this, pointing out there would be grooms and security men in our entourage and it was not the sort of event that would attract photographers from the national press.

She was confident and she was right. We all went for lunch that day at the home of a friend whose children were also competing. There was a large swimming pool behind a wall by the entrance to the house. Diana and I and the boys went down for a swim in the afternoon. I remember the day especially because I had grabbed the wrong swimming costume when I was packing and was obliged to wear an old one left over from school — a very brief pair used for racing which seemed to have become briefer with the years. Diana just roared and roared with laughter. For some reason she thought it was the funniest thing she'd seen. Later she posted me a pair of swimming shorts and enclosed a document which I had to sign promising never to be seen in public in my 'Millfield thong' again.

But as I looked at her as she sat at the edge of the pool in her bikini that afternoon, her skin fresh and tanned, her body in athletic shape thanks to her diet and workouts, her expression so full of joy and free of worries, I reflected that she had come a long way — *we* had come a long way — from the bulimic girl I first encountered. And I thought that if I did nothing else in my life, I had at least played my part in helping the woman I loved regain her health and happiness.

You have to cherish moments like this while you have them — you can never tell how long they will last. I knew as we horsed around with the boys in the pool that this would be the last summer we would spend together for at least two years. My Regiment was going back to Germany and I was going with them.

I was only too aware that by going to live in Germany my relationship with Diana would suffer. She needed me very much, emotionally and physically, and a voice at the end of the phone was not going to provide the level of support she had grown accustomed to. But I had little option. I was 31 and my commanding officer had given me the chance to take charge of a Sabre Squadron of more than a hundred fighting men. I wasn't hugely talented as a staff officer, I was much more suited to regimental duty and I relished the opportunity of working with the men again. After two years commanding a tank squadron in Germany, with the right tick in the box, my career could advance and I felt I might be in with a chance of commanding the Regiment one day.

But I couldn't, at that moment, bring myself to tell Diana that I was leaving and ruin a perfect day.

Before that I had volunteered for P (Parachute) Company at Aldershot which was generally known to be one of the most demanding courses in the army. It was a series of trials of stamina and endurance, the theory being that the only true test of a soldier is how he behaves when he is drained to his physical limit.

After the first two weeks there was a 'mill' in the big gym which soldiers came from all over Aldershot to attend. A temporary ring was set up and each man on the course had to take part in a boxing match. In the case of the 'Ruperts' as the officers were known, the opponent was usually the biggest regular soldier that could be found. Mine was no exception, an Irishman a full four inches taller than me and a good few stone heavier. I decided to go for him and hit him hard on the chin. It had little effect, other than to find a fist come flying back into mine. It put me flat on my back with blood pouring from my nose. It was the only time in my life I've actually seen stars. I managed to pick myself up and we scrapped viciously for the next five minutes. The contest was actually judged a draw.

'I thought you were meant to be an officer and a gentleman, sir,' the training sergeant observed afterwards, 'but I'm not so sure about the gentleman bit.'

There was an exeat that weekend. I returned to Devon and Diana came down to stay. After she had finished teasing me about my pathetic black eyes, she was very caring. She massaged my exhausted body and generally looked after me. It was a different situation for us to be in — it was at times such as this that the caring side of her nature came to the fore and I could see what made her such an irreplaceable mother.

We had temporarily stopped riding while I was away with P Company. The final phase of this was two tough weeks in the Brecon Beacons in South Wales, culminating in a stretcher race. There were quite a few Gurkhas who were serving within 5 Airborne Brigade and were taking the course. I learnt a little Gurkhali and used to help them out a bit on runs and marches. They, in turn, would put up my basher when we camped at the end of the day and cook our rations with lashings of chilli powder. This was a way of working together that seemed to me the army at its best.

When we resumed our rides in Windsor Great Park I knew I would soon have to break the news to Diana that I was going to Germany. But it wasn't necessary — she knew already.

'Why didn't you tell me?' she asked.

'I thought you would be upset,' I said.

'You were right,' she replied sharply.

She was insistent that there was no real need for me to go, making the point that the Parker Bowles were never sent abroad. This wasn't true. I said that Andrew had served in Africa. However, Diana was insistent that Camilla had remained in England and this was a subject she knew only too well.

She said that she was sure that she could speak to Sir Christopher Airey who would find a way of keeping me in England — soldiers were always being sent on special postings or assignments.

I told her that she must on no account do this. It would be an act of absolute madness. For one thing it would have the effect of making our affair public knowledge — at least in court and army circles. People may have speculated about it but if she were to make a request like that their speculation would be completely confirmed. I had to think of my career in the army. My job in Germany would be to command a Sabre Squadron. It was precisely what every cavalry major should strive for. I had no choice.

'Don't you think about me?' she demanded.

'All the time,' I said. 'You know that.'

'But not this time,' she came back. She was in a very bitter mood.

'It's only two years,' I pleaded, 'and I can get away from time to time.'

She shook her head. 'That won't work. You promised you'd always be here for me and now you've broken that promise.'

I suppose I had. We had never had a row before and I feared that all the good things that had come out of our relationship were just going to be blown away. 'I'm sorry,' I said. 'We can always talk on the phone.'

'That's not enough,' she replied. 'You know that. Don't phone me. I'll get in touch when the time is right.'

We finished our ride in almost complete silence. It was to be more than three months before I heard from her again.

# 5

My second tour of duty in West Germany was to prove very different from my first. I was now an acting major and Squadron Leader of A Squadron, one of the three tank Squadrons of The Life Guards at Athlone Barracks in Sennelager under the command of Lieutenant Colonel James Ellery.

It was familiar territory. The nearest town of Paderborn was twenty miles south of Detmold where I had been stationed ten years previously. Again we were one of the first lines of defence against any offensive action from the Soviet Bloc with the East German border less than sixty miles away.

Dressed in plain clothes, we had gone and reconnoitred territory closer to the East German border for pre-designated defensive positions if the communists were ever to go on the offensive. I had studied Russian military tactics on courses at Bovington and Warminster. Their tank drill was fairly inflexible due, not least, to a shortage of radios. But they were intimidatingly strong in terms of numbers. Regular issues of *Threat* magazine provided us with up-to-date information of the likely formations of an advance by a Russian tank division. Our plan was defence in depth. We would absorb the onslaught, slow down the advancing tanks and channel the Russians into AKAs — Armoured Killing Areas. We expected any such engagement to be very messy. It used to be felt that if ever Russia unleashed the full force of an attack, it would be NATO who would be first to employ battlefield nuclear weapons.

We knew the barracks must be an earmarked target in the event of a missile attack from the East, so we would regularly rehearse call-outs. In the middle of the night a siren would go off. You had to get into combat gear and move the tanks out of the barracks in the shortest time possible. We would assemble in a secret 'bug-out' area where the tanks could be well hidden in the woods from any attack or surveillance.

In the big NATO exercises of the late 1970s, when the Russians were seen to be a very real threat, heavy armoured vehicles, including our tanks, would head for the rendezvous areas by the shortest possible routes, going through farms, along autobahns, across cultivated fields, even into school playgrounds if necessary. But now that the threat was less immediate, we tried to operate in a manner that would cause minimal disruption to the local population.

The political situation was changing faster than any of us expected. Seemingly every day in October 1989 we would learn about mass demonstrations in East Berlin and other East German cities. The people wanted free elections and Erich Honecker, the Communist who had run East Germany for eighteen years, was ousted from office.

Like most of the rest of the world I watched the television pictures on November 9th as East and West Germans danced on the Berlin Wall. It was the most amazing time — it seemed almost unreal. The celebrations in Sennelager and Paderborn went on day and night with parties and fireworks, horn-blowing and all the locals deliriously drunk. The soldiers were confined to barracks to prevent any possible incidents but since I lived in Sennelager I was able to mix with the Germans and observe for myself.

In hindsight, the demolition of the Wall meant the demolition of the Communist Bloc as a potential enemy. For the first time in forty years East Germans were free to leave their own state and travel to the West. Their rickety Trabant cars soon became familiar sights on the streets of Paderborn and chugging along the autobahns. East German roads had so deteriorated that the drivers took new delight in the smooth highways of the West. And quite a few British officers took advantage of the absurdly low cost of the cars judging by the increasing number of Trabants in the car parks of various Officers' Messes.

But it didn't mean that the British Army of the Rhine would immediately pack up its bags and go home. To begin with we were required to be more vigilant than ever — a nation in turmoil could explode in the most unexpected way at the most unexpected time. However, it was not the time for large-scale exercises and although our work on the ranges continued as before, we deliberately lowered our public profile as an occupying military force.

The other two tank Squadrons in The Life Guards — B and C Squadrons — were part of a separate Battle Group which included two Companies of the Royal Green Jackets. In the summer of 1990 it was their turn to fly out to the British Army Training Unit at Suffield in Canada.

My Squadron continued with duties in Germany, including operating as a site guard for American nuclear weapons. We also had to look after the security of the barracks and learn new responsibilities in a rapidly changing political environment. I remember on one occasion I had to put on a field demonstration for a visiting Russian General and his party — a year previously we might have been firing shells at them rather than for them. I also remember the General's astonishment that two of my subalterns were able to converse with him in fluent Russian. We had been well prepared for the Cold War conflict.

I threw myself tirelessly into my work. I had telephoned Diana after I had settled in Germany but she had not returned my calls. I had seen her do that to other friends but ours was much more than a friendship. When eventually she did call back it was not to apologise but to reprimand me. 'You let me down,' she said. It was a phrase she repeated in subsequent calls and each time it stung. On one occasion we tried to discuss the matter rationally. She felt let down because just at the moment when she was getting stronger and was on the mend and had found someone to love, I had disappeared. I couldn't deny that. She cited Ken Wharfe as saying that she was a different person when she was with me — happier and stronger. I was her medicine and she was not yet ready to stop taking her medicine.

I suggested we could talk more frequently by phone — I reminded her that I had tried to contact her but she had failed to reply. She said she couldn't see how that could be a substitute for what we had. We both sensed that things were not as they were, yet neither of us wanted to do anything to hurt the other. I think Diana knew that I was always there for her. But at the same time I was anchored in Germany and she had new friends.

I had no serious involvements although I did have occasional girlfriends. Elizabeth, whom I had met at polo and had known for some time, came out to stay with me for a week. One morning when I was at the barracks the phone rang in my flat and she answered it.

'Who is that?' inquired the voice at the other end. As Elizabeth said who she was, it dawned on her who she was talking to.

'What the hell are you doing there?' demanded the voice. 'Get your hands off my man.'

Elizabeth was still pretty upset when I got home that evening. She knew I was friendly with Diana but had not been aware of the nature of our relationship. I apologised to her — I thought I had been granted a certain degree of freedom while I was in Germany. But secretly I was glad to discover that Diana's feelings were still running as high as my own.

Communism was crumbling in Europe but suddenly a crisis was looming in the Middle-East. Saddam Hussein accused Kuwait of bringing down the price of oil by producing much more than their OPEC quota and also accused the sheikhdom of stealing more than $2 billion of oil from the Rumaila oil field which Iraq claimed they owned.

Kuwait refused to back down and on August 2nd 1990 Iraqi troops invaded the country. The Kuwaiti Royal Family managed to escape to Saudi Arabia. Immediately the United Nations Security Council ordered Iraq to withdraw its troops. Predictably Saddam Hussein ignored them.

Very often these resolutions can prove toothless but in this instance Saddam Hussein managed to outrage world opinion by saying he would use Westerners in Iraq as human shields to inhibit any air bombing of strategic targets.

Margaret Thatcher was foremost amongst Western leaders in pledging her armed forces to remove the Iraqis from Kuwait. The world had seen the way she had reacted in the Falklands and knew she backed up her words with action. In September the Defence Secretary announced that 7th Armoured Brigade was to be sent to the Gulf. American troops were deployed in Saudi Arabia. There was almost certainly going to be a war.

Naturally we all wanted to know whether or not we would be sent. It seemed to me that The Life Guards stood quite a good chance. In the desert a tank offensive would inevitably lead the assault on entrenched enemy positions and we had a fleet of Challenger tanks in first-rate condition.

They were in too good condition, as it turned out. It is in the nature of an operation of this size that the first troops deployed should be brought up to full battle strength with the best equipment available and our tanks were requisitioned for The Royal Scots Dragoon Guards who were among the 7th Armoured Brigade.

We helped our fellow regiment in the hand-over and maintenance of the tanks in Fallingbostel, north of Hanover. Back at Athlone Barracks another set of tanks in less battleworthy condition awaited us. Every tank regiment has a Light Aid Detachment of Royal Electrical and Mechanical Engineers and they now came into their own as they led the intricate task of fitting and re-fitting the Challengers so that we could get them out on the range as soon as possible.

The intense work that was going on in the barracks was in sharp contrast to what was happening in the rest of the country. Germany was at play. At midnight on October 3rd, East and West were reunited as one nation after 45 years. There was dancing in the streets of Sennelager until dawn, and for many more dawns after that.

Our tanks were virtually ready to go out on the ranges to fire their weapons and test their accuracy, when I was summoned to see the Commanding Officer, Lieutenant Colonel James Ellery. I was half expecting him to ask me to convey his commendation to my men for the speed with which they had prepared the tanks.

There were two doors to the Commanding Officer's office, one from his adjutant's outer office and another that led straight in which was normally only used by senior visitors and Squadron Leaders. I knocked on this door and a crisp voice from within said: 'Enter.' I did so, clicking my heels in the traditional salute to the Commanding Officer and said, 'Good Morning, Colonel.'

James Ellery asked me to sit down. We were friends, having known each other for several years. We had flats near each other in Sennelager and frequently dined together in the local restaurants.

He smiled broadly. 'Congratulations, James. We've been informed that more troops are to be sent to the Gulf and it's been decided that A Squadron will go.'

I was delighted. This was the news I had been hoping

for. The rest of the details were still at an evolutionary stage but it seemed probable that as we were a tank Squadron we would be in the front of any Battle Group advance on Iraqi positions. For administrative and training purposes we would work with the 14/20th Hussars, another cavalry regiment currently in Germany. The plan was that B and C Squadrons of The Life Guards would come to the Gulf at a later date as Battle Casualty Replacements.

James Ellery confessed that he was deeply envious of the opportunity that faced me and my Squadron. He said that he wished he could come as one of my gunners or drivers just to have the chance of seeing some action in the Gulf. I knew he wasn't joking. I thanked him and left the room with his favourite piece of advice ringing in my ears: 'Fortune favours the brave.'

I felt an incredible adrenalin charge as I walked out of the Headquarters building. This was what my 15 years in the army had been about. All the exercises and training were now to be put to the test in a real battle situation. At the same time there was a slight apprehension as I thought through the reality of the situation. There was a risk of being killed, but to die in battle would be a noble death. It is something that every soldier must be prepared for from the moment he joins up.

I normally only saw my entire Squadron at the 8.10 a.m. parade when they would learn their duties for the day. In the afternoon I would dictate Daily Squadron Orders to a Squadron clerk which would then be posted on the notice board at 4.00 p.m. but the CO's news was too important to be imparted in this fashion.

So I had the Squadron Duty Corporal dash round the barracks and the tank park where people were working on the tanks in hangars with orders that the Squadron was to assemble on the drill square.

There was a tangible air of expectancy when I came out to address the Squadron. I suspect the more experienced men had a fair idea of what I was going to say. It's best to get to the point straight away on these occasions. I told them that we were going to the Gulf. There was an immediate rousing response. I said I didn't know when — it could be before Christmas — and I didn't yet know where we would fit into the Order of Battle. We were at the call of the Divisional Commander, General Rupert Smith, and we would be fighting alongside the Americans. I explained to them the reason we were going out there — to carry out a United Nations Mandate to eject a bully who had unlawfully occupied an ally's country. It was akin to the Falklands operation but this time, because it was desert warfare, tanks would be vital in dislodging the enemy. From this moment on it was our duty to make ourselves supremely fit and our tanks and other vehicles ready for war.

As we would not become part of General Smith's formation until we reached the Gulf, I drew up a new training programme myself. I had to revise Squadron tactics. In Europe, because of the terrain, it was sometimes impossible to see another tank that was 200 yards away. So the tank commanders had been operating more autonomously — although always under my overall command. In the desert in daylight we would be able to see for miles and make effective use of co-ordinated action. The important thing about a Squadron of tanks is that, where at all possible, they should be used together. The best way to bring a good weight of fire down on an enemy position is to employ all 14 tanks in a co-ordinated action.

The main armament of a Challenger tank is a 120 mm rifled bore gun. It fires a variety of different rounds. The most effective against other tanks is the armour-piercing discarding Sabot. This is a long-rod penetrator which is encased in three petals that spin away when it exits the barrel.

You don't want to be an infantryman lying in front of a tank when this happens. If you got one of these petals in the back of the head you'd certainly know about it — it could kill you. The Sabot travels through the air at something like 1300 metres per second — the optimum range is a thousand metres — and its weight and speed create a kinetic energy that will defeat most armour. With a Depleted Uranium tip, it will eviscerate most things in its path.

The other main round for the Challenger is a HESH — High Explosive Squashed Head. This is useful against 'softer-skinned' vehicles. It flies at a slower pace than the Sabot and splats like a cow pat on its target sending shock waves through the armour. This causes huge splinters to fly around the inside of the vehicle or tank rather like a dicing machine.

We trained for long periods on the ranges with live ammunition. The targets simulated those we would be likely to encounter in the Gulf. However, there has been more than one unpopular officer in the BAOR [British Army of the Rhine] — although never in my Squadron — who has had his car towed out to the ranges and used as a target. Once it has been hit by a Sabot, it is not easily recognisable.

We had an idea of the tanks and armoured cars we would be facing from pictures in manuals compiled by the Intelligence Corps. But now the British Army had managed to get their hands on a series of Russian vehicles and they were assembled on a stand by the range. It was the first time that most of us could get a close look at the T55 and T72 battle tanks and have some hands-on experience of them.

It was known that the Iraqis had used chemical weapons in their war against the Kurds, so NBC (Nuclear Biological and Chemical) training became much more comprehensive. Soldiers don't like wearing the mask and clothing — they're cumbersome and difficult to operate in. Now, with the Iraq war imminent, they sat up and paid attention to the lectures from the chemical warfare experts from Porton Down. Trying to learn the variety of nerve agents was always a complex subject but people's minds became much more focused. However, one always had to keep the matter in perspective. There's a great deal of myth attached to chemical warfare — soldiers can become fearful that every time they see a cloud, they're going to die. This is rarely the case.

A decision was made to send me to Canada to observe the manoeuvres that B and C Squadrons of The Life Guards were carrying out on the Prairies which were much closer to desert warfare than anything we could approximate in Germany.

I was due to fly from Hanover to Heathrow with our Brigade Commander in Germany, Brigadier Julian Browne. We set off in his staff car but half-way down the *autobahn* he discovered he had forgotten his passport and we had to go back for it. We made the BA flight with a few minutes to spare but some mean-spirited souls wouldn't let us on it. The Brigadier was livid. I got on the phone and chatted away to everyone I could think of — including some people in London — and somehow managed to procure two Business Class tickets on Lufthansa. Whenever I subsequently encountered Brigadier Browne he always reminded me of this coup.

We were not due to fly on to America until the following day so at Heathrow Brigadier Browne offered me a lift into town. I thanked him but I said I was travelling in the opposite direction. He asked me where I was off to and I told him I was going to stay with friends in Gloucestershire.

In fact, I was going to stay with *a* friend in Gloucestershire. Ever since Diana had caught Elizabeth on the telephone she had maintained more regular contact. She knew how much I hoped I would be sent to the Gulf and used this as a pretext to call me and ask if there was any news. When she heard I was going, she immediately became very concerned and caring, insisting that I come and stay when I could next get away from Germany.

She was waiting at the door of Highgrove to greet me, just as she always used to be. She gave her familiar school-girl grin.

'How's the war hero?'

'I haven't been yet,' I said.

It was as if nothing had changed and there had been no interruption in our affair. We went in and had a drink

— she permitted herself half a glass of champagne, I permitted myself rather more. I didn't talk about anyone else and she didn't talk about anyone else. She asked after my sisters and told me that she had been on the phone to my mother to tell her not to worry and that I would come through the Gulf safely. In fact, I knew that already. My mother had called me and told me that Diana had spoken to her. I was glad they still had a good relationship.

At dinner Diana said she would never be able to live with the thought of William or Harry ever being sent away to war. She said it wouldn't be fair to her as a mother. I pointed out that all soldiers had mothers. She was silent for a bit and then said that her sons were special because they were the only men in her life. I asked her how things were with Charles. She looked at me and I could see the pain in her eyes.

'There are times when I can't bear to be in the same room as him,' she said.

'I'm sorry.' I regretted having asked the question but I knew it was something that would have come out sooner or later. I genuinely hoped they had reached a less bitter accommodation

Later we sat by the fire and talked about days gone by. She said our happiness had got her through some of the darkest periods in her life. I told her how frequently I thought of the times that we rode together and how much I missed them. She said she had a confession to make. I braced myself.

'I hated every minute I spent sitting on a horse,' she said. 'I only did it for you.'

I laughed and so did she, and we held each other. She said that she loved me very much. I told her that I had never for one moment of one day stopped loving her and that I never would.

I had to leave early the next morning to get to RAF Brize Norton for the flight to Washington. Diana told me that when I got there I should sit for a moment at the Reflecting Pool and think of her. I promised I would try to do that.

---

'And if you don't come and see me before you go off to your war, I'll come out and shoot you myself,' were her parting words. She always had a nice line in gallows humour.

Brigadier Browne, perhaps not wanting to repeat our experience at Hanover, had arrived early for the flight. He asked me if I had had an enjoyable evening and I said that I had.

We were joined by another passenger, Brigadier Iain Mackay-Dick, whom I knew already. He was an expert on desert warfare and had actually written a book on the subject. So the flight provided me with a perfect opportunity to benefit from his expertise. He was at pains to point out how important camouflage was in the desert — there were no trees or hills where you could hide. It was wise to take the glass out of all your vehicles since any reflection would give away your position to the enemy. And he warned me to be prepared for the sheer speed of the battle. In muddy European terrain tanks often trundled around quite slowly — but on flat, hard sand you could find yourself going into action at 40 miles an hour. It was a bit like the cavalry of old.

Thanks to my two high-ranking colleagues, the three of us were allocated good seats with plenty of leg room beside one of the exits on the RAF VC 10. Both Brigadiers were excellent company, generous with their anecdotes and firmly of the opinion that next year would see a massive land war in the desert.

I had never been to Washington before and Iain Mackay-Dick offered to share a cab with me to take a look at the sights. The White House was much smaller than I expected it to be. We paid tribute to the Vietnam Veterans' Memorial with the names of the 50,000 killed ominously inscribed on it. From there we went up to the Lincoln Memorial. As we sat on the steps we could see right across the city to the Capitol.

I asked the Brigadier what the large oblong of water was that lay in front of us. He told me that it was the Reflecting Pool. I gazed down at it and my thoughts returned to the previous night.

After stopping for two vast all-American hamburgers, we went back to the airport where we parted company. I had greatly enjoyed the Brigadier's companionship. Subsequently he went on to become the Major General commanding the Household Division in London.

I boarded a domestic flight for Salt Lake City. There I changed planes for Calgary in Canada where I spent the night. After a hearty Canadian breakfast, I set out by road for the town of Medicine Hat. The name had a very Indian feel about it — from the map I could see that the next two staging posts on the road were Swift Current and Moose Jaw. It was strange to think that the previous morning I had been travelling along the winding roads of cultivated Gloucestershire. Once you come off the foothills of the Rockies, the province of Alberta seems to turn into an unbroken prairie, as flat as it is wide.

There were some familiar faces at the British Training Unit at Suffield, where there is a transit camp for troops who are going on to exercise on the prairie. People wanted to know when my Squadron would be off to the Gulf and I told them it would most probably be December.

Although I was expected, there was no vehicle for me. 'We haven't got one,' shrugged the corporal in charge of transport. So I went on the hunt and found an old 432 — a tracked vehicle with a top speed of about 30 mph downhill with a following wind. However, it was the only thing that was anywhere near suitable and that could be fitted with radios — essential if you're in an area where they're firing live ammunition. So I managed to commandeer it for my use.

Having found my transport, it transpired there was no qualified driver available. The main crew complement for a 432 is a commander and driver. I needed to be on the top of it with the hatch open, following the action with binoculars and by radio.

The only driver with an A vehicle licence in the camp was currently in jail. He had tried to go on a joyride and had made it as far as Montreal, a couple of thousand miles, before he was picked up. I went to visit him in the Guard Room. He seemed an okay chap, so I said: 'Right, I'm signing you out. You're coming with me and don't you dare run away.'

I blistered on to Giles Stibbe's Squadron and shadowed his manoeuvres.

The training at Suffield is about as close as you can get to warfare without actually being in a war. You send out a recce to discover the enemy positions. When they are pinpointed you then call down artillery fire just as you would in combat. And it's real fire, so you need to get your map references right or it could land on you. Then the Squadron and Company Commanders, while still on the move, have 30 minutes to devise a plan — a flanking movement or perhaps a head-on assault.

The attack is carried out with direct fire both from stationary positions — which tends to be more accurate — and also while moving forward. Some of the targets are painted screens with sensors attached to them which give off puffs of smoke if you make a direct hit. But the most fun are the hard targets — old tanks — you see quite a flash if you connect with one of those.

It was bitterly cold out on the prairie at that time of year, minus 20 going down to minus 40 with the wind-chill factor. The 432 became my home for a couple of weeks. In fact, it was quite comfortable — we slept in the back at night.

It was less comfortable first thing in the morning. Except in the jungle, where the scent of soap or shaving cream might give you away, it is standard discipline in the British Army that every man must wash and shave every morning. Not only is hygiene important, you need to shave in order to ensure an airtight seal on your NBC respirator. So we would heat up some water and it was a race against the ice to try to wash and shave before it froze over.

Rifleman Cooper, my driver, was true to his word and made no effort to run away. Unfortunately just before the exercise finished he caught his arm under a falling hatch and was evacuated out to an army hospital. We'd been an effective team. Cooper was an excellent cook and a good companion. I taught him how to tune the radios and a certain amount of voice procedure which he picked up very well. I haven't seen him since that day but I hope things have worked out for him.

I went immediately back to Germany when the exercise was over. Believe it or not my Squadron was completing the refurbishment of yet *another* set of tanks, the last lot having been requisitioned for despatch to the Gulf. Preparations were well advanced. The crews had been issued with gallons of paint. They taped over the sights and episcopes and whatever parts of the tank needed to remain paint-free, and then blasted the vehicles with spray guns. Previously the tanks had been painted black and green in a disruptive pattern which was appropriate for Western Europe, but now they were entirely sand-coloured for the desert.

The sense of war came closer. It was essential to bring up the basic military tank skills to a supremely high standard so that we could do virtually anything anywhere. Then things that may otherwise surprise you become less of a problem. It's second-nature soldiering that's important.

It was important that we became battle fit. I would run the six miles from my flat in Sennelager to Athlone Barracks and then embark on another run and PT with my men. By the time I had run the six miles home at the end of the day I was in good enough shape to run a marathon.

We worked hard on our AFV [Armoured Fighting Vehicle] recognition. It was vital not only to recognise Iraqi tanks but to distinguish between them and those of our allies, not always a simple task in the heat of battle. I supervised my men filling in their next-of-kin forms. The majority of them took out life insurance. People were given advice on the correct way to draw up their wills. And, something that wasn't usually practised on exercises, people were instructed on how to bury soldiers in the field.

The men were keen to go to war. One or two hadn't

been with the regiment long enough to get the ethos but they soon absorbed it from the others. There was one attached soldier — something of a barrack room lawyer — who was always questioning the validity of our enterprise, saying we were just going to bail out the oil barons. I simply had him removed.

Overall, however, it was necessary to increase the number of men to bring the Squadron up to the Orbat [Order of Battle] for an operational wartime footing. Anyone on leave or on secondment had been recalled. In peacetime a Squadron has only one captain who is second in command. In wartime there is a second captain called a Battle Captain who looks after some of the administrative duties and is equipped to take over if the first two officers are taken out — killed, injured or captured.

I went through the Orbat with the Commanding Officer and we tried to identify suitable names to fill the vacant places. I asked Colonel Ellery if I could have Rupert MacKenzie-Hill, a Life Guards captain who was currently serving with the Pathfinders in Aldershot to be my Battle Captain. Rupert was a good soldier and an excellent sportsman (we had often played on The Life Guards polo team together). More than anything, he was a fantastic chap to have on your side if you were up against it.

The Commanding Officer agreed that he could come on board and Rupert, when told, seemed only too eager to have a crack at the Iraqis. He came out to Germany as quickly as he could and was soon polishing up his tank skills.

At the end of November Margaret Thatcher — who had been a powerful voice in the need for military action in the Gulf — unexpectedly resigned, after failing to get an outright majority in the Conservative leadership election. She had always been a popular figure in the army, somebody who took difficult decisions and stood by them. John Major, her successor, continued her policy and on November 29th the UN Security Council gave an ultimatum to Saddam Hussein — get out of Kuwait by January 15th 1991 or we will drive you out. War now seemed more certain than ever.

My twin sister, Caroline, was due to be married in December to Peter Bayley, a financier who had already put his life in her hands since she had taught him to ride. I told her I doubted if I could make the wedding — all leave was on hold except for emergency situations. But then I thought I was damned if Saddam Hussein was going to keep me away and bagged a late flight to London. I had to take a bus to Exeter and a milk train on to the family home, The Sheiling. I thought it would be a nice surprise but when I got there at two in the morning the lights were out and everyone was asleep. I threw some pebbles at my sister's window but it was to no avail so I spent the night in the barn, curled up in the hay.

The wedding went splendidly — I had never seen Caroline so happy. It was great to be among friends and family. My father came home again to give the bride away. We hadn't seen each other for many months but we had spoken on the phone. He was always full of wise counsel, pointing out that not many men at the age of 32 had the opportunity that stood before me. He had brought me a present — a hand-portable Satellite Navigation System — reckoning that if it was good enough for ships at sea it would be useful for tanks in the desert.

'Take care of your men,' he said, 'and they will take care of you.'

There were several ex-military men at the wedding including an uncle-by-marriage, Colonel Archie Murray who had commanded the Black Watch in the desert in World War II. He was getting on a bit now and was quite a character. He called me over and said he had a bit of advice for me. I was all ears. 'Don't forget to take your shotguns with you,' he advised, 'you'll be able to shoot some sand grouse out there.' In fact, I followed his advice and did indeed take one with me but the sand grouse, unfortunately, were nowhere to be seen. I let the soldiers use it on the range and we managed to have some fun shooting bottles and tin cans.

The bride and groom left in true style in a splendid old

car, the first stage in exchanging the chill of an English winter for the warm beaches of Barbados. I had to be on my way, too. While people continued drinking and chatting in the marquee, I went up to my bedroom to change out of my morning coat and put my things together for the trip back to Germany.

I looked round my bedroom. Although guests used it while I was away, my mother had kept it very much as it was when I was a child with pictures of school teams and rosettes from gymkhanas on the walls. This was the last time I would be there until I got back from the Gulf. We had been warned to prepare for at least six months out there.

I picked up a picture of my mother and my sisters taken at a horse show and put it in my case. And there was an old photo inside my wardrobe door of my father in uniform, taken while he was serving in Korea. I packed that, too.

'When will you be going?' My mother was at the door.

'I've got a lift up to London this evening,' I said.

'No,' she replied. 'I mean to the Gulf.'

'That's classified,' I teased her.

'Not from mothers,' she said.

I laughed. 'They'll let us spend Christmas Day in Germany — mainly for the benefit of the married soldiers — and then my advance party leaves as soon as they can.'

'I'm glad Rupert's going with you,' she said.

'Me, too.' I agreed. I could see she was a bit distressed. 'Listen, ma, it's very unlikely we're going to have to go in,' I lied. 'It's just some damn great exercise. The Americans want to give their forces an outing. But their missiles will take out Saddam long before any ground war starts. They can bounce the things off his nose.'

She looked at me. 'J, don't forget I was the wife of a soldier. They've made plans to clear out hospital wards all over the south of England to take the casualties. I spoke to a doctor in Plymouth. His hospital's been requisitioned, too.'

I put my arms around her and planted a kiss on her

forehead. 'I wish you could see my men,' I said. 'They're the best. It'll be all right.'

In London I had only one appointment. Diana knew I was in England and insisted that she should say goodbye. Caroline had telephoned her and asked if she would like to come to the wedding but Diana had thought it might be a bit too public. She later told me she had been terribly tempted to come but she thought weddings belonged to the bride and she was aware that her presence had a tendency to unbalance things.

We met at the house of a friend. She wanted to know how we could keep in touch. I said I doubted if my mobile phone would work in the desert but the British Army had a first-rate postal system that was second to none in time of war. All she had to do was go along to a Post Office and pick up some 'Blueys' — the military term for an air mail letter. She said she couldn't possibly do that. I told her the good news was that it wouldn't stretch her bank account, there was no need to put a stamp on it.

She laughed and promised to collect as many Blueys as possible. 'I could be writing to a cousin,' she said. 'I'm sure there must be some relatives out there.'

It was a very affectionate farewell and very tearful and emotional and full of promises — some possible, some wildly impossible.

Back in Germany the final countdown had begun. Various experts from the Intelligence Corps arrived to bring us up to spec on last minute information about the Iraqis — their equipment, their modus operandi and their likely morale. They had been at war with Iran for the past eight years. It was thought they were certainly battle-hardened by that. We were told they were well-equipped, highly motivated and expertly trained — none more so than the élite Republican Guard. Several of their officers, in fact, had been at Sandhurst.

We had to brush up on the Geneva Convention and how to deal with prisoners of war. In the event of being captured you were obliged to give no more information than your name, rank and number. You were also obliged to do your best to escape — there were lectures on escape and evasion.

Brigadier James Rucker, Brigadier Royal Armoured Corps, who was pretty well in charge of anything to do with the cavalry in Germany came to see how we were getting on. He seemed satisfied and asked me if there were any problems. I told him that this was the third lot of tanks we had prepared and I wanted these to be the ones we would have in the desert. He said he couldn't make an absolute promise but he would do his best to ensure that this would happen.

Captain James Astor, who was then my second in command, oversaw the mounting of the tanks — the movement of all our vehicles by low loaders and then rail from the barracks to ships on the Kiel Canal. From there they would sail to the Gulf. It was one of James's last duties — his short service commission had come to an end. He was sad to have missed the opportunity of action. Captain Robin Tarling, who had been with me for a couple of months, would become my second in command when we got to the Gulf.

Shortly before Christmas I gave a party in the NAAFI at Athlone Barracks for the whole Squadron — eight officers and 120 men and their wives and girlfriends. There was plenty to eat and drink and a karaoke machine which seemed the ideal distraction to jolly things along.

When the time seemed right I stood up and made a short speech. I said that we were going to fight for what I thought was a just and worthwhile cause. There was no sign of Saddam backing down so we would be going in some time after January 15th. There were estimates that the war could last 6 to 8 weeks but that depended on the effectiveness of the aerial bombardment and the resources of the enemy. I thought it might be shorter but however long it was I was certain we would emerge victorious.

I thanked everyone there for their support and understanding. I promised the wives and girlfriends we would try to keep them informed of how we were doing on a day-to-day basis. And that we would be grateful for anything they might write to us or send us by way of encouragement. I told them I was very proud of the Squadron. We were all members of the same team and we would take care of each other. And I gave them my solemn promise that I would endeavour to look after everyone in my command and I would do my best to return with them all.

It was well received. There were cheers — and tears. People were very emotional. At that time nobody had any idea what the cost in human lives was going to be.

But the words of Saddam Hussein were never very far from people's thoughts. This was going to be the mother of all battles.

Diana visiting a mosque in Cairo, Egypt.

Dressed for a ceremonial occasion, in Mounted Review Order.

*Inset*: Aged five with my twin sister Caroline *(to my right)* and Syra, my elder sister.

*Top*: Polo at Windsor with Prince Charles. We met frequently on the field, both being keen players.

*Bottom:* Drinks with Diana, Prince Charles and the chairman of the Guards Polo Club.

*Top*:  A Squadron Life Guards 4 Brigade beat seven 7 Brigade for the
Golf polo Trophy – they are all 'Desert Rats'.

*Bottom*: Manoeuvres in Canada with 2 Troop.

A picture that became world-famous. Diana presents me with the Captains
and Subalterns Cup.

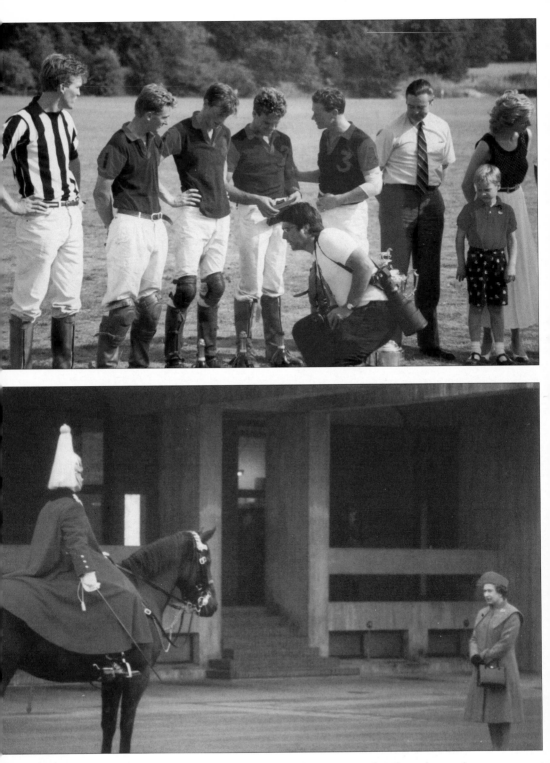

*Top*: A line-up for the photographers on the day we won the Captains and Subalterns Cup. I'm talking to Rupert Mackenzie-Hill. Milo Watson and Christopher Mitford-Slade are the other team members.

*Bottom*: A salute for the Queen on my charger, Foxhunter.

The Life Guards in action, guarding the Queen and President Banda of Malawi during a Windsor state visit. I am closest to the carriage on the right.

*Top:* Diana, Princess of Wales.

*Bottom:* Me and my crew in front of a destroyed Iraqi T55 tank.

# 6

It was arranged that I should fly to the Gulf on Boxing Day 1990 with a small advance party of officers and senior NCOs. This enabled the men who were married to spend Christmas Day with their families in Germany. Those of us who were single — about eight officers in all — went to a popular Schloss near Paderborn where we had a Christmas lunch consisting of typical German fare. I was aware that it would be quite some time before we would be able to enjoy another meal like this — it was going to be army catering and rations from now on. Not only that, Saudi Arabia was an alcohol-free zone as far as British troops were concerned so this provided an excuse — if an excuse were needed — for the wine to flow freely.

In the late afternoon we visited friends and families in the area to wish them Happy Christmas and to say goodbye. It was a very positive day. Morale was high. We felt we were about to embark on a worthwhile enterprise. I remember sleeping soundly that night.

We went by a British Caledonian flight from Hanover to Akrotiri in Cyprus. The air stewardesses were dressed in tartan, an appropriate costume since we were due ultimately to join up with The Royal Scots as part of their Battle Group. In Cyprus an RAF transport squadron was in charge of getting people out to the Gulf. There was a chap in charge with a huge badge on his upper arm with a swallow as an emblem and the motto 'Swift to Move' who managed to assemble about 200 of us on the hot tarmac — the sun was quite fierce — and kept us waiting there for what seemed like hours with the promise that a plane would be ready any moment. 'What's this "swift to move" crap, then?' said some wag at the back of the crowd.

It was the middle of the night before we reached the airport at Dharan, which is on the east coast of Saudi Arabia. We were guided into a hangar and officially processed so that those in authority knew who was in theatre. On the coach on the way to Blackadder Camp we passed an Arab airbase and for the first time, for real, I saw the awesome power of the US airforce — row upon row of giant B-52 bombers. Although it must have been about two in the morning, hundreds of people were busying around under the floodlights, and climbing over the planes like ants.

The British name for the movement of our forces in the Gulf was Operation Granby, after the Marquess of Granby who had fought with distinction in the Seven Years War. His name was apparently chosen at random by a Ministry of Defence computer.

Operation Granby was the biggest deployment of British forces since the Second World War. 45,000 men and women served under the command of Lieutenant-General Sir Peter de la Billière of whom 35,000 were ground troops under Major-General Rupert Smith. These were known as the British 1st Armoured Division and were divided into two Brigades, 7th Armoured Brigade under Brigadier Patrick Cordingley and 4th Armoured Brigade under Brigadier Christopher Hammerbeck.

4 Brigade was broken down into a series of Battle Groups of battalion strength and my Squadron would ultimately be attached to the 1st Battalion The Royal Scots under the command of Lieutenant Colonel Iain Johnstone.

Initially, however, we trained with three tank squadrons of the 14th/20th Hussars under the command of Lieutenant Colonel Mike Vickery. We made them up to a four squadron regiment which meant — strange but true — they were in a substantially better position in the desert hierarchy to be serviced and get spares. In fact, it had been suggested we should be called D Squadron but I was adamantly opposed to that so we were always known as The Life Guards Squadron.

Overall the Americans were running the show with nearly half a million armed forces in Saudi Arabia under the command of General Norman Schwarzkopf — known to the press as Stormin' Norman.

The name 'Blackadder camp' had not been chosen by computer. Its old green canvas tents made it look like something out of World War I and the troops had christened it Blackadder after Rowan Atkinson's extremely funny television character who had ended up in that war.

Blackadder was the protected base that acted as a staging post for most of the British troops. The camp had been created from scratch by bulldozing flat a sandy base, surrounding it with razor wire and putting up various makeshift structures. There was running water, Portakabin loos had been installed and the Engineers had erected field showers made from pinewood and plastic.

There was also an ingenious electricity supply. A black cable wire ran through the place and you just clipped on to it if you wanted power for a lamp or a radio. Rupert Mackenzie-Hill had been appointed war diarist for the duration and he approached his duties in a very modern manner by bringing a video camera with him. He was able to recharge the batteries by plugging them into the cable.

However ramshackle it looked, it was important that the place be kept clean and tidy — hygiene can soon deteriorate in a situation like that. There were separate

messes and accommodation for officers. The Army
Catering Corps did its best to provide familiar food —
there was always bacon and eggs for breakfast — but they
could do nothing about the UHT milk which we all found
tasteless at first but which we eventually got used to.

Our first concern was to set up facilities for the rest of
the Squadron when they arrived. At the same time I
managed to get hold of a Land Rover soon after we
arrived and Rupert and I made it our business to find out
just how the military system was working in the Gulf. It
was a curious combination of British and American
administrative personnel but they seemed to harmonise
well. We made a point of visiting all the various
headquarters and made contact with any people who
would be useful to know when we were on our own out in
the desert.

The American presence in the port of Al Jubail was
pretty impressive. They seemed very much in control of
the situation and made their own imprint on the town,
with a noticeable number of good-looking female soldiers.
The mood was very gung-ho — they fully intended to put
Saddam Hussein in his place. There were places serving
hamburgers and Coca Cola and the like. Rupert and I
stopped at a stall for a couple of hot dogs and when we
offered to pay the young woman just smiled and said: 'It's
on Uncle Sam.'

We also familiarised ourselves with the lie of the land.
I needed to find an area where we could exercise and
practise. We drove far out into the desert and logged the
co-ordinates of suitable locations on our maps. My troops
arrived all in one piece but my tanks didn't. They had
been held up somewhere between the Kiel Canal and the
Suez Canal. It was impossible to get an accurate estimate
as to when they would arrive.

The situation looked grim. I could think of nothing
worse than the ground war starting and The Life Guards
not being part of the action because we had no tanks.

On my travels I had come across more than twenty
'ghost' tanks in a dust bowl in the desert. They had been

so stripped down for spares, and with no armaments looked like carcasses. But I was also aware from trips to the docks that there had been substantial new shipments of spares from Vickers, the company that makes the Challenger tanks. So I spoke to Colonel Mike Vickery of the 14th/20th, who was my commanding officer at this stage, and told him my men were well-practised at assembling tanks and that I would rather start work on the 'dust bowl' tanks than wait for our own to arrive. He was happy for me to go ahead.

I instituted a shift system so that the tanks would be worked on 24 hours a day. The dust bowl was about four miles from Blackadder and as the coach brought back one batch of men to camp for a shower and a sleep, another batch would go out to continue work. Vickers were marvellous — spares were coming in as they never had before. The engine packs were supplied by British Leyland. These were multi-fuel although we ran the tanks on diesel which is less powerful than petrol but a lot safer if you're hit.

Each commander has to do a CFT (Commander's Functional Test) on each tank to decide when it was battleworthy. It's essential to check things like the oil levels and establish that the episcopes (the mirror sights) aren't moving. With the threat of chemical warfare from the Iraqis still very probable, it was imperative that the tanks were 'hermetically' sealed with proper rubber fittings around all the orifices so that the fan in the NBC (Nuclear, Biological and Chemical) pack could provide a higher air pressure inside the tank than outside. We achieved overpressure in all the tanks, meaning we could unmask and fight without the need to wear respirators, which can be very restricting.

I reported to Colonel Vickery when the tanks were battle ready and we went out to Devil Dog Dragoon Range, which had been set up just north of Al Jubail by gunnery staff from Germany, to test out our armaments. It was essential to bore-sight and ensure the guns were firing accurately. You had to achieve a certain amount of rounds through a hole at 1,000 metres. There was an assessment of speed of acquisition of targets — they pop up and you are timed on how quickly you pick them up and destroy them. Finally you do a battle run, which combines all the skills with fire and movement. Every armoured squadron went through the range and we managed to get one of the highest scores, even with our rebuilt battle casualty replacement tanks. I couldn't have hoped for better confirmation of the talents of my soldiers.

Although I attended regular briefings with Colonel Vickery we were fairly autonomous. We trained and lived on our own in the desert, although always in radio contact with the 14th/20th HQ which itself would move position every so often. All our radio traffic was recorded so when the time came to move west and position ourselves for the assault on Iraq, our radio conversations from the east would be continually rebroadcast to give the listening Iraqis the impression that the attack would come from there. It was a deception that was to prove effective.

The desert was frequently sunny but initially, in January, not that hot. There was a cooling wind most of the time and the nights were quite cold. Some days there would be dense fogs and these gave us ample opportunity to practise our navigation. A magnetic compass does not give an accurate reading inside a tank (you have to factor in so many variables) so the commander has to get out and walk about twenty metres from the tank, otherwise it would affect the magnetic pull of the compass. This was hardly practical in the middle of combat. We also practised navigation by a sun compass during the day and the stars by night.

The ship's navigation system my father had given me in England proved useful in giving read-outs in longitude and latitude but now we had been issued with four American Magellan Satellite Navigation Systems (SATNAVs). These are common technology today but in 1991 they were brand new. You just punched in the co-ordinates of where you wanted to go and you could get there without the aid of a map. However, when the satellites were on the wrong side of the world they proved ineffective and we had to revert to basic navigational skills.

We found the fastest and most efficient way to traverse the terrain — it was scruffy, hardened sand desert not mountainous Beau Geste stuff — was in twin lines of seven tanks each. I would be at the front of one and would usually navigate thanks to my SATNAV, and Robin Tarling would lead the other — these were the two Headquarters tanks. In case of trouble there was a step-up system. If I was killed or taken out by injury, Robin would take command and Rupert would take his job, and if both of us were taken out Rupert would become Squadron Leader. So both men needed to practise doing my job.

In all, our Squadron comprised more than 40 vehicles. There were fourteen tanks followed by Rupert's 432 (sometimes he would go ahead and navigate), two ambulances, a Land Rover, two Ferrets (one for the liaison officer Captain Toby Masterston and the other for the Squadron Corporal Major), two Armoured Recovery Vehicles, four other tracked vehicles and four four-tonners for the Light Aid Detachment, and last and extremely important the Squadron Quartermaster Corporal — Corporal Major Ormiston, a good-hearted Geordie — who had about eight vehicles for stores, rations, fuel and the like.

I attended an O (Orders) Group in the second week of January where we were told that the Prime Minister, John Major, was coming out to visit the British forces. I was given the co-ordinates of where to be and when for the rendezvous. It was to be a pretty spectacular assembly with most of 4 Brigade massed to impress on the PM the physical size of the ground forces and we were allocated specific 'parking slots' for our vehicles.

Actually getting there proved to be a valuable training exercise. We had set out in the early hours of the morning, there was a dense fog and, for much of the time, a sand storm. We travelled with just the tanks and the Fitter Section. Visibility was down to a few metres and those vehicles without SATNAVs had great difficulty navigating. We were in radio contact but they became very disorientated. So when I came to a recognisable landmark, a sand hill with a small hut on it, I ordered the other leading tanks to stop and for all of us to rev our engines as loudly as we could. This gave the vehicles that were lost a beacon of sound on which they could converge. It worked very well.

When dawn broke another pitfall lay in store. I hit the edge of a Sabbqua. This is a large lake of soft sand of indeterminate size and depth. I'd been in one before. It was crossable in a 54-ton tank but on that occasion the hull had completely sunk into the sand, leaving just the barrel and the turret sticking out. Before the various squadrons became more familiar with the landscape, quite a lot of tanks were completely submerged in Sabbquas in training and had to be dragged out. It was threatened that commanders would be relieved of their command if they lost their tanks in one of these but I don't think this penalty was ever imposed.

It was possible but very time consuming to look for a way around and we were behind schedule. I ordered the tanks to go into a 14 line astern, took a deep breath and moved forward. We were quite close to the rendezvous and I had visions of John Major circling in his helicopter and seeing 14 Challenger tanks stuck in a mammoth sandpit. At least we would make a memorable impression on him.

But we made it through unscathed and hit our parking slots on time. All except Corporal Major Nicholson who pursued an independent route through the Sabbqua and whose tank got stuck in a soft spot. He missed Mr Major's speech and so he later wrote him a letter saying how sorry he was not to have heard it, informing the Prime Minister that if he'd only looked over his left shoulder he would have seen him and his men in their stranded tank.

This sort of gesture was characteristic of the witty spirit of my men and it was equally characteristic of the Prime Minister that he later sent a hand-written letter to Corporal Major Nicholson saying how sorry he was he had been so uncomfortably detained and wishing him all the best.

---

Iraqi troops were dug in all along Saudi Arabia's northern border with Kuwait in the east by the Gulf and further to the west along Iraq's own border with Saudi Arabia. I knew it would be some weeks before we would 'go in', so it was important to establish a disciplined routine in the desert. While we were exercising in the afternoon, I would send the Squadron Corporal Major ahead to recce a new position for us to move to that night. He would radio back the co-ordinates. Ideally it would be in a dip where the ground would offer a certain amount of protection and ensure we did not stand out in the landscape.

We had pretty good intelligence that the nearest Iraqi armour was well dug in, so the most likely form of attack would be by missile or possibly small groups of lightly armed men. This led to the formation of the Squadron Hide being a square with four groups of three tanks forming triangles at each corner and Headquarters being a rectangle of vehicles in the middle. People would sleep within the camouflaged triangles and the box so no one was exposed to the outside.

Sentries were stationed in trenches on the perimeters. Inside we would put up bivouacs. A tent with a straight back goes up against the bazooka plates of the tank, a ground sheet is laid and people sleep in sleeping bags. When the Scud missile attacks started coming from the Iraqis we would be warned by radio. Everyone would have to wake up and get dressed in their NBC clothing and respirators. Early on this happened three times in one night and periodically thereafter. It seemed to me illogical that we should wake and put on our NBC suits every time a Scud was launched. The men had been working hard, day and night. I thought that sleep should be a priority. So I called the officers together and said that I thought that any Scuds would be aimed at Al Jubail or one of the bigger conurbations, not at some lone tank squadron in the desert. So I took the decision that we would ignore Scud alerts unless we had very good reason to think we had been singled out as a target. Happily no Scuds hit us.

---

But we were in a position whereby we could get into the vehicles without exposing ourselves to the outside of the box in the event of an attack from the ground or from missiles. The traditional time for an attack is in the half hour before sun up or sun down. This period is known as Stand-To in the army and I made sure that every soldier was in position then. It's very easy to become disorientated in the desert and this gave each day a regular programme and kept people on their toes.

Every few days Squadron Quartermaster Corporal (SQMC) Ormiston would be despatched back to Blackadder or Headquarters for supplies. Robin would ask me when I wanted a 'Replen' and the SQMC would set up his vehicles. He would radio his co-ordinates and the direction from which we should approach and the tanks and other vehicles would go through the Rendezvous in a straight line, picking up from the Quartermaster's Bedford 4 tonners fuel, ammunition, rations, including water, and miscellaneous things like special oils or lubricants for the guns, or boots and extra clothing.

Sometimes mail would be distributed in this fashion. On other occasions the SQMC would bring it by special delivery and ask if it was a good time to distribute it to the men in the Squadron Hide. It is impossible to overestimate the effect that letters from home had on morale. However harmonious we were as a Squadron — and we got on very well — letters from friends, family and loved ones would lift our spirits and, at a time when everyone was experiencing doubts and fears, would give people renewed faith in the day when the war would be over and they could go home again.

A few soldiers didn't get any letters, or very few, and I made sure that our allocation of letters that had been written by a member of the public to 'A Soldier in the Desert' would go to them. They could be just as effective. There was a huge amount of support, urged on by the media. Women's Institutes and Wives' Clubs would send food parcels and these were distributed amongst the men.

Rupert said to me that nearly everyone whom he'd

ever met in his life seemed to write to him in the Gulf, such was the atmosphere of the time. It was created, in part, by the fear that some of us weren't going to come back.

My father wrote me letters of enormous affection and wisdom and comfort. His generation are not the sort who show great emotion face-to-face — certainly that was the case with him — but he had fought in Korea and knew what was passing through my mind as we waited for battle and his words often moved me to tears. My mother and my sisters wrote with love and concern and there were a surprising number of letters from old friends and old girlfriends. Many of them asked if there was anything I needed but Francis Showering, who had been at school with me, didn't need to ask and despatched a well-disguised square parcel from Fortnum and Mason containing a bottle of Jameson's Irish Whiskey encased in polystyrene. That tended to make me very popular at coffee breaks when people welcomed a drop.

In the early days of exercise, the driver of my Land Rover, Trooper Doyle, would set up the Squadron Leader's tent for me directly behind my tank. It was useful to have a place with some privacy if I needed to write orders or get officers in to talk about things. It was also the place where I usually read and wrote letters. True to her word Diana had managed to lay her hands on a supply of 'blueys' and wrote regularly to me. It was quite amazing, really. Sometimes she would write as many as three times in the same day. In all she must have sent me more than 120 letters when I was in the Gulf. Many of these I sent home in packages to my mother. Sadly others, like some very moving ones from my father that I wish I could read again, I had to burn with the rest of my identifying documents on the eve of the attack.

Diana had contacted my mother to find the address to send letters to. It was quite easy:

Major James Hewitt,
Life Guards Squadron,
(14/20 + 1),

O.P. Granby,
B.F.P.O. 648.

Less easy was the sender's name and address which
you were required to write on the back of a British Forces
Aerogramme. To put 'HRH The Princess of Wales,
Kensington Palace, London W8' might have attracted
attention, even among the tens of thousands of blueys
coming out to the Gulf and certainly with SQMC Ormiston
when her letters were arriving in batches that sometimes
accumulated into double figures. So she put the name of
her dresser, Evelyn Dagley, on the back and used what I
presume was her home address in Rugby, Warwickshire.
The fact that all of E. Dagley's mail was posted in
Kensington or Paddington was probably too small a
discrepancy to cause comment. I never met Evelyn,
although I heard Diana speak fondly of her, and I am
grateful to her for lending her name to ensure privacy.

Diana always liked to borrow names. Whenever she
would ring me at the Officers' Mess, especially at
Combermere Barracks in Windsor, she would put on her
'harlot's voice' as she called it and ask for Major Hewitt.
When the NCO who answered the phone inquired who
wanted to speak to him she would say: 'It's Tracey.' So the
poor man had to interrupt me in front of my fellow officers
and say: 'There's a Tracey on the phone who insists she
must speak to you, sir.' I did get a few old-fashioned looks
from some of the more stuffy members of the mess.

Her preferred name for the letters to the Gulf was Julia
or, sometimes, just J. And beside it she would draw a small
smiling face, very much her trade-mark. I don't know why
but those little faces always made me smile, they were so
innocent and almost childish and entirely Diana.

The letters were written with discretion, with Prince
Charles referred to as C — things seemed to have reached
an all-time low in their marriage — and the Princes
usually referred to as 'the youngest son' and 'the eldest',
although she would often forget this and talk about Harry.
But it wouldn't have taken a Sherlock Holmes to work out

who the author was — not many 'Julias' spend their lives performing official engagements or worrying about the effect they have when a bunch of naval officers go weak-kneed on meeting them, nor do they have to wear black in mourning for the King of Norway.

Diana had a real gift as a letter-writer. Her approach was direct and cheerful and cheeky when she felt like it but she could make mundane things like being in bed with a cold an event. This was as a result of a night out at a charity musical — 'you'd have laughed as the audience sat in 10 degrees below as the air conditioner was on and we froze to death and all that could be heard from the front row was the chatter of teeth, even Ken [Wharfe] was in pain.'

Ken would go with her and sometimes the boys as well to visit my mother — 'your Mamma' as Diana always referred to her — and Syra and Caroline in Devon, literally to compare notes and letters. Diana would make a point of taking some orange vodka — she had done so the first time she came to stay and it remained a sort of symbolic offering. The fact that she was so close to my family meant a great deal to me.

She could make something as mundane as a trip to the movies into an amusing moment. She wrote once that she had taken William and Harry to see *Three Men and a Little Lady* at the Odeon Kensington and they had been practically the only people there apart from the obligatory members of the Royal Protection Squad whom she described as sitting around looking like child-molesters.

She wasn't afraid to commit her emotions to paper. 'God the worry is simply dreadful bordering on agony for you all,' she wrote in an early letter. 'I do hope that you're home soon — dream on, I suppose. I think of you constantly and I've got the youngest son doing the same now and every tank on the news contains you as far as he's concerned!'

And as important as the contents of her letters was the 'Dearest James' at the beginning and the way she would sign herself off, often boosting my confidence by telling me how my men were fortunate to have me as their leader followed by an impassioned farewell: 'All my love and thoughts and prayers. Julia.' This was followed by a string of kisses and that little smiling face that would stay in my mind's eye until I fell asleep that night.

Some of Diana's letters have obtained a notoriety because they were stolen from my safe in 1998 — as I shall relate later in the book — but I truly think it is a tribute to her to present just a flavour of them in the context in which they were written. It was a remarkable correspondence which revealed her concern not just about me but for all of those serving in the Gulf which revealed the true heart of Princess Diana at a time when many around her were trying to paint her in an unflattering light. The letters from my family and the letters from Diana fortified me in the dark days when I and my men had no idea what our fate might be.

It was actually quite difficult to find things to write back about. There are only so many ways that you can describe sand and I must have used more than enough since Diana, at one stage, wrote back 'bet you'll never go on a beach holiday again' and threatened to send me a bucket and spade so I could make a sand castle. She observed that I would have had lots of practice looking at Windsor Castle when I was at Combermere Barracks. With no scenery to describe, and writing about the grid co-ordinates of our position being a little less than fascinating, I would tend to tell her about the men in the Squadron.

She already knew Lieutenant James Gaselee, one of my troop leaders, since he was Prince Charles's godson. His father, Nick, was one of Prince Charles's race horse trainers and James certainly got one bluey from the Prince, wishing him luck and safety.

The three most important men in Diana's life, she used to say, were William, Harry and me. So I told her about the three men who shared every waking moment with me and, when we got closer to combat and dispensed with my Squadron Leader's tent, every sleeping moment — such as they were.

An enduring sense of comradeship regardless of rank

grows up between the four occupants of a tank, much heightened in time of war. For weeks on end you live together in a small confined space with the unspoken knowledge that if you take a direct hit in the wrong place you will most probably die together.

Trooper Stafford, my driver, hadn't been in a huge amount of time and was barely out of his teens. He was shortish, a Northerner, very keen on rugger and a hard-working grafter. Tanks require continual maintenance and Stafford would assiduously do interior and exterior checks at every stop, especially oil levels and hub caps. At the end of the day the driver has to carry out dedicated maintenance to make sure the tank will get up and go in the morning. Stafford never let us down in that respect.

The commander's closest relationship is with his gunner and I had worked with Corporal Bebbington since I had taken command of the Squadron. He was in his early twenties, an articulate and educated man who made a point of studying the Koran while we were in Saudi Arabia. He loved his gun, he was always tinkering with it. I couldn't get him to leave it alone. But he was consistently accurate. The gunner sits in a seat directly below the tank commander. In periods of quiet, when we were waiting for movement orders, Bebbington and I would join up a couple of Nintendos and play tennis on them. It was a good way of sharpening up our reactions.

Corporal of Horse Roberts — known to us all as Robbo — doubled up as radio operator and loader. He was a family man, the same age as me — 32 — and good to have in the team. In Germany he used to be slightly out of condition but he put his mind to it and became very fit, actually winning the regimental cross-country on several occasions. Robbo was a signals instructor who could have built his own radio if he was called on. He was also greased lightning when it came to loading.

I told Diana there was always a debate as to who should make the coffee and do the cooking in the tank. So I arranged a coffee-making competition in which I came a miserable — and deliberate — last. Thus I was let off coffee-making for the rest of the campaign, although I did provide some coffee that was better than the army stuff (not least thanks to a food parcel from her).

Robbo won the coffee competition and also the cooking one. Although there was a small boiling vessel in the tank, we tried to eat outside where possible and we had an old-style petrol cooker which he actually managed to master. He would mix in curry powder to enhance the flavour of corned beef hash. One of the advantages of being in a tank is that you carry around a supply of eggs and other rations — an infanteer can't do that as they would smash — so we would sometimes have bacon and eggs and fried bread. Delicious!

Diana had met Rupert Mackenzie-Hill at polo when she had presented me with the Captain and Subalterns Cup at Tidworth and Rupert had been on the winning team. I told her how important to me it was to have Rupert with me. He was absolutely fearless — he had been on target to join the SAS before I asked for him as Battle Captain — and our friendship firmed very strongly in the Gulf.

Rupert had used his video camera not just to record our life in the Gulf but for the soldiers to send messages back to wives and girlfriends in Germany. It was in many ways worse for them — there were a lot of press scares about high casualties. So we didn't want it to be too solemn a tape but to show them we were confident and in good heart. Corporal of Horse Camp donned some green lycra leggings — goodness knows where he found them — and ran round the Squadron Hide in the manner of Anneka Rice in television's *Treasure Hunt*.

'Now let's see who's behind this camouflage net,' he would say, 'is it Corporal of Horse Godson or is it Corporal Major Ormiston?'

The messages, however, were usually moving. It didn't take many words. One man just said to his wife: 'It can't be long. I love you. We're fine out here.' Another, talking to his daughter, said: 'Be a good girl for Mummy. I know you will. If I don't come back, look after Mum.' Things like that.

Diana wanted to see the tape but I told her she would have to go and visit the families in Paderborn to do that, and this she managed to do. She was desperately keen to come out to the Gulf to 'do her bit' as she called it. But the 'grey suits' in the Palace were having none of that. She did, however, manage to get hold of a video of the Prime Minister's visit and wrote to me: 'There is a very brief glimpse of one Major! so great excitement. You look horribly pale but we can get over that!'

On January 17th 1991 at 3.00 a.m. Saudi time the aerial bombardment began. Diana said she watched television all that night. 'My mind constantly wanders off to where you are and what you're thinking,' she wrote the next day. 'I know you're on the move — Kate Adie told us!'

Diana was terribly moved by John Major's address to the nation that night and sent him a letter saying so. Two days later she told me: 'John Major wrote me the loveliest of letters in reply to mine — I was so touched that he made time to do that.'

# 7

I doubted if Kate Adie was actually referring to us, but we *were* on the move again. Now the air war had begun it could be a matter of days rather than weeks before the land war followed. Much of the initial battle would probably be fought at night where we believed we had superiority over the Iraqis. The most significant advance in my fifteen years in tanks was the introduction of TOGS (Thermal Observation and Gunnery Sight) which meant we could operate much more efficiently at night. Everything out there emits a heat signal and shapes and figures can be seen on a small computerised television screen. In addition, the commander inputs details such as ambient temperature, wind direction and air pressure into his Improved Fire Control System (IFCS) which increases the probability of a first-round hit.

It became a co-ordinated action. Both the gunner and I had separate sights. When there was a dot on my sight on the target, I released my switch which up until then had been overriding the gunner's. He could then take over the movement of the turret and the gun, which was actually still moving because the loader was ramming the bag charge and chosen round into it. When the breach is shut and the gun is stable he shouts 'Loaded'. The gunner then shouts 'Lasing' as he presses the laser switch. The laser beam hits the target and instantaneously a figure will appear on the crystal screen of the commander's Range Read Out. Now the commander has to think fast. Is it a reliable figure? Or did the beam hit some battlefield debris or dust or smoke? Should he release?

If he's happy with a read-out of, say, 900 metres he will respond: '900. Fire.' The gunner is already at work on the hand controls. He finelays the gun sight on the target and when he's about to fire shouts 'Firing Now' to let people know there's going to be a big bang in the tank. You quickly learn to go with the movement of the tank as it recoils in case you smash your forehead into the sights or some other part. Not surprisingly, a lot of people who have served in tanks have a bit of a problem with their hearing.

We practised these manoeuvres night after night until the use of TOGS and all the equipment became second nature to the tank commanders. We also had to prepare for the eventuality of the enemy attacking our tanks from much closer. The commander has a General Purpose Machine Gun (GPMG) which is mounted on the turret and can be operated from inside — not that easily with its small hand controls. Although it wasn't particularly accurate, it could come in very useful if people started clambering on your vehicle. Everybody had a personal weapon — I had a 9mm pistol which I kept in a holster in my belt for close-quarter fighting.

We did PT in the mornings and, after necessary maintenance, would set out across the desert, polishing our navigation and tactics. One day, to give the men a break of sorts, we went right across to the Gulf coast. We managed to relax there a bit. Some men swam in the murky waters. There was a rumour that it might be polluted with zinc but none of them were any the worse. We set up a small range of cans and bottles in the afternoon to fire our GPMGs and do all the small arms testing. I even gave my shotgun an airing.

We would come across Americans as we moved about the desert. They were warm and optimistic. A friend of mine who was a vet had the job of testing the water at artesian wells. I remember a big one that was pumping gallons out and the Americans had filled a huge black rubber swimming pool so that we could all fill up with drinking water.

One evening I came upon what amounted to an American fort from which they directed the Patriot missiles. It was an encampment full of trucks and trailers. They had clearly used bulldozers to create a fifteen-foot sand berm (the local term for barrier) around it, with well-fortified wire entanglements. The only entry was through the manned gate. I went in and introduced myself. I was immediately given a cup of excellent coffee and a guided tour. There were several female officers all of whom seemed to be computer buffs. One of them pointed to a screen littered with flashing images. 'See all these blue dots, James,' she said, 'every blue dot here is a friendly aircraft. But this red one — he's not so friendly.'

I figured that if these Americans couldn't defend themselves against incoming Scuds nobody could so we leaguered (camped) near there for several nights. This had the added attraction of being able to go across for a shower in the mornings. When we had to move on we exchanged presents, giving them regimental berets and shirts and a pair of wings and receiving some very useful green desert parkas in return.

I wrote to Diana about this and the way the Americans have of making you feel you're an instant friend after just a short acquaintance. I also told her about how one of the padres — a man of my own rank — had asked if he could talk something over with me. I said 'sure'. He asked me if I thought there would be a ground battle and I said I was fairly sure there would be. He said he didn't think he could believe in God any more if this happened. He was agitated and frightened and seemed convinced he was going to die. We talked. I told him we were part of the best-prepared army ever assembled and if God was on any side it would be ours. I think our conversation helped him a bit — he said it did.

Diana's faith remained resolute. 'I forgot to mention in my last letter [sent the same day] that I lit a candle for you in church this morning. Thought you'd like to know.' She had become in her own words 'an expert on this war. I watch all the military briefings on the box and probably know more than maybe our boys out with you. Does someone keep you informed or is it the World Service that does that? Saddam H is looking v. drained and exhausted on our news, which brings hope to us this end.' As well as boosting morale, she usually had a bit of entertaining trivia. 'Kate Adie lost her pearl earring in the sand and, believe it or not, that gem (pl. note the pun!) was in print in the newspapers.' She had sent me a parcel with some coffee and good batteries (the army ones had very short lives) but more precious than these were her words — 'I miss you something rotten.'

At the end of January there was a full-scale rehearsal for the ground invasion of Iraq. The idea was to create a 'Breach' in Iraqi lines, first by pounding it with artillery and then sending in the armoured bulldozers of the American 1st Mechanized Infantry Division, familiarly known as 'The Big Red One' which would clear the minefield. American cavalry would go through first but then our tanks and those of the 14th/20th would lead the infantry of 4 Brigade. We would punch due north into Iraq and then each Battle Group would swing to the east in turn for the fight through the positions of Iraq's 12 Armoured Division, the main counter-attack in the area, then be prepared to head north to destroy the Republican Guard.

As we approached the Breach it was an impressive sight looking back — an entire Brigade stretched out in a huge line that stretched back over the horizon. Because nobody could calculate the exact timing of an operation like this it was decided not to give us the grid references of our 'Drop-off' points since they would undoubtedly vary. So it was the responsibility of the American Special Rangers to guide us to this initial location. It was getting dark as we went through the Breach. I was in the leading tank and I could see we were in the right designated channel with a recovery vehicle in the centre of the Breach for pulling out any tanks that got stuck. We linked up with our American guides in a HumVee, a strange squashed little reconnaissance vehicle, and duly followed them.

About half an hour after we had exited the Breach I got an uneasy feeling. It seemed to me that we were going too far east. Also our guides had stopped a couple of times and I wondered if they were quite sure where they were going. The minutes were creeping on and we were getting close to the time of our final Rendezvous (RV). We had no radio contact with the HumVee so I said to Stafford: 'Just put your foot down and catch up with them.' At first they thought it was a race but then they allowed us to come up level.

We both stopped. I opened the hatch and jumped out of my tank and four black guys emerged from the HumVee.

They were very friendly. 'Gee, it's good to see you, sir,' the sergeant said.

It was clear he was in charge. 'Where exactly are we going?' I asked.

'I'm not rightly sure, sir,' he replied. My heart sank. 'We're meant to be following an Asmath,' he went on. 'I think you call it a bearing.'

This seemed more promising. 'Fine,' I said. 'What's the bearing?'

He pointed to a light in the distance that flickered intermittently. Goodness knows what it was, it could even have been a star. Almost at once it disappeared completely.

It seemed to me there was no point in bothering with the Drop-off point. We would head straight for the RV for which I had co-ordinates. I was determined we would get there in time.

I told the sergeant what I intended to do and that he could follow us if he wanted. I got back in the tank and got on to the radio to the rest of the Squadron. 'There's been a slight confusion here. Follow me. Make the best speed. Out.'

We had to track back through various people who were being correctly guided. It was like driving your car across an eight-lane highway.

A senior officer came on the air and wanted to know what had happened to our guides. 'I caught them up and I'm afraid they were geographically embarrassed,' I replied.

'What's your situation, then?' he demanded.

'Have you ever been up a creek without a paddle?' I asked.

The banter was a way of relieving tension but I was determined to reach the RV on time. An American colonel, who was listening, came on the air and insisted we go back and do it again.

'It's your responsibility,' I responded. 'It's your chaps. You sort them out.'

The complaints continued but I was determined to make our RV and we did just about on time. I feared I was in for some trouble but my Battle Group Commander, Colonel Iain Johnstone, stood by me and said I was absolutely in the right.

That apart, the rehearsal went well but I was very aware that as a single Squadron we seemed too frequently to be in last place in people's priorities compared to the regiments. SQMC Geordie Ormiston noticed it, too. He was having a hard time, any spares were going to the 14th/20th. Much of what he demanded just wasn't happening and when he got things it was after everybody else had got theirs.

This was even true when we started to have injections against possible biological agents. I nearly managed to get a Life Guards medical officer Lieutenant Colonel Charlie Goodson Wickes (later MP for Wimbledon) forward to my ambulance. He was more than willing. He wanted to be at the front and managed to get to see me. But when the head of medical services heard he was there, he was recalled to some hospital.

Matters came to a head during a running replenishment at Battle Group level with The Royal Scots. Not only were we the last to go through but when we reached the fuel tanks they had run out. All their Warriors were topped up to the gunnels but our fourteen Challengers, who would lead any assault, were left with no fuel. I jumped out of my tank and demanded to see the Quartermaster, who was a major in The Royal Scots and completely blew my top. I pointed out in words of four letters that his system made nonsense of the whole concept of our battle plan.

Afterwards I felt a certain amount of remorse at having lost my cool. It was late at night and I was tired. These things could and should be handled rationally. But I noticed that the system changed dramatically and my Squadron never went short again.

I don't think there was any delay with our mail, though. Several former Life Guards officers wrote to me wishing me luck, including Major Ronald Ferguson who had once commanded A Squadron in Palestine and who said that he had heard good reports of our training. I wrote back to him suggesting that after the war it might be fun to have a polo match between the two British brigades. There was Mike Vickery, Rupert and I and a few other players in 4 Brigade, and I was sure Patrick Cordingley could put together a team from 7 Brigade — which he did, bringing in Prince Charles as a reinforcement.

Somebody had rumbled the Fortnum and Mason whiskey packages. Diana had even managed to send me one but it was shortly after that that I think the store was warned not to send any more to the Gulf because of Islamic law. But I reckoned this was one law that was made to be broken. After all, we weren't benefiting from the Islamic law that permitted us to have four wives, so whiskey found its way to the men in shampoo bottles and, of all things, chocolate boxes. It was good for morale and never abused.

When I was in Germany you used to be able to get Benson and Hedges Oval Turkish cigarettes in the mess. I became rather partial to them but for some reason they were made illegal by the European Community. So I switched to Camels and Diana kept me well supplied in the Gulf — 'I've sent an enormous parcel with camels, haven't you seen enough?' she joked. She also purchased copies of *Playboy* and *Penthouse* which went rapidly round the Squadron. They didn't know who had sent them but I would have liked to have been a fly on the wall on that shopping trip.

I, in turn, had sent her a present — the pair of emerald earrings which I had promised her if she would stop biting her nails. They had gone missing en route to her but now they had arrived. They went down well. 'I'm speechless and thrilled to own something so beautiful,' she wrote. She was aware they had not been inexpensive and remarked, 'There are ten years of army pay hanging on these ears ... How you do spoil me and how special I feel.'

The timing could not have been better. She was clearly in a very depressed state which she was unable to disguise. 'At the moment I've lost the fight to survive in this set-up. I'm tired by all my battles.' But, typically, she was off to help other people — in this case very special other people — the Gulf wives, who were left behind in Germany including the families of The Life Guards in Paderborn and Sennelager. 'I hope it goes alright and that I am able to be of some comfort, to take their minds off what their husbands are doing.'

Even with her private life in such a depressed state, Diana seemed determined to outdo the rest of the Royal Family when it came to commitment to the war. She swore off unnecessary entertainments, preferring to follow events on television, and refused to go skiing. In Paderborn she was shown round by the popular Brigadier Julian Browne — the man for whom I had procured the Lufthansa business class ticket. 'It was very strange going around The Life Guards reception and not being able to mention those I knew in The Regiment, like my friend,' she wrote. 'How proud I am that you're out there and I can't wait until you come home — so many of the wives told me how difficult it was not having a return date to set their eyes and hearts on and I longed to say — too right! I think of you all the time and I pray for you every night.'

There was talk in the Squadron in the days that followed of her visit to Germany. The effect she had on the hopes of the families back there was apparently enormous and enduring. I listened a lot but I said nothing and I wondered if she really knew the incredible impact she was capable of making on people. It was as if some spiritual presence had moved among them and inspired them.

It was so important for the men to know that their families were not overburdened with worry. The fact of being in the desert and filling the days and many nights with exercises meant that we were sufficiently occupied not to dwell too much on the dangers ahead.

Things took a bit of a down turn, however, with a visit from Brigadier Christopher Hammerbeck. Everyone was assembled to hear his talk. He crouched down and assumed a sort of 'matey' posture. He told us there was going to be a tough fight ahead. The war could last anything from 60 to 90 days as we fought all the way to Baghdad. He suggested that each of us should think of something that would get us through it. In his case it was religion. This made good sense. But then he seemed to want to get the troops used to the idea that they would be seeing people being blown up and badly injured and killed next to them. He asked us to look around and to realise that some colleagues might undergo that fate. We had to take on board the fact that there might be up to 30 per cent casualties.

It wasn't so much the Brigadier's message that was unwelcome — we all knew the risks involved — but, although he had the best of intentions, he wasn't a natural speaker and the way he delivered it and his timing did our morale little good. All my troops knew the consequences of battle — I used to show recruits an American training video called *Medic in Vietnam* when I was at the Guards Depot at Pirbright and that showed the effects of fighting — arms blown off, ghastly burns, terrible head wounds. In fact, it was so strong the Commandant had asked me not to keep using it, but it did bring home the impact of war at the right time and made men less likely to suffer from shock.

I suppose the Brigadier's speech had one particular effect on me. Originally I had kept Diana's letters in my tank suit. 'I'm deeply touched by where the letters are resting,' she wrote when I told her. 'I'm privileged to have made it to the top pocket.' But they had been coming more and more numerous in the last few days and she herself joked in one of them that 'if you keep all my letters, you'll have to carry around a trunk at this rate.' In fact, I had sent some packets of them home to my mother for safe-keeping. We had begun to use Shirley as a sort of clearing post office. For a while I wrote to Diana at Kensington Palace — a discreet JLH in the top left-hand corner meant the bluey was unopened by secretaries or staff.

But I feared that some of the things I was writing might do her no good if they reached other eyes so I enclosed my letters to her in ones home and my mother sent them on in a plain white envelope. The system often frustrated Diana who would ring my mother on an almost daily basis and ask if there was a letter for her. On one occasion she asked her to open it and read the contents over the phone. Shirley firmly refused, saying the contents might be rather personal but such was the power of Diana's persuasion that she eventually capitulated.

However, I had accumulated several letters which I kept in a folder beside my radio, which was just above my left shoulder in my tank. And mindful of Hammerbeck's warning I thought the time had come to make sure they would be destroyed if I was killed. In the five years that I had known Diana, Simon Faulkner was the only person in the army in whom we had confided. Even Rupert, who was becoming a trusted friend, knew nothing whatever about it. But I knew that if I was taken out, it would be Robin Tarling who would assume command.

I asked him to accompany me for a short walk into the desert. 'Robin, there's something you should know,' I said. 'I've been getting blueys from Princess Diana. She's a friend — well, she's more than that. They're in my papers. If anything happens, can I rely on you to get rid of them?'

He was very understanding. 'Of course you can,' he said — and didn't ask any questions. It was a slightly surreal moment but it had a bonding effect on our friendship which has lasted long after we both left the army.

Like the rest of my family, Diana kept the parcels coming — sweets, copies of *Horse and Hound* and a buff-coloured jersey from Turnbull and Asser with a scarf to match. She also sent me a gold cross which was identical to the one she had on which these words were engraved: 'I will love you for ever'. I wore it next to my tags which had the rather more prosaic JL Hewitt 505268 C of E. This was the maximum information you were meant to give to the enemy if captured. There were two of them so that if you were killed one would remain with the buried body and the other could be attached to the cross or other grave marking.

The army was very aware of its relationship with the press during the Gulf War. After all, CNN was giving commanders news of the effect of their bombing in Baghdad before they learnt it from their own information channels. A number of British newspaper correspondents were allowed forward to the front line and Michael Vickery at an O group said that one of them had asked to spend a week or so with The Life Guards.

So Richard Kay and his photographer, Mike Roberts, came to observe and photograph the work of the Squadron. There was no room for them in the tanks so they either rode with Rupert in his 432 or we found them room in the back of the ambulance. In the event of any attack they would at least be protected by armour.

Kay seemed an amiable enough chap. He said his main job was writing for the *Daily Mail* but in the case of the Gulf there was a pool arrangement whereby certain articles might appear in other papers. He asked me questions about myself and my command and I tried to answer them as best I could.

I'm fairly certain the two of them were with us when word came through that the land war was about to commence. The actually day for going through the Breach was G day, which remained a secret, but we knew it could only be a few days away.

Kay said that he had a satellite phone back at his hotel for sending urgent despatches and suggested I might like to use it to call home before going in. I leapt at the chance. I summoned Trooper Doyle and my Land Rover and with Kay we drove what must have been more than 60 miles to a small desert town. Kay had rooms in a rather beaten-up looking hotel and in one was several thousand pounds' worth of expensive satellite phone. He seemed very eager for me to use it.

I spoke to my mother. It was a very emotional moment. She knew we were going in and she was clearly very upset. I tried to cheer her up as much as possible. I told her my men had never been better trained or more motivated. We would be okay.

Then I rang Diana on her private line. Paul Burrell answered.

'It's James,' I said.

He seemed very pleased to hear from me and was anxious to know how things were going. I told him we'd soon find out.

'Good luck,' he said. 'I'll just see if the Princess is in.'

Of course, he knew whether or not she was in, although maybe she had told him she wasn't taking any calls. But I soon got my answer as I could hear female whoops and shrieks in the background. She came breathless to the phone. I was too blown away by the emotion of the moment to recall the words we used but she smothered me in hugs and kisses from the other end and said how much she missed me and I said how much I missed her. She, too, knew this would be the last time we spoke before the battle and she said how she knew how I would be safe as she prayed for me all the time and she was certain her prayers would be answered.

She said she just wanted to be with me. I said that if that was the case she would have to marry me and she said she would love to do that.

I felt perfectly at peace as we drove back to join the Squadron. Whatever lay in store in the days ahead, there was a contentment inside me that made me completely prepared to face my fate.

I thanked Richard Kay for letting me talk to my family. He said it was his pleasure. What I didn't know was that he was the Royal Correspondent for the *Daily Mail*. Nor did I know that he was in possession of much more information about me than anyone in the Brigade might have suspected.

# 8

The ground war was coming closer. Our tanks were sent ahead on low loaders and we flew by helicopter about 200 kilometres west to Assembly Area RAY, a point 40 kilometres south of the Iraqi border where the Division was assembled for the assault. I looked down at the desert beneath me. The sight was amazing — thousands upon thousands of Allied troops and vehicles as far as the eye could see. This certainly looked like being 'the mother of all battles'.

Nobody, apart from the high command, was sure exactly when G Day (the start of ground operations) — would be, so there was an opportunity to fraternise with some of our American allies. I arranged an exchange morning with a squadron who came over in their Abraham tanks. These were very impressive vehicles but much too thirsty for the desert — they ate up a lot of fuel. However, inside they made ours seem very antiquated. The interior was white and spacious with a drawer for the ammunition.

The Americans, in turn, had a roam over our tanks. One of the last things we had done in the desert was to bolt layers of secret Chobham Armour on to our tanks which was meant to give them extra protection against anti-tank rounds and explosives. It had been a bit like knights of old putting on their armour to go on the crusades, only it had taken 48 exacting hours to assemble the stuff. In order to improve our range — who knows when we might get a Replen — we had strapped two great 50 gallon drums of diesel fuel on the back of each tank. This caused an American sergeant to remark: 'These tanks look a lot like Russian T72s.'

This was a rather disconcerting observation since that was the main Iraqi tank and the possibility of being hit by friendly fire — a blue-on-blue, as it was commonly known — was a very real fear. All Allied vehicles had inverted 'V's on them for identification but in a war fought at night or in the bad visibility we had already experienced in the desert, they wouldn't be much use.

The time waiting at RAY was an uneasy period. There was no opportunity for exercises. We could clean our weapons and prepare our vehicles but there was a lot of just waiting and thinking. We were not allowed to take anything into combat that might identify us so we had to burn our passports and papers, all the vehicle documents and any letters that we had with us. I had to set fire to some incredibly moving ones from my father and my mother which I bitterly regretted doing and many from Diana, too. We buried the remnants in a pit in the sand.

Just when we were certain that it would be a matter of hours rather than days before the land war began, something quite unexpected happened. Word spread through the assembled troops that after a last minute peace initiative from President Gorbachev, the Iraqis had offered to withdraw from Kuwait. The rumour was that Colin Powell had agreed there would be no invasion if this took place. Someone said on the radio there had been a deal. It looked as if the land war would never take place.

Although I attended O groups, I was no better informed than most soldiers. These negotiations were being conducted in secret at a high political level. Men in my Squadron asked me what I thought and I replied, quite honestly, that I thought we would still be going in. I had always maintained that since we were in Germany. But a confused mix of emotions went through my mind as they must have with everyone else. One was utter relief that we might be going home safely. But this gave way to a huge wave of disappointment. This is what I had joined the army for, this is what we had trained hard for, this was a war we were going to win. To have it taken away at the eleventh hour seemed a cheat. There are those who, for professional reasons, really wish to fight on the basis: all that training and never the test. With such a build-up, not to have gone in would have been an anti-climax. Against this was the horrific realisation of the enormity of it all and the fact that people would die. But this roller-coaster ride of emotions eventually settled down and there was a return to the professional calm that we had trained ourselves to maintain.

As it turned out, any hopes had been raised in vain. No satisfactory agreement was reached. Saddam Hussein was not to be trusted. At 0400 hours on Sunday, February 24th 1991, President George Bush announced to the world that the land war to drive the Iraqis out of Kuwait had begun. In the east the American marines began to fight their way towards Kuwait City. In the extreme west the American XVIII Corps commenced a broad sweep through the desert.

In the south — we waited. First there was a sustained artillery attack on the Iraqi positions at the Breach and then VII Corps began to fight their way in, with the 'Big Red One' following, ploughing their way through the 'Berm' (a bank of sand intended to defend a position) and surrounding minefields, ultimately creating a sixteen-lane highway from Saudi Arabia north into Iraq.

We moved down to 60 minutes notice to move. By 0745 that evening my tanks were lined up nose to tail in 'Staging

Area 4' waiting to be led over the Breach by American
Scouts. We learned that the American Breach crossing had
been extremely successful and they had moved faster and
deeper into Iraq than they had anticipated.

In the light of this, plans were rapidly changing. VII
American Corps had successfully ring-sealed the area of
the Breach. In the rehearsal British 4 Brigade had gone
through the Breach first, mainly because it was 'infantry-
strong' and better suited to fighting its way through this
type of defence. Now it was thought that this was more
likely to be encountered deeper into Iraq. General Rupert
Smith ordered 7 Brigade who were more mobile to go first
and take up positions further to the north.

At 1230 hours on February 25th we finally moved out
from our staging area. We followed our allotted highway
'Route November' and at 1415 crossed the Breach into
Iraq. The weather was closing in and the visibility bad.
Unlike the rehearsal, the real Breach was surprisingly
undulating and it was impossible to see vehicles very far
ahead of you.

I hadn't heard much in the way of bombardment so I
wasn't anticipating any action during the crossing.
Nevertheless we were on constant alert and all garbed in
our NBC suits in the anticipation of encountering chemical
or biological weapons. Our intelligence was that the Iraqis
had 3,500 tons of mustard and nerve gas and we knew
50,000 Kurds and Iranians had been killed or poisoned by
the use of these agents.

But to my surprise, when we had cleared the far end of
the Breach, I saw an American soldier sitting on the top of
his tank, with the hatch open, chewing gum. I cautiously
opened my hatch and asked him if there had been any
reports of chemical warfare. He shook his head.

So I made a personal decision. I had reckoned that if
the Iraqis were going to hit us with chemical weapons at
any point the most likely would be at the beginning so I
took my NBC suit off and it remained off. It was much
easier for me to operate without it. I didn't ask any of my
Squadron to do the same and we continued to observe

strict NBC precautions within the tank.

The Americans had done a very good job. As long as we were in a convoy moving north, there was minimal chance of immediate Iraqi attack — we were too far down the line. But as each Battle Group splintered off to the east, they were on their own. The pattern of every attack on successive positions would be the same. We, as the tank Squadron, were at the front and would be the first to engage the enemy, destroying the heavy weapons and then supporting the infantry as they went in to fight and clear the trenches.

General Rupert Smith had devised a new concept of operation to try to make the most effective use of his forces. He was a parachute officer with a brilliant military mind — both forward thinking and lateral thinking. He probably believed that he didn't have sufficient forces to move in a sweep east. So using the information gleaned from satellite pictures, he created a 'trace' of our objectives — a sheet of tracing paper one could put over the map of Iraq and Kuwait with little potato-like shapes drawn all over it to pinpoint the significant enemy positions. He had used the names of metals as code-words for each: bronze, copper, brass, steel, zinc, platinum, lead, tungsten and so on.

By and large, 7 Brigade was to attack positions to the north and we in 4 Brigade those to the south. But by not attacking at the same time, General Smith was able to pool all of his divisional artillery and bring down a maximum amount of fire before we went in. It was clever, well-calculated and enormously effective.

As we reached our Forming Up Position the sky was alive with missiles from the MLRS launched to our rear. Almost immediately word came over the radio that due to the speed of the advance we were to take in an additional objective. I was summoned to an O group at Colonel Iain Johnstone's Battle Group HQ. Since my tank Squadron was the furthest forward I had to make my way back to him. This presented a complication. We were parked on the far side of a minefield. I didn't want to end my war by stepping on an anti-personnel mine, so I carefully jogged along the tracks my tank had made going through. It was night and I prayed that the batteries on my torch wouldn't give up. They didn't and I sent a little prayer of thanks to Diana for sending me the Duracell batteries that saw me through.

Lieutentant-Colonel Johnstone's briefing was well under way by the time I joined it. There was a different atmosphere in the O group — tense, determined, no time for small talk. I noted the co-ordinates of Objective Bronze and hot-footed it back to the Squadron.

We were well en route to the Way Point when Iain Johnstone came on the net asking: 'Where are you?'

I reported that we were about two kilometres short of the Way Point. He replied: 'That's strange because we're there and we didn't overtake you. Are you sure? Confirm.'

'Roger,' I replied. 'Making good ground.'

But when we got to the Way Point in a few minutes there was nobody else there. Something had gone wrong. I got on the net to the Colonel to try and untangle it but his second-in-command, Major Kirk Gillies, had been listening in and immediately spotted the mistake that had been made. There was not only a new Objective but a new Way Point (although the Objective was assailable from the original one). I had joined the meeting after the new Way Point co-ordinates had been given out and there was no recap at the end. He now gave them to me in code over the air.

I cursed my bad luck — it was nobody's fault — but I was determined to lead the attack on Objective Bronze. I told my commanders over the net: 'Listen. We're going a different way.' I gave them the co-ordinates and ordered them to follow me.

We had to swing around and virtually go back in the direction from which we had come. And this meant going full tilt through our own troops and vehicles which were now advancing on us. It was pitch black and a very hairy situation.

I could see the sweat on the back of Robbo's neck as he drove towards this advancing army who would have no idea who we were.

'What a way to go, Robbo,' I said, only half-jokingly. 'Blue-on-blue. Pity.'

'Yes, it is, sir,' came the tight reply.

'Give us a fag,' I said. We both lit up Camels. Smoking may be bad for your health but at that particular time neither of us was immediately worried by that.

'You remember that conversation we had, sir, about you not wanting to fly the Squadron Pennant,' Robbo ventured. 'Well, I've got it here in the bin. Should I put it up?'

It remained up for the duration of the war. We made it to the Way Point unscathed and reported in to Iain Johnstone. 'Well done,' he said. 'Sorry about the cock-up.'

Now we were safely reunited with the rest of the Battle Group we embarked on our first assault on the real enemy. The Life Guards Squadron moved ahead in two files of seven tanks each. It was after midnight and the weather was getting worse and worse. Two commanders reported that their Thermal Imaging had broken down and even for those of us who could still make use of it the rain degraded the images so it was hard to be sure what lay ahead. It was very much a journey into the unknown.

I counted down the distance to the Objective over the net to the rest of the tanks. At 4,000 metres we went into line abreast and continued forward. It was almost eerily quiet — just the noise of our tanks and minimal radio traffic. No response from the enemy. I was beginning to wonder if the Objective was manned. I just wished the Iraqis would let us know where they were.

I knew the men were feeling on edge and tense. I had to do something to give them a little bit of spirit so at 1,000 metres I gave the order to fire the machine guns.

The Battle Group Commander came on the net and demanded: 'What on earth are you doing? What is the situation?'

I told him we were putting down searching fire. The words were barely out of my mouth when all hell broke loose. The guns that we were told were going to be there were there, and a wall of fire came in our direction. I gave the order to open up with our main armaments. On my left 3 Troop Commander reported: 'Contact ... tank, no two tanks.' To my right 4 Troop reported: 'Contact ... infantry.' The whole area lit up and battle commenced. We engaged the bunkers with our high explosive (HESH) rounds and began to advance again, driving over trenches as we went.

On the thermal imaging screen on my TOGS I could see Iraqi infantry advancing towards us. I felt curiously removed from the actual blood and guts of warfare although men were being cut down and dying. We lived with the awareness that we could take a hit from an Iraqi tank and the fear of chemical and biological weapons remained very real. The noise of battle was deafening. It was impossible to determine whether the weight of fire was coming from their side or ours but I felt confident we were in the ascendant.

This was confirmed when a message came through from 4 Troop that some infantry were waving a white flag in an apparent attempt to surrender. I ordered the tanks to stop firing and reported the situation to Battle Group HQ.

We needed to know whether it was just a few individual units who were surrendering or the whole emplacement. Things fell very quiet so after a while we flashed our headlights and slowly Iraqis began to emerge from their positions, their arms held up in surrender.

I told HQ that we were accepting prisoners — not a task that tanks are well-equipped to perform. 'What do you want us to do with them?' I asked. The order that came back from a higher formation was: 'Shoot them.'

This order was not carried out and quickly countermanded by a senior officer who firmly stated that we should abide by the Geneva Convention. The Royal Scots began to flush out the trenches and bunkers and round up the prisoners in tank scrapes. The Major in command wanted to ask the artillery to put up some white light which would turn night into daylight. I asked him not to as it would silhouette the tanks and make them extremely vulnerable. Such a clash was understandable —

both of us wanted to protect the safety of our men. They compromised with some two-inch mortar light which is not as strong but was not weak enough for me. I ordered the tanks to move off. 'Where are you going?' demanded the major.

'To regroup and throw a ring of steel round your position,' I responded.

It had been a good start. More than a hundred enemy were killed or wounded, many more taken prisoner and at least a dozen vehicles destroyed.

At 0300 we were ordered to head on to Objective Brass. It was going to be a busy night. Busier than expected if our Thermal Imaging was to be believed. We had moved four kilometres towards the Objective when I picked up the heat signal of about 20 vehicles in the distance. I contacted Battle Group HQ and asked if there were any friendly forces in the area. They came back and confirmed that there were not.

The adrenalin was running very high in the Squadron at this stage. We had won our first engagement comprehensively and with no casualties. People were hungry for another. Their blood was up and they were maybe a little trigger-happy. But I didn't want to find myself in an attacking position without being able to identify whom we were attacking. We moved forward another three kilometres. Through my SATNAV I knew exactly where I was. I took a bearing on the unknown vehicles and then lased them to get an accurate feedback from the range finder. Using a backbearing I now contacted Brigade HQ and provided them with a grid reference.

'Confirm there are no friendly forces in this area,' I radioed.

Again they came back and confirmed this. Moreover, they wanted to know why I was moving so slowly. I was holding things up. 7 Brigade had already gone through Objective Copper to the north.

James Gaselee on my left-hand side reported vehicle movement and requested permission to engage. I told him no, I was not convinced that these were enemy vehicles.

For one thing they were on the move and the intelligence reports were that the enemy in this area was completely dug in.

Battle Group HQ came on the radio. 'Are they firing?'

'Yes,' I confirmed.

'Are they firing at you?'

'It's difficult to tell.'

'Are you being hit?'

'No.'

'Well, get on with it,' I was told. I was left in no doubt that if I didn't get on with it, they could find someone who was prepared to.

This was a dilemma that I did not want. But as I calculated the odds it was solved for me with a voice from Battle Group HQ shouting through my head-set: 'Stop! Stop! Stop! There are friendly forces to your front.'

The relief was enormous. I closed my eyes and started to breathe again for the first time in 45 minutes. What had happened was that Brigade HQ had asked everybody to verify their positions and this squadron had verified theirs incorrectly. They had been moving to their Forming Up Point (FUP) and firing to the north so we would have hit them side on with God knows what catastrophic results.

As they moved north to their correct position, we set out for our FUP for the attack on Objective Brass. It was down as a position of battalion strength supported by T55 tanks. Intelligence suggested that some of these may have been destroyed and the artillery barrage would certainly have caused some consternation in the rest.

Unfortunately there was more than a little consternation in my own tank. The main armament was out of action and we had a mechanic working furiously trying to find the fault and repair it. So there were five of us in the tank as we approached the objective.

It was a sweaty situation. Troop leaders were reporting: 'Contacts, tanks to our front,' and I couldn't even fire at the things. But I didn't want to relinquish command and I was still able to send accurate ranges to my oppo (Robin Tarling). There were three Iraqi T55s well dug-in in shell scrapes, their hulls were hidden and you could just see the turrets above the sand. They didn't seem to be expecting us quite so soon. We moved in in a shock wave. Pip Earl took out two tanks and Robin Tarling removed the third.

But it was a well-fortified position and we came under fire from the bunkers and trenches. James Gaselee's tank was hit. Some of his Chobham armour was blown off. He asked permission to use his grenades. I readily gave it. With no main armament, this seemed a good idea. I threw open my hatch and lobbed a couple of grenades into a trench myself. Almost at once I came under fire from men emerging from it. I got hold of my GPMG and returned it. An Iraqi soldier who had been rushing towards us snapped backwards and lay motionless on the ground.

I had never killed a man before. Within thirty seconds I had killed another. We had to go in hard. It was our duty to clear the position and get them to capitulate. Then we accepted their surrender. Until that moment it was a kill or be killed situation. I have never been traumatised by those individual killings. I feel I can live with myself because we did the least possible to achieve the most.

The two Companies of the Royal Scots moved through and joined the engagement. They were a magnificent fighting force — well-trained, efficient and extremely brave. We continued with fire, flushing out bunkers and attacking Iraqi armoured vehicles — more than thirty tanks and MTLBs (armoured personnel carriers) were destroyed.

By 1000 hours Objective Brass had been secured. The Squadron immediately went firm on a line south-east to fire the 14th/20th into their next enemy position. We had been on the move or engaged in combat for 24 hours non-stop and we badly needed a Replen of fuel and ammunition. There was a brief opportunity for sleep but with adrenalin levels running so high it was difficult even to doze. I was fearful about how we would last the predicted 60 days at this rate, but I doubted if it would be that long.

We were gathered in a semi-circle with our tanks

pointing towards the enemy to allow the infantry to accept people surrendering. Battlefield smoke hung over the position creating quite a thick haze. There was a good feeling in the air. We'd made a decent start. SQMC Ormiston and his men arrived with food, fuel and ammunition. He was warmly greeted — it was our first contact with non-combatants and my men were eager to get news of the bigger picture. Evidently the attack to the north had gone well, too. In fact, we had moved so quickly that 7 US Corps had yet to plan our next operation.

I was sitting on top of the tank — feeling very stiff after 24 hours in the same seat — with a cup of 'Irish' coffee, puffing a Camel and talking to SCM Evans. My head-set was round my neck. Suddenly I heard it crackle into life. I put it to my ear. 'Contact — Wait out.'

There was no need for a call sign. I recognised the voice — it was Corporal of Horse Godson, who was commanding a tank well to my right. I picked up my binoculars. 'Contact' meant an enemy sighting and, sure enough, there was an Iraqi T55 tank moving from left to right.

Godson — an experienced gunnery instructor — didn't need me to tell him to fire. He immediately let off a Sabot that went just a cat's whisker over the top of the tank. By now most of the gunners were trailing this through their sights. Godson came on the air again: '900. Out.' This let them know he had fired with the 900 metre point on his sight and people would have to relay at 850.

He obviously wanted to fire again but his oppo, Lance Corporal of Horse Douglas, was too quick for him. There was an enormous explosion — Douglas must have opted for a Sabot with a DU (Depleted Uranium) tip which had a much bigger bag charge since it needed more explosive to propel it. The trajectory of this thing was almost direct and one hundred per cent accurate. It hit the tank between the hull and the turret ring which shot twenty feet or more into the air with a huge explosion of gas and flames.

Not for nothing were these DU tips known as 'Jerichos' — they would make any wall come tumbling down. The Iraqis wouldn't have known anything about it. They must have been completely vaporised. Some men cheered. I just smiled and thought 'you naughty boy'. People had been under orders to save the DUs until we came up against the Republican Guard. But — who knows? — this might have been one of them and the moment was too good for morale to deflate it with a reprimand.

In the afternoon I went for an O group at Battle Group HQ. People were satisfied with the work done so far but nobody was feeling smug. There was a long way to go. The next move was 30 kilometres east to form up for a night attack on Objective Tungsten, which promised to be the hardest objective so far. It was reported to have two regiments of artillery, three mechanised infantry companies and two ordinary infantry companies. An additional squadron of tanks from the 14th/20th was requested to group with B Company of The Royal Scots.

There was a substantial obstacle in our way in the shape of an oil pipeline. The tanks would have to cross this 'belly-up' which is always the most vulnerable and dangerous position to be in — the underside of the tank being where the armour is at its thinnest. This would present a natural attacking position for the enemy.

Nobody had discounted the possibility of the Iraqis saving their chemical weapons for this stage. Rupert, who had NBC detection sensors, led the Squadron in his 432 for part of the way. Suddenly there was a loud explosion and the side of his vehicle lifted off the ground. There had always been the risk of friendly fire from the American airforce and, if this happened, the fairly obvious rule was to run away from the vehicle. So one of his radio ops got out of it and began to run.

'Come back,' Rupert yelled at the man. The guy turned in amazement. 'We're in a minefield,' Rupert explained, pointing to a fist-sized hole in one of the tracks of the vehicle.

He filled me in on the situation on the radio, wanting to know what to do. With other commanders I might have suggested he retreat back along his tracks but Rupert had little fear and great judgement.

'I'd like you to push on,' I said.

Which he did unquestioningly, although he later claimed he had spent the rest of the crossing with his fingers in his ears and his feet well off the floor of the vehicle. Fortunately they hit no more mines and we followed safely in their tracks.

When night fell we were obliged to halt for a couple of hours in a holding position. I was exhausted — I had taken to opening my hatch and jogging on my seat to try and stay awake. Now seemed a good time to give the Commanders a chance to rest. I got them all in and said that they should get some sleep and leave it to their seconds in command to take over — this would involve organising the sentries, getting the trenches dug and laying the wire.

I lay down beside my own tank and closed my eyes. Just an hour's sleep would be a salvation. But it was not to be. After I don't know how many minutes I was awakened by Lance Corporal Roberts. He had been given the task of putting sentries out and had first cleared the area with another man, both carrying machine guns. To their amazement about 50 Iraqi soldiers appeared from seemingly nowhere and surrendered to them.

'I've got this group of prisoners back here, sir,' he said. 'Do you want to interview them?'

I got up and took a look at them. They were frightened and dishevelled and ill-clad. Many didn't even have a decent pair of boots. All of them looked hungry.

'I think one of them's a political officer,' said Roberts, indicating a better dressed man to the rear.

But I didn't believe I would learn anything from any of them other than that their morale seemed rock-bottom.

There was a tank scrape, dug for an Iraqi tank, nearby. 'Put them in the scrape,' I said, 'and then go and get Corporal of Horse Barry to inform HQ we've got another 50 prisoners.'

I congratulated Corporal Roberts on his initiative. It

was a very fine piece of soldiering.

I gave up all hope of sleep. It wasn't long before we had to move on again. In the middle of the night we passed two batteries of Multiple Rocket Launch Systems (MRLS). I had never seen them in action so close before. It was an awe-inspiring sight as the rockets streaked off into the air. And confidence-inspiring, too. I got a report that they had landed on their objective, now about five kilometres away.

The pipeline proved less of a hazard than I feared. It was banked on either side in the form of a sand Berm. We crossed this under the cover of our own smoke screen using well-rehearsed Squadron defile drills, covering each other as we went across. Now we were only 1,500 metres from the western perimeter of the objective. We moved into line abreast and advanced bringing maximum fire to bear on the first position.

There are several parts to each objective and when we had got about halfway through and there was an awful lot of firing, I needed to evaluate how much was coming from the enemy. I feared we might be getting a little too confident and trigger-happy and could be wasting too much ammunition.

I ordered that people only fire at identified targets. This had little effect, so I told them: 'Only fire when you're being fired at.' This brought the rate of fire right down, almost to a halt. I said: 'Let's draw a line here.' We were now well into the Objective and hadn't been replenished. I didn't want anyone to go beyond their reach or be surprised or get outflanked.

However, on my right flank I could see on my TOGS a lone tank motoring along, firing away.

'Bloody well stop!' I yelled. 'Who is that call sign?'

It took no notice. I thought: 'Bugger, I've lost contact with one of my tanks.'

Still the lone Challenger kept advancing and firing although there seemed to be very little response from any enemy.

The errant tank had passed quite close to James Gaselee's position. He came on the air and said: 'I think it's call sign One Four Charlie.'

That was the tank a senior officer used. Evidently he could not have had the time to get on to my radio net. I got on to the Battle Group HQ and told Iain Johnstone that we were unable to move forward or engage the enemy as the situation had been confused somewhat by One Four Charlie.

This was sorted out and we continued to work our way through the remaining positions of Objective Tungsten. It's very hard to explain the emotions one felt on a night like that. We were exhausted. People were living on adrenalin. The fact that some of the positions in Tungsten had put up weak resistance didn't mean that round the corner there wasn't an intact tank position ready to blast away at you.

At 0530 our attack was called to a halt. We were needed elsewhere. A convoy of Republican Guard were reported 25 kilometres to the north. This, I knew, was going to be our toughest test. The Republican Guard had T72 tanks which were comparable to ours and we knew they were the best trained and most aggressive soldiers with the best equipment. We were hardly at our most mentally alert to take them on — but, there again, perhaps neither were they.

However, we never had the opportunity. We drove north to a blocking position and were then ordered to halt. Instead they sent in American A 10 planes known as 'Tankbusters' which can fly very low with 20mm cannon which despatch 2,000 rounds a minute. When they came back from their mission it was reported that they had managed to destroy 90 per cent of the enemy in a mere 22 minutes.

Our new orders were to move 65 kilometres to the east to a position just north of Kuwait City to prevent the enemy from withdrawing northwards. But later in the day these orders, too, were countermanded and our fast drive was halted some 30 kilometres into Kuwait.

The news that came over the military network was to stop and await further orders. But Rupert had been monitoring the BBC World Service in his signals 432 and put his microphone to the radio so that everyone in the Squadron could hear.

It was 0800 hours on February 28th 1991. A ceasefire was confirmed. Saddam Hussein had surrendered. The Gulf War had been won.

# 9

I don't think I have ever experienced a moment of such complete and utter satisfaction. We had done it. We the allies, we the British Division, we The Royal Scots Battle Group and we The Life Guards Squadron.

Confirmation of the enemy's capitulation came over the radio net. This didn't mean that every Iraqi knew about it so I reminded my commanders that although we had ceased to fire we were still in a battle situation. We went into a position from which we could reply to fire and attack and advance if we had to.

But there was time to celebrate. It was such an incredible occasion. A few bottles of scotch miraculously appeared and everybody wet their lips and toasted each other. I told the men how highly I thought of them and what they had done and the professionalism with which they had gone into battle and carried out their duties.

The operation had lasted 96 hours and for more than

half of that time we had been in combat or contact with the enemy. During the advance we had covered more than 300 kilometres, we had attacked ten positions, possibly killed or wounded as many as a thousand men, and destroyed more than 40 tanks and armoured vehicles. We had finished the operation as we had started with fourteen battleworthy tanks. None of my Squadron had been killed or injured. I had fulfilled my promise to their wives and families and for this I closed my eyes and gave thanks to God.

I went back to HQ for an O group where Iain Johnstone passed on congratulations from the top. Evidently 4 Brigade had taken more than 5,000 Iraqi prisoners. The Royal Scots had acquitted themselves with courage and distinction. It was a cause for further celebration.

After the adrenalin of war it wasn't easy to come to terms with the pattern of peace. Nobody had really slept for the past four days. I remember Rupert saying that the constant fear prevented one from relaxing into any depth of sleep and, if you did doze off, you woke up to find yourself still in your worst nightmare.

It wasn't easy to sleep now. It took several days to adjust and much longer than that to get back into a normal routine. It wasn't just the war that had changed us — the weeks of training before we went in had been so strenuous and stressful that it was hard to adapt to days that were less so.

There was an enemy position quite close to where we had stopped at the ceasefire. We went back to it and my men buried the dead. In some cases they had to look for legs to go with the corpses. They didn't put crosses on the graves but made sure that they all pointed towards Mecca. We eventually handed the relevant papers and dog tags back to Battle Group HQ but I doubted if the Iraqis knew or cared who had died and who hadn't.

I had informed HQ that James Gaselee had had some of his Chobham armour shot off in one engagement and that I had noted on my SATNAV where I thought it might be. They provided us with a helicopter to go and look for it. On the first trip they put the co-ordinates into the helicopter's navigation system and we couldn't find it but the next day we went again with my own SATNAV and we did. However, the heavy armour was too small for the Gazelle helicopter so we went back a third time with a Lynx to pick it up. I persuaded the pilots to land at some of the objectives we had been through so that Rupert could record them with his camcorder for his Squadron War Diary. It was bizarre to see them in daylight. They were more spread-out than they had seemed during combat, most of them were utterly decimated with the artillery and armoured vehicles completely disabled. In several, unburied bodies still littered the ground. Not a pleasant sight.

It was fascinating to look round the Iraqi bunkers. Some of them were stacked with brand-new Kalashnikovs. The officers' quarters were well equipped with marble floors which made them very cool in the heat of the day. By March we were beginning to feel the force of the desert sun. I liberated a handsome leather desk-chair from one, put it in the back of my Land Rover and got it back to Athlone Barracks where I presume it remains to this day. I also found a nicely finished 9mm pistol with an ivory handle. We were obliged to hand weapons in with the firm promise that they would be returned to us in Germany, but I never saw it again.

A fellow Life Guards officer, Tom Thorneycroft, was working in 4 Brigade HQ and he and I took my Land Rover down the Basra Road. It was before the Engineers got there. It was quiet and rather eerie. The whole strip was littered with burnt-out vehicles, civilian and military. There was a stench of rotten flesh with many mutilated bodies, some with severed heads and limbs. I almost joined them. We stopped to investigate a Russian BRDM with a SAGA missile on top. As I stepped out of the car I very nearly put my foot on a cluster bomb which would have deprived me of my left leg, at least. Disaster averted, I lobbed a grenade into the BRDM which gave off a very big bang.

The desert where we were now camped — about 15 kilometres west of Kuwait City — was more undulating than our training areas. The Squadron site was camouflaged as usual, although now as much to give protection from the strong sun as any enemy. It was a huge administrative problem to get everybody out of theatre. 7 Brigade rightly had priority in going home — many of them had been in the Gulf since well before Christmas. It was essential to keep the men active. Whilst the tanks were brought back into perfect condition, we kept physically fit with various sports and games of rounders during the days and frequently films at night.

Army rations didn't get very much better but there were plentiful food parcels from home and these added lustre to the meals. We would share them out. My mother had sent jam and coffee and chocolate for the men in my tank and, although they didn't know it, they enjoyed the soup and oatmeal biscuits from a hamper from Diana, leaving me to savour the caviar.

A backlog of letters were delivered, many of mine from the 'Kensington Palace War Correspondent'. Most of these were written before we had gone in. She had been to the Guards Chapel for Sunday Service. 'I do love that place more than I should,' she wrote. 'Apart from anything else I feel closer to you so hopefully God will hear my prayers.'

She had been following events in the Gulf as avidly as ever — '7th Armoured Brigade tend to be on the news a lot with Martin Bell, who doesn't look happy in his situation!' And whenever possible she had been to see and talk to the wives of men serving in the Gulf. Diana was very aware of the lift she could give to people's spirits by being a good listener with a warm smile. She did as much as she possibly could to help people during the war. She tried her hardest to come out to the Gulf but she wasn't allowed. I hope future historians will take account of her deep concern and total commitment when they write about her.

She'd also been to see my family a couple of times

down in Devon and wrote with delight of my phone call from the desert. 'You sure know how to make a girl's day. I just couldn't believe it when your voice came through on the telephone this morning — it must have been God listening to my prayers.'

As soon as she learned the ground war had started she went to church and lit a candle and 'prayed very hard for your safe return'. But she was aware that my position was far from safe and that there was always the danger our tank could be taken by the enemy. 'Please can you burn my letters after reading them now,' she wrote, 'in case they get into the wrong hands.'

The war was over before I received her request and I had already told her that I had sent a bundle back to Devon. She was relieved by this — 'your parcel of letters have returned to base so that was quick,' she wrote to reassure me.

Diana's joy was unconfined when she heard the war was over. As had frequently been the case, she had been watching television all night. 'I heard Bush, 5 in the morning our time, telling us of the ceasefire and because of the ghastly time of the morning there was no one to celebrate with! The whole country is upside down with elation. A lot of drunk wives on the TV. Champagne bottles everywhere! I long to know when you're coming home.'

There was such sadness in the thought of this bird in a gilded cage being unable to get out and celebrate that when I received her letter I used up a favour with a friend in signals to make a quick call to England I didn't tell him to whom. Our conversation was too brief — we were cut off — but I think it helped.

It was time to part company with Iain Johnstone and The Royal Scots. He had been a fair and pretty fearless Battle Group Commanding Officer. There was always a good reason behind his orders and he knew we had to hit continually hard at the enemy, even when they appeared weak or disorganised, because we never knew for certain what we were going to come up against next. He gave me a generous amount of leeway and I thanked him for that.

I was never quite sure what Colonel Iain made of me. What I do know is that some months after we had returned to our respective barracks in Germany he invited me to a Royal Scots Mess Dinner and after the meal the Regimental Band played 'Here comes the galloping Major' with various made-up verses about me which all the assembled officers sang. That gesture meant a great deal.

The Squadron moved further to the west and joined up again with the 14th/20th Hussars under Colonel Mike Vickery. All of us had seen action. We put up some tents and generally tried to make life in the desert a bit more comfortable since we didn't know how long it would be our home. There were spirited games of rugby between the four Squadrons.

I would go to the Regimental HQ for a daily conference. We would get details of the bigger picture and usually deal with matters of logistics, how we would get the equipment out of the desert and then the men.

On one particular day the adjutant took me to one side and said he would like a quiet word. I asked him if anything was wrong and he simply handed me a copy of a newspaper. It was the *News of the World*. I looked at the front page. The headline read: I LOST MY LOVER TO DI. There was a picture of Diana and beside her one of Emma Stewardson, an old girlfriend who had written to me in the Gulf.

I just froze. This was the moment I had been dreading for more than four years, and it was more heart-stopping than anything I had come up against in the past weeks. I took the paper out into the desert and sat on the far side of a Bedford eight-tonner to read it. Today I am a little more acquainted with the ways of the tabloid press and accept that much of it is pure fiction. But then I was an innocent and I believed what I read, that Emma Stewardson had gone to the *News of the World* and said that she and I were lovers (this wasn't true — we *had* been lovers but the relationship was long over) but I had transferred my affections to Princess Diana.

There were pages of the stuff and Emma had been

dressed up to look like Diana — same hair, jewellery, same pose. I wondered what had possessed her to do this. She had often been changeable in her moods when I knew her but she had never been downright spiteful.

I don't know whether or not Mike Vickery had been waiting for me but he was there when I went back inside. 'I'm very sorry about all this,' he said. 'Let me know if there is anything we can do.'

I was able to take him up on his offer straight away. I had to talk to Diana. I told the adjutant, Jonty Palmer, that I needed to speak to England. This was not at all easy from where we were in the desert but there was a Ptarmigan field telephone that linked up with other connecting nodes which could eventually be patched through to London.

Fortunately Diana was at home. I told her I had just read the *News of the World*. She said that she'd seen it, too. I told her I was terribly sorry — I wanted to know what the reaction had been there. She said that nobody was saying much. She wasn't too worried about it. In retrospect, she seemed remarkably cool. She said that she hoped that I wasn't going to get too much stick about it. I said my worst concern was just sitting here in the desert not being able to do anything to help. Diana told me not to be worried and we both sort of reassured each other that it would blow over and everything would be all right. But we knew this would not be so. The cat was out of the bag.

In the days and weeks that followed I was very aware that my fellow soldiers knew what people were reading back in England. The press had been waiting for someone to make the first move. Now it was open season. Whatever my men read in newspapers or in letters from home, they remained entirely discreet as we concluded our business in the Gulf. I believe that Robert Fox, generally regarded by the troops as one of the best war correspondents, and who recently covered Kosovo with considerable insight, wrote one or two pieces that included the sentiment 'leave this guy alone, he's been in a war' and I'm grateful to him for that.

In preparation for the move back to Germany we flew

south to a camp near Al Jubail. It was necessary to debomb our vehicles and give the surplus ammunition back to the quartermasters.

We were now that much closer to home. British newspapers were more readily available and, although I avoided them like the plague, the sight of them was enough to plague me. I desperately needed to get away, if only for a couple of nights.

At Millfield, I had been the fag of a cousin of the King of Saudi Arabia, Prince Walid Ben Said. I now made contact with him. He was pleased to hear from me, appreciative of the British contribution to the liberation of Kuwait and, with typical Arab generosity, offered rooms at a hotel in Bahrain for me and any friends I wished to take.

I put this proposition to the squadron leaders but they didn't want to be away — there was always a chance our flight might be brought forward. But Robin Tarling, who had been aware of my personal situation since I had entrusted him with destroying the letters, insisted that I go. He would take charge of the Squadron.

Rupert didn't take much persuading to accompany me so we managed to get hold of a Toyota Land Cruiser. There were lots of them in the Gulf, donated by the company, all painted dusty yellow with an optimistic inverted V on the bonnet. It was necessary to obtain an official pass to cross the causeway to Bahrain. We began at the British HQ in Al Jubail and were passed on to people from the Pay Corps. They wanted to know the purpose of our trip. I told them it was an important Public Relations mission, we were under the command of Colonel Mike Vickery of the 14th/20th and arrangements had been made by Prince Walid of Saudi Arabia. Both these last two facts were true, the PR bit less so!

A pass was produced but then a voice stopped us as we were going out of the door.

'Major Hewitt?'

'Oh shit,' I thought. 'Nearly made it.'

I turned. The man at the counter was holding up an envelope. 'Your daily allowance,' he said. 'The Bahrain dinar is worth approximately £1.75.'

I thanked him and turned again to leave. 'Captain MacKenzie-Hill,' came the voice. Rupert stiffened. 'Don't you want your allowance, as well?'

I've always suspected that people in those jobs get their pleasure from ragging marginally dodgy situations like ours — this seems fair enough.

Still in our combat gear and Dinar-rich we stopped at an American gas station to fill up the Toyota. When I went to pay, they said there would be no charge.

We barrelled down the coast to the causeway. The Toyota was programmed to go 'bing, bing' if one exceeded 70 mph so the journey was done to the non-stop sound of 'binging'. If you've been driving around in a Challenger tank, top speed 40 mph, the temptation to put your foot down is too great.

After nearly four months in the desert, it was an eye-opener to see green grass being watered and banks of flowers and trees along the road. Bahrain seemed like a paradise. We checked into adjoining rooms at the hotel. After the bliss of warm showers we made straight for my mini-bar. The first cold beers since Christmas tasted like nectar. And the champagne wasn't bad, either.

We had given our clothes to the laundry and within an hour they came back immaculately pressed and smelling so sweet. I was grateful for my daily allowance at the end of the trip to pay for all our extras. Rupert took off to check out the terrain, but I wanted to slip between the sheets of a freshly-made bed and I drifted into the most carefree sleep I had enjoyed in months.

We stayed in Bahrain for three nights. We had brought civilian clothes with us and explored the old town and bought trinkets and souvenirs to take home. We swam in the clear blue pool of the Sheraton and had most meals at the hotel buffet. There was an enormous spread and for a single payment you could eat as much as you wanted. I don't think they had taken into account the amount that would be eaten by people who had been on army rations for as long as we had.

Prince Walid was not there but an English friend of his who had a large house with a swimming pool invited us to a party. Bahrain, it turned out, is the air-stewardess capital of the Middle East and it was just great to have some female company again.

I began to unwind. Life seemed to be getting back to normal. Or nearly normal. There were quite a lot of British officers about, mainly RAF, some still in uniform. They occupied the bars of most hotels. By and large the atmosphere was friendly and convivial — we had won the war and we were going home. There was plenty to celebrate.

But one evening I overheard an army officer saying some rather rude and untrue things about Colonel James Ellery. I waited for him to stop but he didn't. So I went across to him and suggested that he should keep his opinions to himself. I had served under James Ellery and he was a first-rate commanding officer and had the highest respect from his men.

The chap, who was a bit drunk, took a step back and eyed me up and down. 'I see you've been written about rather a lot lately,' he said.

I sensed every head in the bar turning to look at me. It was time to leave town.

Ellery had passed over the command of The Life Guards to Lieutenant Colonel AP De Ritter. The second-in-command at Athlone Barracks was now Major Peter Hunter and it was he who contacted me before we finally departed from Dahran. He told me not to get into the buses when we landed at Hanover Airport. He was sending the commanding officer's staff car to collect me. 'The newspapers are very keen to get hold of you, James,' he warned. 'We'll try and get you away from the aircraft before anybody notices.'

It worked. I managed to arrive at Athlone Barracks just before the rest of the Squadron. Behind those gates I was safe. You couldn't but be moved to tears by the welcome home. There was a guard of honour, two mounted dutymen and the band playing. Every tree seemed to have a yellow ribbon round it. People just fell out of the buses and into the arms of their loved ones. It was hugely emotional. There had been such fears in the weeks before Christmas and now there was such unconfined joy and happiness.

Several wives thanked me for bringing their husbands safely home. In normal circumstances I would have made light of it but such was the atmosphere of this incredible reunion that I found I had no words with which to respond. I just thanked them and tried to button back my emotions as much as I could. I was proud of my men. We had served our country in battle. Nobody could ever take that away from us.

Still wearing combat gear, we repaired to the Officers' Mess for tea, and tea eventually turned into a tremendous dinner. It was a day to remember.

The following morning I was back at my desk handling the administrative task of getting people away on leave. We tried to get those men who had no family in Germany back home to England by the fastest means possible.

I had telephoned Diana on my return. She said she was desperate to see me and demanded to know how quickly I could get away. I promised I would be with her in three days.

The following morning I set off in my little TVR sports car to drive to England. It was only five hours to Calais if you got a move on. I stood on the deck of the cross-Channel ferry and watched the white cliffs of Dover come into view. It was grand to be home — but I was fearful of what lay in store.

I had made an arrangement to meet Paul Burrell, Diana's butler, at a small railway station just south of Cirencester. I telephoned ahead and he was waiting there in an anonymous Ford Orion which he was driving himself.

He greeted me warmly and said how glad he was to see me back. On the drive I asked him about Diana. He told me that she had been consumed by nothing else but the Gulf all the time I was away and she was over the moon that I was home safely.

As we approached Highgrove House he warned me that nowadays there were often photographers hanging about the back entrance (which everyone used). The police were unable to do anything about them. He said he would call in and see what the situation was. If there were paparazzi, he advised me to slide down out of sight in the back seat. But the coast was clear.

I can remember the first words she shouted at me from the door.

'You've got rid of it!'

I wasn't sure what she meant. 'Got rid of what?' I asked.

'That ghastly moustache,' Diana laughed. She had seen photographs of it from the Gulf and already expressed her disapproval in her letters.

She dragged me inside, full of laughter and joy. It was the most loving and passionate welcome home any man could ever have experienced.

We talked far into the night. She said Harry had been her constant companion during the war, wearing his army uniform, sleeping in her bed some nights so they could follow the Gulf on television. William, for most of the time, had been away at what she referred to as 'prison' but she was so proud of the way he was turning out.

She had seen my family regularly when I was away and said they had had some good laughs. She was less at ease with her own family — she argued a lot with her mother and her grandmother when they were together. This was understandable, given the state of her marriage.

It was coming up to her tenth wedding anniversary and also her thirtieth birthday and Diana had been determined that this summer should be a watershed. She had known for a very long time now that Charles would never give up Camilla and she could see no point in their marriage continuing.

But the timing she had worked out had been thwarted by the fact that the marriage of Prince Andrew and Sarah Ferguson was also on the rocks. Sarah had been on the telephone to Diana wondering what to do. There was no way the Palace was going to let both royal couples announce they were splitting up at the same time. Diana had been informed in no uncertain terms that the effect on the Royal Family would be disastrous.

This was not the news that I wanted to hear. In her letters Diana had repeatedly expressed her belief that July would be the month when her life would change. Her determination to be free was so strong that I had formed a real hope that some time in the future we could be together. She had written wistfully of visiting a friend in Wantage for Sunday lunch and had so much wanted to be like her and her husband — a normal happily married couple. She said that she had prayed for that for so long she was certain that God must be aware.

In her letters she had promised that when I came home she would take me to see Pavarotti at Covent Garden and then we would go to dinner at Claridges. It had been a wonderful notion and had sustained me through some of my lowest moments in the Gulf. And it would have been possible — in the company of friends, as we had done before. But now the *News of the World* revelations had put a stop to even that. Our relationship had been subject to continuing speculation in the newspapers since then. I apologised to Diana for this. She replied that it was hardly my fault and it hadn't caused her 'too much grief'.

She seemed to be more concerned for her brother, Charles, who had been caught by the press in what she termed 'a legover situation'. She loved Charles very much and was greatly protective of him. She blamed herself for the press coverage, saying that if she hadn't been who she was nobody would have been much interested in his infidelity.

But she was who she was and the future of our relationship was what concerned me. I knew that when Paul Burrell had suggested I duck down in the car if there were photographers ahead it must have been something he had discussed with Diana. As a result of the *News of the World* and all the subsequent coverage in the press, it was madness for us to be seen together for the immediate future and maybe for the not so immediate future.

I told her that I had to return to Germany. She said that surely I could take some months off — I had done my duty. But it wasn't as simple as that. I had an important job ahead of me to try and keep up morale in my team in the aftermath of the Gulf. It would be letting the men down if I were to do otherwise — now was the time we had to stand together for support.

She understood that. But the very fact of my return to Germany made future meetings even more problematical. There was a fresh vigilance in the press and weekends at Highgrove were likely to be heavily monitored. And the chances of her coming down to my mother's house unnoticed as she had in the past were now reduced to nil.

'Don't let's talk about it, things will change,' Diana insisted.

'How can you be sure?' I asked.

She gave me a schoolgirl smile.

'I know,' I said. 'One of your soothsayer women told you. A lot of good they are.'

'Leave them alone,' she laughed — and shut me up with a prolonged kiss.

Later she said that one day she would come and live in Devon, by the sea. I told her that I would look forward to that.

'Are you prepared to wait for me?' she asked. 'Do you love me enough?'

'I have always been there for you, you know that,' I said. 'I'll love you for as long as I live.'

Polo with Prince Charles at the Royal Berkshire club, summer 1991. The red rat denotes 7 Armoured Brigade and the black rat the 4 Armoured Brigade (the Desert Rats).

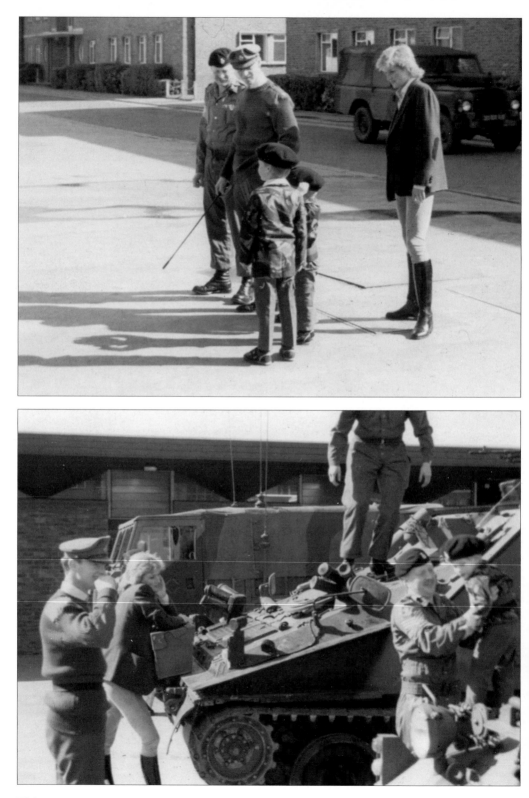

This was a great day out for the boys, looking around Windsor barracks. They are wearing the little uniforms I had made for them.

Another of the photos given to me by Diana. It is rather crumpled at the edges since I carried it everywhere.

*Top:* On exercise with the French in 1980, driving an AMX30 of the Premiere Curassierf.

*Bottom: A* photos taken during exercises with the regiment in Germany shows my tank Commanders.

*Top*: Letter-writing in my tent during the Gulf War.

*Bottom*: A photo taken shortly before *News of the World* broke the story of our love affair.

The squadron line-up in the Gulf.

*Top*: Eversfield Manor, where I hoped to run a successful equitation centre.

*Bottom*: Cross-country on Murtoca in France.

Skiing in the Zermatt – another pursuit that Diana and I both enjoyed, though sadly not together.

# 10

After a week's leave with my family I was back in Germany and back at work. Of course, it was something of an anti-climax to go out on tank training exercises again after the real thing, but there were new people joining the squadron and new techniques to be learned and practised.

At a personal level I was feeling pretty mixed up. The stories in the papers about me and Diana — true or false but mostly false — continued to come out. They turned our telephone conversations into damage limitation exercises as much as anything else and I knew they were eroding the prospects of my having a decent career in the army.

The rest of 1991 turned out to be a fairly bad year. When I was away in the Gulf I had forgotten to renew the BFG (British Forces Germany) number plates on my car and on my return to Germany I was slow in doing anything about it. It had always seemed to me a little silly to go around advertising yourself as a British serviceman with IRA and other terrorist cells about, but it was army law.

So I was stopped one day by a corporal in the Royal Military Police and asked why I wasn't driving with the correct plates on my car. I was annoyed by this and I thought he handled the situation in a rather rude manner. But I wasn't too tactful myself. I asked him if he hadn't better things to do with his time and also inquired if it was the custom in the RMP for officers to be saluted as it certainly was in my regiment. That just about did it. From that moment my card was marked. The RMP were on the look-out for me. I didn't get my BFG sufficiently quickly. The matter was reported to my commanding officer.

Fair enough — I had been in breach of a rule. This was something that could be dealt with internally but, to my astonishment, Lieutenant Colonel De Ritter chose to refer the matter to the Brigadier and it was then referred on to General Wallace, the Divisional Commander in Germany.

So I had to travel down to the headquarters in Bielefeld where in service dress and Sam Brown I was marched into the General's office. Lieutenant Colonel De Ritter was standing behind him and a military assistant read out the charges.

General Wallace looked up. 'How do you plead?'

'Guilty, General,' I replied.

'Do you want to accept my award,' he asked, 'or do you wish to elect to go for trial by court martial?'

I said that I would accept his award. He asked me if I had anything to say and I mentioned that the matter had got a bit out of proportion and maybe I was being victimised slightly. General Wallace tore me off a strip for not accepting my award in silence, fined me £700 and gave me a severe reprimand which would stay on my army record for the next five years.

I accepted the punishment but I did reflect, as I drove back to Athlone Barracks, that I had managed to discipline my own men for the past five months without referring them to a higher authority.

On June 23rd 1991 the following was published in the *London Gazette*:

> *By the Queen's Order the name of Captain James Lifford Hewitt of The Life Guards was mentioned in a despatch for Distinguished Services. I am charged to record Her Majesty's high appreciation. Signed Tom King, Secretary of State for Defence.*

It was an honour to be mentioned in Despatches but one that was tinged with disappointment. I had put forward various names including Robin Tarling, Rupert Mackenzie-Hill, James Gaselee, SQMC Ormiston, Corporal of Horse Camp and others whom I thought had performed under duress and beyond the call of duty in the Gulf but none of them received an award. 1st Battalion The Royal Scots fared rather better — they were given a dozen awards. We had the consolation of adding Gulf War 1990–1991 to the list of Battle Honours on The Life Guards Regimental Standard.

True to his word, Ronald Ferguson took up my suggestion of a post-war polo match between 4 Brigade and 7 Brigade. It took place at Brian Morrison's club, The Royal Berkshire. Major Ferguson did all the organising and persuaded Prince Charles to play which helped to raise interest in the event. I learned that Ronald Ferguson was approached by people who thought it was better that I shouldn't play. But he had told them that it had been my idea in the first place and that I would definitely be playing.

Prince Charles was obviously consulted, too, and evidently he had no objection. He played for 7 Brigade captained by Arthur Denaro. Mike Vickery captained 4 Brigade and we managed to win a hard-fought match. Prince Charles was generous in his congratulations. On the occasions when we spoke he was very chatty and friendly.

My father came to watch the match as did General Sir

Peter de la Billière and a very large crowd. The Duchess of York gave away the prizes. We managed to bring in £250,000 for the Gulf Trust, to help widows and orphans in Kuwait.

Back in Germany out on exercises I continued to work with Lieutenant Colonel De Ritter and he seemed quite keen on occasion to pick up a few things from my experience in BAOR and the Gulf.

On another occasion he was less well disposed to me. We were at the annual regimental firing camp at Hohne. The various squadrons were camped behind the ranges. De Ritter was anxious that we should be reported on well during our firing period and said there was to be no walking out over the weekend.

Robin Tarling was still with me. He was a first-class Gunnery Instructor, the only Grade A since 1953 and we had benefited enormously from his experience in practice. I asked him if it was okay if he looked after things for a bit and he was pleased to.

So I took off for Jimmy's Bar in Hamburg to watch England play Ireland in the Five Nations Championship on TV. I managed to squeeze in a party in the evening as well and stayed the night in the city.

When I walked back into HQ on Sunday there was, to say the least, a frosty hush. I was summoned before De Ritter. I knocked on his door, went into his office, clicked my heels and said: 'Good evening, Colonel, I understand you want to see me.'

'Don't you come into my office like that,' he bellowed.

'I've been in The Life Guards for fifteen years and that's how I always have,' I replied. I'm not sure I was doing my cause a lot of good.

So I had to go out and come in again, marching smartly, unusually for an officer, and giving a salute in the conventional manner — with the hand.

De Ritter wanted to know why I'd disobeyed his order to remain on the range over the weekend. I said I thought they didn't apply to Squadron Leaders and I had left my men in much more capable hands than mine.

He said my behaviour was disgraceful. Would I accept his award or go for court martial. I agreed to accept his award and he fined me £400 to be paid into regimental funds.

In recounting both these infractions I am not particularly proud of my behaviour — I believe in strong discipline — but I did feel that people might have learnt a little bit from the Gulf about flexibility and working together.

Brigadier Julian Browne had told me that I would not be required to take my promotion exams to make my acting position of major (which I had held for more than five years) a permanent one. But somewhere along the line someone thought differently and I was obliged to sit them in the autumn of 1991. There were three papers, with the main one on battle tactics, of which I had first-hand knowledge. I was told I had failed each paper by one per cent.

But I knew my card had been marked quite some time previously. I was not so naïve as to think that the authorities didn't discuss my situation with regard to the heir to the throne. It would be much more convenient for all concerned if I simply resigned my commission.

But I didn't and throughout my final year in Germany I hope I led my men with decency and consideration. They certainly indicated so when I left.

However, I was not sorry to return to Headquarters Squadron at Knightsbridge. The Commanding Officer there, Lieutenant-Colonel Gordon Birdwood, was a universally popular man. As Headquarters Squadron Leader my job was largely administrative including, for some reason, families officer. The army cut-backs had begun and I was also redundancy officer — working out courses for men to go on to prepare them for a new career. I knew it was only a matter of time before my own name would be on the list.

Diana kept in touch, although we both knew there was no question of being seen together in public. She would ring my office and Caroline Snowden who came in to help me was taken aback to hear a familiar voice saying: 'Just tell him I rang.' On a couple of occasions I went across to Kensington Palace to have lunch with her. It was good to see her but I was never sure whether our relationship was merely on hold until she disentangled her future or whether it was just a thing of the past. I don't think she was sure, either.

In June 1992 the *Sunday Times* began to serialise the Andrew Morton book *Diana: Her True Story*. Morton had written to me asking if I would talk to him about the Princess but I had declined. Diana's attitude had always been: 'Do what you like.' The book alluded to my friendship with the Princess and related how she was entertained by my parents in Devon while the boys went riding with me. I suppose if I had spoken to the author I could have told him that my parents had long been separated and the boys didn't go riding with me. But I would also have had to lie constantly to him about my relationship with Diana.

Some of Diana's friends did speak to the author. Carolyn Bartholomew, who had known her since they were at school, seemed to be the person who gave the most sympathetic account of the Princess's problems. She knew all about Diana's illness, the disaster of her marriage and most things about her relationship with me. When the book was published and people wanted to know whether Carolyn had let Diana down by talking to the author, Diana made a point of going along to Carolyn's house and embracing her for a pre-arranged press photo.

But the truth was later to emerge that the main source for much of the book was Diana herself. In fact, it seemed most likely that the whole project was her idea. She recorded a series of tapes which a friend, Dr James Colthurst, then passed on to Andrew Morton.

The revelations were instrumental in at last securing her separation from Prince Charles at the end of the year. I telephoned her and said I was happy she had found her freedom. She said she would have liked to move abroad but she wanted to devote herself to her sons.

The following year I became involved with Sally Faber, the estranged wife of a Conservative MP. We had met while hunting and she expressed a desire to ride out from Knightsbridge Barracks — an opportunity that was given to the friends and relations of soldiers serving there. Sally was an accomplished horse-woman and I would travel with her to one-day events. But the time was not right for a serious relationship and our romance gave way to a strong friendship.

Colonel Mel Jameson of the Royal Scots Dragoon Guards who was in charge of officers' postings telephoned me in early 1993 with the expected news that I was on the list of army redundancies. At the time I was back at Combermere Barracks in Windsor where Simon Faulkner was now the commanding officer of the regiment. He had allocated me the non-post of Officer without Portfolio. I said to him that clearly he didn't want me about. He acknowledged this and suggested that I take some 'gardening leave' before the actual date of my redundancy.

My future looked uncertain, to say the least. It had been hard to scale down what had been a very active existence in the army. I felt that if I set myself a challenge that was both physical and where I had to live off my wits I could best prepare myself for the changes to come.

It was my good fortune that my close friend, Francis Showering, was also contemplating a change of career and felt the need to see a bit of the world.

Over lunch and maps one Sunday we drew up a plan to drive from Devon to Mombassa in Kenya through Spain, Morocco, Algeria, Niger, Nigeria, Cameroon, Zaire and Uganda. We reckoned the journey would take us from October until Christmas.

Together we bought a long wheel-base Land Rover and customised it for the trip with such things as a roof rack, additional windows, extra gerry-can holders, sand ladders in case we got stuck in the desert (we did) and a fridge which we could cram full of goodies.

Francis did much of the engineering while I tried to get the necessary papers and visas in London. This was not very successful. The advice from many embassies was that they could not guarantee our safe passage through their country. We weren't expecting them to, but there's nothing like a bit of opposition to make you determined to press ahead.

I wrote a letter to the Military Attaché in Rabat whom I knew from the army. Not only did he ask us to stay but he introduced us to high ranking officials — even ambassadors — for the relevant African countries and after a week in Morocco I had most of the essential paperwork.

We kept diaries of the trip and perhaps one day we will type them up for the amusement of our families. Suffice to say here that the journey through Africa was considerably tougher and more arduous than either of us could have contemplated. But if it hadn't been, maybe it wouldn't have worked. You needed day-to-day problems abroad to clear out the ones you were trying to get away from at home.

Some of the advice we got was sound. We avoided the route through Mauritania as we were warned the border was mined. In other cases maybe we were lucky. We heard stories of the nomadic Taureg who dominated the trade routes in Southern Algeria stopping whole convoys and stripping them of everything. One night in the Sahara the road petered out and a few oil drums were all that indicated the possible way ahead across the desert. The last thing we needed was an encounter with the Taureg — but we got one. However, they seemed happy to share a supper of tinned sardines before indicating the route we should take in the morning and then riding off into the desert on their camels.

The most intimidating people in each country usually turned out to be the border guards. In Niger they combed through the Land Rover and discovered my army boots. Although our passports said we were 'company directors' these guards with their Kalashnikovs were convinced we were spies. Francis was taken away while I attempted to protect the vehicle. An hour and a half later he returned with the thankful news that we were free to proceed. I asked him how he managed it. 'I gave them your boots,' he said.

Using a SATNAV we set off in what we thought was the correct easterly direction to progress through the country. But our friends from the border didn't seem to like the route we had taken. They came after us in a jeep with a Pintel-mounted machine gun, firing over the roof of our vehicle. At least, we *hoped* that was where they were aiming. We were told in no uncertain terms the road they had decided we should take.

Normally the border guards just wanted more money on the pretext that our papers were invalid or that there was a tourist tax or a vehicle tax or even a tax on cameras. At the Zaire border we just point blank refused to pay any more. There was a stale-mate with the guards sitting it out as we waited all day in the burning sun. Eventually, however, they went off duty. We gave them some time to disappear and then lifted the barrier and drove into the country.

For two days it looked as if we had got away with it. But as we were boarding a raft for a river crossing, some very unpleasant officials with the inevitable Kalashnikovs came out of nowhere and arrested us. The bush telegraph had been at work. I was taken to a well-guarded villa and hauled up in front of some Idi Amin character. It looked like we might be stopping in Zaire for a year or two more than we had intended but he was more interested in cash than incarceration and decided to fine us all the money we had.

But my main memories as we drove into the heart of Africa were really warm ones. People went out of their way to help us find food and water. Whole villages would just stand and watch as we put up our tents and bedded down for the night. We came across Belgian nuns in Zaire who took us in and looked after us. And everywhere there were children who had so little to smile about — some were so incapacitated with polio that they just dragged their bodies along on their forearms — but never seemed to stop smiling.

Sometimes, in the evenings, I would open the car door and turn up the stereo and encourage the children to dance to the music so that we had a spontaneous party. At the end of it I would make them line up for their 'party bags' — Bic biros until we ran out of them and after that Cadbury's biscuits.

We met people from widely differing cultures, most of them very poor but eager to show friendship — even if there was no common language — and usually ready to give a hand when our vehicle got bogged down. When it was possible we would ask them to eat with us in the evening. We rarely spoke the same language and I can't explain why but we nearly always ended up laughing.

I have a vivid memory in Zaire of the rain coming down in such a solid wall that the window-wipers were of no use at all. We hadn't had a decent shower in weeks so we grabbed bars of soap, took off our clothes and stood by the side of the road washing ourselves. I really had a sense at that moment that the clutter of normal life was taken from me and I was somehow being purified by Africa.

In fact, just by travelling through the continent, you realise more than ever that you are a mere speck in the universe. There are many greater problems in the world than your own petty problems.

In one respect the expedition had failed. I had been unable to get Diana out of my mind, let alone out of my system. I knew I never could and never would. But I was able to put things into perspective. She called me early in 1994 and said I had to do something about all the innuendo that was recycling itself about us in the papers. People felt free to invent what they wanted. According to one paper Diana and I were living together for some of the time at my cousin's house in Chesilton Road in Fulham. In fact, she didn't even know the place existed. My solicitor put me in touch with Geoffrey Robertson QC to see what I could do to stop such stories. His advice was not optimistic — there was nothing Fleet Street would like more than for me to go to court over such a lie because it meant that Diana would have to be subpoenaed and have to appear. Was I prepared to do this? I said that I wasn't. Geoffrey pointed out that the press knew that and that was why they kept going after me. I was a soft target.

Diana urged me to give an interview to Richard Kay of the *Daily Mail* in the hope that this would put a stop to the speculation. After my experience in the Gulf I wasn't sure. But I did want to help Diana so I gave a long interview to Anna Pasternak (whom I knew through friends of friends) in the *Daily Express* about myself and my friendship with the Princess. This was an error. I was held up to ridicule by other papers for the fact that I had said nothing new — merely repeated the same old story which they knew to be false. The Palace, the police, Downing Street, Fleet Street and many others were all aware of the true facts of our relationship.

Indeed true facts were coming out all the time. Prince Charles had been giving interviews to Jonathan Dimbleby for a book and television programme revealing his side of events. He acknowledged his marriage had long broken down and he had had a subsequent affair, and the importance of Camilla Parker Bowles in his life. We had moved into a time of open government — people were more likely to forgive you if you told the truth. Anna Pasternak said there were other books in the works which undoubtedly would harm everybody concerned as they would undoubtedly contain fabrications presented as fact. With both Diana and now Charles having put their position in print, was I going to remain the silent victim of rumour for the rest of my life?

She said she would like to write a book which would present Diana and myself in a sympathetic light without any tabloid spin. She assured me it would do us both good and set matters straight.

I thought about it for several days and nights. Nothing could be as bad as the press I was now getting. And I couldn't just keep lying. Truth, I reasoned, must be the best way forward. So I agreed to do it. In the atmosphere of those times it seemed a sensible way to put an end to the lying. But it proved to be the biggest mistake I have ever made in my life.

---

Anna was pleased. She thought I had made the right decision. She only needed two more days of interviews and access to a limited amount of private papers. She would write the book under her name as she had the articles. As with them I trusted her and had no desire to see anything she had written. I told Diana that Anna Pasternak was doing a book on me. She seemed unconcerned.

After Anna had submitted some early material to the publishers, they came back and said it wasn't what they wanted. They needed much more detail. Anna said she was certain she could find a way round this. She wrote very quickly — a new draft was submitted in just over a month. She rang me to say that the book was no longer a documentary account of my life and Diana's role in it, but had become more of a love story. I said this sounded wrong to me. We should meet as soon as possible.

Anna was accompanied by her mother, Audrey, when she arrived at the village which was a halfway point between our houses. The three of us sat in the corner of a field and she explained what she had done to the book and we discussed it backwards and forwards. I said that I was not at all happy about this. I had also spoken to Diana and neither was she. I didn't want it published. I was quite prepared to give the publisher's advance back.

Both Anna and her mother were now in tears. Anna said the book had gone too far and it was too late to stop it. She asked me for Diana's telephone number and said she would call her and assure her that the book would not be harmful. I didn't give the number to her, but Anna's desire to do this and the fact that both she and her mother had such utter conviction that what Anna had written would be nothing but beneficial was finally persuasive. So I agreed that I would not try to stop it being published — not that I legally could since I had no contract with the publishers.

But I knew in my gut it was wrong. The story broke in early October 1994 that a book was about to be published in which I confirmed I had had an affair with Diana and the press were on my back as never before.

This time I had less cause for complaint — I had brought it on myself.

There was no place to hide in England so I got in my Land Rover and drove to Plymouth. My mother insisted on coming with me, although I tried to persuade her not to. But my powers of persuasion were not very strong at that time.

We crossed to Cherbourg and stayed in various small hotels and *pensions* on the Normandy coast and then went south into Bordeaux country. The book was published that week in Britain. It caused a sensation far greater than my worst fears.

I got hold of a day-old copy of the *Guardian*. Under the front-page headline ROYALS MADE LAUGHING STOCK, the paper reported that the whole print run of 75,000 copies of *Princess in Love* had been sold out in a day and — to my amazement — that the publishing director of *Burke's Peerage* had announced: 'We are extremely close to the end of the House of Windsor.'

As I got further reports from home on my mobile phone matters seemed to be going from bad to worse. One paper accused Anna of being the most hated woman in Britain (she subsequently sued them for libel and won). The press needed to talk to me to find out my involvement and to keep the story going. I was 'sighted' in Spain, America, Australia and Argentina.

Actually some journalists were closing in, thanks to a leak in my credit card company. When I used the card to pay a bill and the transaction was processed in London, a reporter would turn up at the hotel or café shortly afterwards.

I was in a state of such extreme depression I couldn't bear to talk to the press. The only way to lose the 'credit card' trail was to stay with someone. But who? I looked at the map and discovered we were less than a day's drive from Saumur where I had attended the Ecole National d'Equitation. I telephoned my former landlady, Christine Cremer. I had no need to explain my plight to her. She had read about it and readily agreed to provide a safe house for myself and my mother.

We stayed there for a week. It was the worst of times. I went for lone walks in the woods, always feeling sick but unable to be sick. One evening I went to the abbey church of Fontevrault, where I used to go with Catherine eleven years previously. Maybe I should never have let her go. If she had come to England and we had married, life would have taken a very different course. But then I would never have met Diana or fallen in love with her — or got myself into this nightmare. I looked at Richard the Lion-Heart lying with such peace and dignity on his grave and I knew what I had to do. I was going to kill myself. If I had been at home this would have been easy with a shotgun but here in France I would have to buy a hosepipe and asphyxiate myself in the car. It was too late to acquire one that night but I would do it tomorrow.

I actually slept more soundly in the knowledge that my mind was made up. But at breakfast the next day I looked at my mother across the table and realised that I couldn't just leave her in the middle of France. It's curious but absolutely true. Perhaps she knew. Her presence stopped me from committing suicide. I owe my life to her — twice.

Eventually I had to get back to England but it would have been impossible to get through any of the ports or airports anonymously. The pursuit of me had become an end in itself for some of the tabloids. But my brother-in-law, Peter Bayley, rang to say he had managed to get hold of a friend's helicopter. He would fly in to Fontevrault with the pilot and I could take his place for the return journey. He could then drive Shirley home in the car.

The plan worked perfectly. At Stansted the pilot radioed to customs and asked if they wanted to see us but they told us not to bother. Daniel Showering, Francis's brother, picked me up at the airport and drove me to Geoffrey Robertson's house in London where I stayed in the room once occupied by the fugitive Salman Rushdie. I played with the children during the day and Geoffrey's wife, the writer Kathy Lette, greatly cheered me up. When the press got nose of my presence I transferred to Lady Showering's house in Hyde Park Gate. They staked that out after a few days so under cover of darkness I headed for Peter and Caroline's house in Devon.

They had not been having a pleasant time. Reporters had been offering cleaners, grooms, handymen — anyone who worked for them — sums of money for stories about me. But nobody said anything.

I just stayed inside for two weeks with the curtains drawn. I was in a downward spiral. There was a copy of the book in the house but I couldn't bring myself to read it and I never have. But I knew there was one thing I had to bring myself to do. I telephoned Diana. I told her I wanted to apologise for what had happened. It had never been my intention to harm her. She said she believed that and was surprisingly understanding.

I couldn't stay inside forever. I eventually got a horse and went out through the back fields on to the wilds of Dartmoor. It did little to raise my spirits. While I was hacking back there must have been some photographer hidden in a hedge and a picture appeared in the papers the next day.

The sole beneficiary of all this misery was a lady who had come to book a riding lesson with my sister. A newspaper took a photograph of her and somehow implied that she and I were a couple. This was an unwise claim since she was a married woman and also an untrue one — we never even met. But today she is £50,000 richer in libel damages.

The storm never passed but it abated. There is always tomorrow's news to replace yesterday's. I managed to get back to the task of selling off the family riding school at The Shieling. Since my sister had married we had always intended to close it down. New roads had made it very hard to ride on to Woodbury Common and I had obtained planning permission to build eight houses on the site of our indoor riding school. I eventually sold it to a developer for a good price.

The tabloids, when they mentioned me, had me in the

role of social leper, outcast from local society. This wasn't so. I was invited to hunt as before and to dinner parties and house parties. Old friends if anything became firmer friends. A few people avoided me but in that manner I found out who my friends really were.

I did have to resign from the Officers' Club and The Life Guards Association. The regiment has to be seen to be loyal to the Sovereign and my relationship with Diana certainly broke that rule.

Just before Christmas I agreed to give an interview to Peter McKay in the *Evening Standard* to try and start the process of rehabilitation. He wrote: 'I read the book and quite enjoyed it. The story wasn't new. We'd read about this friendship in gossip columns for years but *Princess in Love* is chapter and verse. The *Times Literary Supplement* likes it better than two other royal offerings this Christmas: Jonathan Dimbleby's book about the Prince of Wales and Andrew Morton's on Diana. Matthew Parris in the *Times* enjoyed it, too, as did Fay Weldon in *Night and Day*.'

McKay concluded: 'If he had kept his love affair with Diana more or less private, books would have mentioned it anyway. If, then, he hadn't denied it, the story would have been told, retold and embroidered over the years. What he did, or what Anna Pasternak did, was to shoot the fox.'

I wasn't going to get a much fairer hearing than that. Somebody in America made a television film of the book but I didn't see it nor did I benefit from it financially. That apart, the story gradually attracted less media attention.

Until November 1995, that is, when Princess Diana appeared on *Panorama*.

# 11

The summer of 1997 was pleasingly busy. We now
had a solid base of clients at Eversfield for whom
we could customise their programmes. It wasn't
immensely profitable work but it was fulfilling. Also I had
built up something of a business buying and selling horses
both at home and abroad. I would travel quite regularly to
Niels Geertsen in Denmark on behalf of British customers
who were looking for horses and also to take stock
of Niels's inventory in order to find buyers for him
in England.

It seemed a less good summer for Diana. I could see
from the newspapers that she was getting a harsh and
unfair press. Since her divorce in February of the previous
year she had seemed to have found little freedom to live
life as a single woman. Wherever she went she was
dogged by photographers. And in the accompanying
stories there was nearly always the spin that she was

behaving in an eccentric or crazy fashion.

I thought she might need a bit of moral support so I telephoned her at Kensington Palace. She seemed very pleased to hear from me. She said she was finding life in England uncomfortable and was trying to do more work abroad, especially for her Landmine charity. But it was important to her to spend as much time as she could with the boys. Her pride and pleasure in them remained immense.

'How's the love life going?' she teased — she nearly always asked that.

'Pretty non-existent,' I said. 'How's yours?'

'About the same,' she replied, 'but I think I'm going to shock the world and run off and marry a big fat black man.'

We joked some more and agreed we would talk and hopefully meet in the autumn when the boys were back at school.

'Give my love to your mother and sisters,' she said by way of farewell. 'I often think of them.'

I was glad I had spoken to her, although I had told her something of a white lie. My love life *was* existent — I had met a girl called Camilla Courage and we had been seeing each other quite regularly during the summer. It was a good relationship, easy-going with neither of us making too many demands on the other.

Camilla had a pretty hectic job at an estate agents in London. She was due a couple of weeks' holiday at the end of August and we agreed to go to Marbella where Rupert's family had a villa. He wasn't there himself but his brother Charlie was down with some friends and there was plenty of room.

Quite often we went our separate ways but we tended to meet up for breakfast. The boys had already found a café down by the sea front that served a really great breakfast of fresh orange juice and delicious coffee and scrambled eggs. We tended to drift down there most mornings.

No more than a hundred yards along the coast from

there was a place where you could get the British newspapers. It was a nice little shop, quite narrow with a single door. It was owned by a little old Spanish lady who, the moment I walked into it, pointed her finger at me and pronounced: 'You are James.'

It wasn't uncommon for people in Spain to recognise me — the ubiquitous *Hola* magazine would often run pictures. But her instant and certain response was probably due more to the display of all the English tabloids along her wall — over the years she must have seen my face on the front of a few of those.

She was a very genial woman with slightly more English than I had Spanish. We struck up a friendship of sorts and chatted each day while I perused the tabloids before buying my *Daily Telegraph*.

'Diana — she is a wicked woman,' she once remarked.

I asked her what on earth made her say that. I told her that the opposite was the case — Diana was a good woman who had been done wrong. Only now did life seem to be turning around for her.

But, as the days went by, I could see that a reading of the tabloids did give the impression that Diana was somehow doing something wrong.

She was pictured on a romantic holiday with Dodi Fayed (who had ditched his American fiancée) on board his father's yacht *Jonikal* in the South of France. Her wickedness seemed to consist of this and the fact that this was her third holiday in six weeks; she was taking too much hospitality from Mohamed Fayed, the controversial owner of Harrods, and she should have been spending more time with her sons or working for charities such as landmines.

I didn't know Dodi but the friends we had in common spoke well of him and I could tell from the pictures that he seemed to make Diana happy. This made me very happy for her. I genuinely had no jealousy. I was with Camilla now. Maybe Diana and I might have had a future together if the timing had been right.

But Diana seemed more than happy. I knew her and I

could tell she was at last winning the battle with her own demons, both those inside her and those outside. She had achieved the position she wanted. She was divorced, she was financially secure and she was accountable to nobody save her two sons. That summer she had sold all her frocks to raise money for AIDS charities — it was a symbolic gesture, liberating her from all those formal occasions where she would have needed to dress up. She was her own woman — and she discovered that she had immense fame without the need to be part of the Royal Family, as was evidenced by her vastly successful landmines crusade. And this fame — this ability to command photographers and press and television like no one else in the world gave her real power. She was a leader and I really admired her for that.

There was no longer any need for her to hide anything about her life. She was free to be the person she really was at last. She could go on holiday with Dodi Fayed or any man she wanted. I doubted if she intended to marry Dodi — it's not the sort of thing you decide on in the first weeks of a relationship. But she was clearly enjoying herself as never before in public. She would certainly know what the papers were printing about her. I remember when she stayed in Devon she would urge me to go out and buy every single Sunday paper. But what was important now was that she read the stuff and she didn't care. They'd castigated her to hell and back but it didn't worry her any more. She had insulated herself from cruel jibes. For the first time in her life I could tell she was utterly, joyously free.

It was an extremely relaxing time in Marbella. We swam, played volleyball with people we met on the beach, explored the local hills — there was an entrancing village called Ronda — and read. On Saturday night we stayed late at a nightclub in Puerto Banus. I had bought some tickets for a local bull-fight the following day. The plan was for us all to have a picnic brunch on the beach and then drive along to it.

I woke up late that day. Charlie Mackenzie-Hill and

Camilla were already at the pool waiting for the rest of us. I emerged — somewhat dozily — and then went back into my room to get my mobile phone. I remember thinking it wasn't really necessary since it had hardly rung all week. I picked it up and dialled in the code to the recall service and found there were seven messages. My immediate thought was that there must be something ghastly about me in the Sunday papers.

One of the messages was from Rupert. I could rely on him to give it to me straight so I called that up first.

His voice on the answering machine didn't really sound like him, he was usually so lively and positive but this was slow and sombre.

'Listen, I know where you are, so you may not have heard this. There's very bad news. Diana's dead. She and Dodi were killed in a car crash in Paris during the night.'

I played the message again. And again. Then I went back out and broke the news to the others. They were completely stunned. I said I would try and find out some more information and returned to my room. I just wanted to be on my own, but I had a small radio and I twiddled the dial to find an English language station. As I did so I could hear that on every station in every language people were talking about nothing else but the death of the Princess. I wandered around my room in a shocked state listening. And then I cried.

I just remained very, very tearful and in a state of shock as I listened to all the reports. People were talking about conspiracy theories or that it was the paparazzi's fault, but I knew it would be a long time before they had all the facts. My mind was racing. I couldn't stay on holiday. I had no desire to go splashing in the sea when the woman I'd been with for five years was dead. But I had to consider Camilla and the other people I was staying with. I knew the fact I'd been seen by British journalists in Puerto Banus meant I would eventually be hunted down. It took them two hours to find me but Charlie asked them to go away. I realised I had to get back.

I telephoned Terrence Rowland at Eversfield Manor.

He was extremely distressed. There was already a gathering of press and television at the gates. He said he didn't know what to do. 'Don't worry,' I told him. 'I'm coming home.'

I managed to get on a flight that afternoon from Malaga to Gatwick. A friend met me and drove me down to Devon. My mother and Becky had arrived at the house which was now surrounded with news crews and photographers.

I knew I had to say something or people would just stay there for days. So I asked Terrence to go down to the main gate and tell them that I would come and make a short statement, but nothing more, no questions.

I sat for a while with a pad and a glass of whisky and made some notes. When I was ready I walked down to the gate. There were large numbers of press and television crews gathered as there had been on other occasions but this time something was different. Nobody was pushy, firing snide questions or telling me where to stand. Instead they seemed rather contrite and very respectful of my feelings for probably the first time ever.

I kept my statement as brief as possible. I just said that like the rest of the world I was shocked and very sad and my condolences went to the families of Diana and Dodi, and the relatives of the driver killed in the crash.

I spent much of the next few days following events on television. On more than one occasion Diana had said to me that the Royal Family needed better advisers as they were frequently out of touch with the emotions of the people. Now her own death was bringing about a change in royal behaviour in a way that she could never have imagined.

I watched the field of flowers in Kensington Palace Gardens grow larger and larger, like a spreading tide. I had an urge to go to London but it was out of the question. It would result in drawing attention to myself and I certainly had no wish to do that. I was astounded at the magnitude of what was happening. I wasn't too sure about 'people power'. I wondered if some people thought they had bought the newspapers that had in some way contributed to her death and this was an expression of guilt as much as grief. I really didn't know. Nobody did. It had never happened before.

In fact, I was laid low by a recurrent bout of sinusitis and took to my bed for a couple of days. I felt numb with sadness. I began to receive letters of condolence from strangers — eventually totalling more than a hundred, some from as far away as Australia and I, in turn, reread some of the letters Diana had written to me over the years and remembered her in my own way. I realised I loved her more than any other woman I ever have or ever will love — and, for some years at least, she felt the same way about me.

One letter was especially poignant. She had written it to me almost exactly eight years previously, in August of 1989, when I had been away in France and she was waiting for me to come back. In it she wrote: 'I have lain awake at night loving you desperately and thanking God for bringing you into my life — you, my darling one, are the most magical and special person I've ever met and how extraordinarily lucky I am to be loved by you — what a difference it's made to me and I just long for the days when finally we will be together for always, as that is how it should be.'

We watched the funeral on television. My sisters left their husbands and families at home and joined my mother and Camilla, who had returned from Spain, and me. My family loved Diana dearly and knew the boys. The moment when the young Princes joined the cortège was too much. I looked round the room and it was just full of grief.

There was a feeling of great sadness that she should be buried in an island grave. It seemed a lonely place to be for ever. I think she would probably have liked to have been with her father. She introduced me to him one night at Kensington Palace, she was so fond and proud of him. Maybe she is, in fact, buried in the family vault in the church at Althorp — only the family would know.

I wrote a letter of condolence to Charles Spencer whom

I had first met when Diana had invited me to Raine
Spencer's 60th birthday party at Althorp in 1989. He later
wrote back and said he had received letters from hundreds
of thousands of people. He thanked me for taking the time
to write and, in an extremely thoughtful letter, said he
knew how difficult this must be for me, too.

I also wrote to Prince William and Prince Harry at
Kensington Palace. I said there was no need for them to
write back to me but my thoughts were with them in their
grief and my sorrow was deep. I just wanted them to
know that I counted myself very lucky to have been a
friend of their mother.

# 12

I first became aware of the Chaos Theory when I went to see the film *Jurassic Park*. The scientist, Ian Malcolm, simplified the physics for the audience: a butterfly flaps its wings in Beijing and the weather in New York changes. The butterfly that brought chaos into my own life was called Anna Ferretti, a beautiful dark-haired Italian woman.

If the Louis XV restaurant at the Hotel de Paris in Monte Carlo had not been completely booked on the night of Sunday, November 30th 1997 I would probably never have met her and the next couple of years of my life might have been reasonably quiet and undisturbed. In the event, the reverse was to be the case.

It had been a fairly miserable November in England. Life at Eversfield had never been quite the same since Diana's broadcast. The people who worked with me noticed that we were attracting some clients who arrived more with the ulterior motive of taking a close look at me rather than improving their riding skills. And at that time of year, when the nights drew in, the number of guests always dropped.

So when Sir James Cayzer — an old family friend — suggested a long weekend in Monte Carlo, ostensibly to celebrate the birthday of the mother of Geoffrey Bunting (an American chum of us both who works in the City), but really to take a break from the November gloom, I took very little persuading. An army colleague, Giles Stibbe, was equally enthusiastic. We had all been away together before and got on well as a group

James, Giles and I had actually booked rooms at L'Hotel Hermitage in Monte Carlo but there had been a mix-up and when we got to the hotel the ones we had requested facing the sea were unavailable. There doesn't seem much sense in going to Monte Carlo for the week-end and not having a room with a view so we managed to rebook at the Hotel de Paris. There was no way I could have known it at the time, but had I stayed at L'Hermitage it was unlikely that I would have become involved with Anna Ferretti. But my room at the Hotel de Paris had a great balcony that looked out over the harbour, crammed with splendid yachts, and the shimmering Mediterranean beyond.

The weather was glorious that weekend. We lunched at La Chèvre d'Or with its magnificent view of the Riviera, we visited friends in the hills behind Nice and went for long walks and shopped for perfumes and oils and other gifts at the famous Soap Factory in Grasse.

On our last night it had been our intention to eat at the Louis XV restaurant in our hotel. I had half assumed that staying at the Hotel de Paris would ensure a table there but when I rang to book that Sunday night there were no tables left. So I made a reservation instead at Le Train Bleu, a less popular restaurant but still a good one. The food proved excellent and the wine every bit as good. We were all feeling relaxed at the end of an enjoyable weekend and found plenty to laugh about.

The only other occupants of Le Train Bleu when we arrived were an oldish man dining with quite a young woman — not an uncommon sight in Monte Carlo. It looked as if our two tables were going to have the place to ourselves. But just after we had finished ordering, two attractive women arrived at the restaurant.

Annoyingly they were shown to a table directly behind me. This gave Giles and James an opportunity to pull my leg a bit and say how I was missing a beautiful view. Tempted, I tried to sneak a glance at them but on both the occasions when I surreptitiously turned my head I was caught by one of them looking directly back at me. I gave them a smile — I was a bit embarrassed — but, as I recall, it wasn't returned. When I later looked round for a third time their table was empty — they must have left by a different door.

After dinner I suggested that we all should go to the Casino for a night-cap but Sir James insisted he was off to bed and the Buntings pleaded that they had an early flight and retired to their hotel. So it was left to Giles and me to go out on the town. Actually I didn't want to gamble, it had been an expensive enough weekend without donating more funds to the Monegasques, but the bar at the Casino is a great place to watch the world go by — all types from Arab princes to Mafia millionaires. Or so they seemed. I think it was Somerset Maugham who described Monaco as 340 sunny acres inhabited by shady people.

Wherever big money is being spent there are inevitably beautiful women to be seen and that night was no exception. I wasn't really surprised to see the two girls from the restaurant there. They were playing the poker machines, something which has always seemed to me the equivalent of throwing coins down a bottomless well.

After we ordered a couple of whiskies Giles gave me a nudge and suggested I should ask the girls to join us.

'Why is it always me?' I said. 'It's your idea, you go and ask them.'

'No, no,' he insisted, 'you go. You may have more luck.'

'Coward,' I said, 'go on.' But he wouldn't budge.

They were clearly on their own so, taking the bull by the horns, I walked over to talk to them. I said *'bonsoir'* and they said *'bonsoir'* back. Then I asked them if they were having any luck and they said no. So I said maybe they would like to join us at the bar for a drink. But they politely declined so I excused myself and let them continue to lose money.

Giles was greatly amused by my failure. 'Okay, you try and do better,' I challenged him. But he excused himself on the grounds that he, like the Buntings, was leaving on the early flight. He finished his drink and said he was going to hit the hay.

But I had an urge to prolong the weekend. It had been such a good one and I reasoned to myself that I hadn't come to Monte Carlo just to sleep. So I made my way to a nightclub called The Living Room. I was greeted by the doorman, who knew me. I had been a regular visitor to the principality since I was thirteen. The father of Francis Showering, who was at Millfield with me, had a house at Cap d'Ail and I had visited it regularly over the years. From the time my face had been featured in newspapers and magazines there I was aware that most front-of-house staff seemed to know me. It's their business not to miss much. So the doorman asked me how I was getting on and we chatted for a bit. In fact, we had a beer together. He said it was pretty dead inside and not really worth my while going in. I took his advice and thanked him and said I'd be back some other time, maybe in the spring or summer.

It was a clear night, warm for November and I decided to take a stroll and enjoy the balmy Mediterranean air before turning in. After about fifteen minutes I was just coming round the corner of the square on my way back to the Hotel de Paris, when I saw the two girls at the bottom of the Casino steps walking down the street towards me. As we passed I said 'Good night' — this time in English — and they said 'Good night' in English and that was it.

I entered the hotel, retrieved my key from reception

and took the lift up to the fifth floor. Once in my room I took a shower and afterwards packed my bag except for the clothes I was going to travel in. We were due to return to London after breakfast the next morning. Wrapped in a big towel I lay down on the bed and flicked through the television channels. There were various French movies on but none of them seemed of much interest so I settled for Sky News and caught up with some of the weekend sport from England. I had dined well and felt peaceful and relaxed.

I was awoken by the sound of the phone ringing. I must have dozed off. I glanced at my watch: it was past one o'clock. I couldn't think who it could possibly be — you always try and make a split-second anticipation in order to prepare yourself.

I lifted the receiver and guardedly said: 'Yes?'

There was a pause and then I heard a woman's voice say: 'Is that James?'

I couldn't place the voice at all — she sounded French so I merely said 'yes' again.

The voice said: 'It's Anna.'

I didn't know any French Annas. I merely repeated 'Anna?'

'We met at the Casino,' she went on.

'I didn't meet anybody at the Casino ...' I began — and then it clicked. The two girls. So I came out with something like 'Oh yes — Anna — right — how are you?'

Her voice remained very calm. 'I was wondering if you'd like to come for a drink?'

I explained that although that would be very nice I was already in bed and it was pretty late. We talked some more and eventually agreed that she would come up to my room for a drink.

I was now fully alert and called Giles. 'You're not going to believe this,' I said, 'but I've just had a call from one of the girls in the Casino. She's coming up for a drink.'

'Do you think she's a journalist?' he asked.

'I'm not sure,' I replied. The thought had crossed my mind. 'Somehow I don't think so.'

'You know where I am if you need me,' he replied. 'Have fun.'

I quickly got up and put on some trousers and a white towelling hotel dressing gown and generally tried to smarten myself up a bit. I was still in the bathroom when the doorbell rang.

I opened it and there was Anna. I did a double-take — she looked utterly beautiful, a million dollars. She was by far the prettier of the two girls to whom I'd spoken earlier: long dark hair, tight-fitting trousers and a white Versace top that did little to hide her eye-catching figure.

I invited her to come in and asked her if she'd like some champagne. She said she would and I found a bottle in the mini-bar which I opened. We sat on the bed and had a sort of frivolous conversation. Her English was limited so we spoke mainly in French. The year I had spent on the riding course in Saumur in the Loire Valley stood me in reasonable stead, although my command of the language was a bit rusty. But we seemed to communicate with ease, especially compared to our curt exchanges in the Casino. The conversation became more flirtatious — *much* more flirtatious. She asked me if I believed in one night stands. I told her that I didn't really but joked that there were exceptions to every rule.

She moved closer to me on the bed and started to play with the cords of my dressing gown. 'Why don't you get out of this thing?' she suggested.

I didn't need persuading. We made love. It was glorious, passionate, exciting, unforgettable. We held each other tightly and silently. The feeling was so good.

After we had made love for a second time, we lay back on the bed and began to talk again — this time a little more seriously. She lit a long, slim cigarette and seemed very relaxed. I was intrigued to find out how she had tracked me down.

'I asked a concierge who is a special friend of mine,' she replied casually. 'I told him I wanted to find the tall Englishman in the blazer who had come in earlier.'

I pointed out to her that no member of staff in a hotel

of this standing would reveal the identity of a guest, let alone the number of his room. It just wasn't done.

'They all know me here,' she explained. 'I lived in the penthouse of this hotel for fifteen years with my husband — Alberto Ferretti. He was Italian, like me. But he became ill and he died. That was more than two years ago.'

She went on to say that she now had a house nearby in Beaulieu-sur-Mer and had come into town to have supper with her sister, Lucia, who lived in Anna's Monte Carlo apartment with her boyfriend.

I asked if Lucia was the reason why she wouldn't have a drink with me in the Casino. Anna shook her head. 'No. That place is full of security cameras, they watch your every move. I am very well known here and I do not want them seeing everything I do and every person I meet.'

I told her that I was leaving the next day but I would really like to see her again. She said that would be very nice — she would like to see me, too. She would love to show me her favourite shops and restaurants. I warned her that if she was concerned about her privacy in Monte Carlo she should know that I sometimes had my photograph taken by paparazzi.

She seemed surprised by this and asked me why. I told her that I had been involved with Princess Diana and took her through the events in my life that had caused me to be of interest to the papers. Anna said she had no idea of any of this and anyway it didn't matter a bit. She wondered why they still bothered with me.

I agreed but explained that it was a fact that a photograph of me with a girl — any girl — could often make money for the photographer. I knew this by the way paparazzi lingered on the bridle path across my property and journalists even offered bribes to people working with me for information about girlfriends.

I think she thought I was exaggerating — but I wasn't. She repeated that it didn't worry her. She would still like to see me again. She slipped out of bed and got dressed. After writing her telephone number on the pad by the phone, she gave me a passionate farewell kiss and then left.

On the plane back to London I couldn't get over how smitten I had been by this woman. I desperately wanted to see her again. My own relationship with Camilla Courage — although neither of us had really wanted to admit to it — had been declining in the weeks since Diana had been killed on August 31st. It had been a strange period for all the world and a stranger one still for me. Once Diana was divorced and had the freedom that she had continuously craved throughout our time together, it was all too late. That hurt a lot. I knew that too much water had flowed under the bridge for us ever to get together again but I also knew that I would never love another woman in the same way.

After the crash there was no escaping her image: every newspaper, every magazine, every television bulletin seemed to remain focused on her. Wherever you turned, there was Diana. My feelings were in turmoil. Camilla was a steadfast and understanding friend but our relationship just slipped away during that period. It was entirely my fault. She was dealing with somebody who was emotionally absent. I liked and respected her enormously and today I'm glad to say we are still the best of friends.

Now, three months later, I saw in Anna Ferretti the chance of a fresh start. She was foreign, she had no knowledge of the baggage that I trailed with me and she was entrancing.

I telephoned her when I got to Devon and asked her to come and stay in London the following weekend. She sounded excited on the phone and agreed immediately.

It was with some trepidation that I waited for her at Heathrow the following Friday. Had I built her up too much in my mind? Our relationship, however passionate, had been — to say the least — fleeting.

But things worked out better than I could have expected. Anna looked more beautiful than I remembered her. We hit it off from the word go. In a curious way the fact that we communicated in a sort of hybrid language of our own made our emotional contact more important than words. I spoke no Italian. She was fluent in French but her

English was weak and ungrammatical. So we swapped between English and French in the same sentence but we seemed to understand each other.

It was the Christmas season in London. The city always takes on a sense of excitement at this time of year and we shared it as we walked hand-in-hand among the shoppers in the West End streets, bright with decorations. The stores all had a bustling Christmas atmosphere and we went in and out of them, buying each other little presents.

We stayed with some friends of mine in Ebury Street in Chelsea and in the evenings dined at the local Italian restaurants which were packed with people full of the Christmas spirit. Our romantic life proved even richer. I loved being with Anna — I was infatuated with her and she certainly showed every sign of being emotionally involved with me.

She told me about her childhood in Sorrento in the south of Italy. Her grandfather had been a very wealthy man but he had not supported her father because he considered he had married beneath him. In fact, Anna said, he had married for love. He travelled widely and eventually made good as an international businessman. She and her sister Lucia were part of a large family. When she was only fifteen she went to Milan to work as a model. It was there, two years later, she met Angelo Ferretti who was a fashion magnate. Despite an age difference of more than thirty years, they fell in love, married and had a son — Luchino. Angelo was an inveterate gambler so they moved into the penthouse of the Hotel de Paris next door to the Casino. And it was in that hotel that he had died of a heart attack three years previously, leaving Anna a widow at only 35.

He left her well provided for and she moved to a villa in Beaulieu-sur-Mer in the South of France. Now she had business interests of her own — she had invested $10 million in a company that was developing a new fabric — something like Gortex — and this took her back to Italy and to the States. She was building the business up in the hope of selling it to the Japanese for several million dollars.

She also told me that there had been no other man in her life after her husband died — not until she met me.

Later in the month she came down to Devon to stay at Eversfield Manor. She had never ventured outside of London before on previous trips to England. She fell in love with the house, saying that it and the wild countryside around it reminded her of a romantic England that she had only seen in movies.

I wanted her to meet the rest of my family. We had tea at Gidleigh Park Hotel with my mother and, later, drinks with Caroline, my twin sister, and her husband Peter at their house, the Old Rectory. I seem to remember she spent a lot of time playing with the children and they certainly gave her a huge seal of approval.

An old army friend, Tony Grimley Grennan, asked us to dinner at his farm. Anna insisted on helping his wife, Marianne, with the washing up and I could hear them chattering away in French like two old schoolfriends as Tony and I sipped whisky and talked by the fire.

At the end of the week we met up with Caroline and Peter again to make up a party for the Mid-Devon Hunt Ball. This was the most eagerly awaited annual event in the local calendar. It was held at Castle Drogo which stands imperiously above the wooded Fingle Gorge of the River Teign. This was, in fact, the last castle to be built in England, the pride and joy of a tea baron, Julius Drewe, who had admired the work of Sir Edwin Lutyens in New Delhi and commissioned him to design his mock medieval home. On the night of the ball there was a dusting of snow on the huge, circular croquet lawn.

Anna was entranced by it, saying it was so English and so different from anything she'd been to before. The Master and some other gentlemen were in white tie and red tailcoats and she said that she would like to have seen me dressed like that.

I told her you had to be awarded the hunt button to be entitled to wear red tailcoats. At the grand hunt balls this was a more common sight. I had hunted a regimental pack of bloodhounds in the Wesser Vale in Germany. But I had

had enough of dressing up in my army days and was far more comfortable in a dinner jacket.

Anna entered into the spirit of the occasion with a great sense of fun. She insisted that I dance every dance with her. She looked gorgeous in a figure-hugging strapless gown, her deep brown tan setting her apart from the winter-white shoulders of the other women.

She was keen to experience English country life so the next morning we set off to join the meet at Drew Steignton. I showed her round the old village church and then we repaired to the Drewe Arms for breakfast. Not a few people were nursing a hangover and Anna soon learnt what the 'hair of the dog' meant. George Lyon Smith, the Joint Master, asked me why I wasn't mounted and I explained that my house guest was not an experienced rider.

Outside the mounted field — most of them dressed in black hunting coats, less formal than the shires — were handed drinks. There were the familiar cries of 'Brandy! Whisky! Come here, Grasper!' as the huntsman gathered his hounds. He blew a couple of notes on his horn and they were off.

We followed by car for a while and got out to watch the hounds draw the first cover. Anna said that she thought it was cruel. I pointed out that she rarely went anywhere without her fur coat. The hunt headed deeper into the country and we left them to their day's work.

Anna took my arm. She seemed very happy. I asked her what she was going to do for Christmas and she said that she had to visit her mother in Italy the following week but apart from that she had no particular plans. So I suggested she might like to return to Devon and join my family. She hugged me with delight and said she had hoped I was going to say that.

So it was that she arrived back at Eversfield Manor late on Christmas Eve. There was limited public transport that night so she had taken a Claridges car from Heathrow. I think the cost surprised her — it was something like £500 — but fortunately I had sufficient cash in the house to cover it. I helped her in with her luggage. I was truly glad to see her and so was my mother who greeted her like an old friend although they had only met for the first time the previous week.

Anna was hungry so I went into the kitchen to make her an omelette and she followed me in. Setting a goodies bag on the wooden counter, she pulled out *pannatone* and champagne and fruit and chocolates like a female Father Christmas. But, more than anything else, she brought warmth.

Christmas morning dawned crisp and clear. I got up early to exercise the hunters and then Anna and I went to a drinks party at Glebe Farm followed by our family Christmas lunch at Peter and Caroline's. Afterwards, as was traditional, we exchanged presents. It was clear that Anna had given a lot of thought in choosing presents, especially for Peter and Caroline's children. There were Kid Cool pyjamas for Hugh and nightdresses for Harriet and Lily. She gave me a fountain pen and expressed delight at the earrings that I had bought for her.

Anna stayed on until the end of December. She eagerly helped around the house and was at great pains to clean my bedroom and reorganise my wardrobe although as far as I was concerned the place was already pretty tidy. However, Anna made it look as if it had been smartened up for barrack room inspection with my shirts freshly ironed and restacked and my suits immaculately ordered. I asked her how on earth she had learnt to do all this if she'd been living in the penthouse of the Hotel de Paris for the past fifteen years. She said that all Italian girls — especially from the south — learned how to 'look after their man'.

She returned to Monte Carlo for a few days and then arrived back at Waterloo on Tuesday, January 6th with her son, Luchino. I took them to dinner at The Ivy that night. It seemed strange for a woman who was only 38 to have a grown-up son of 21. He had been educated in America and spoke American English. Now he was intending to become a student in London. We went out to lunch and dinner several times that week but I never warmed to him.

He was the beneficiary of a substantial trust fund administered by his elder step-brother Mimmo, the son of Angelo Ferretti by a previous marriage. He had acquired an indulgent lifestyle.

So it was something of a relief after dinner on Thursday when Luchino announced that he was going off to stay with friends and at last Anna and I were able to be alone together.

My father, John Hewitt, was in hospital in Exeter recovering from a small operation. I had been unable to see him over Christmas and now was a good opportunity to do so and to introduce him to Anna. I had told him a lot about her over the phone and he was intrigued to meet her.

He was fully dressed and sitting by his bed when we entered his hospital room. He stood up and welcomed Anna warmly. Whether he was in pain or not, he certainly didn't show it. As a former Royal Marine, it was his style to make light of any situation. He told her this was an excellent opportunity to practise his French and surprised her with his fluency in the language.

My father always has a great sense of humour, on occasion too great. Sweeping Anna's fur coat off the bed he pulled it over his head and proceeded to do an imitation of Flannagan and Allen singing 'Underneath the Arches'. I curled up in embarrassment as — between snatches of the song — my father tried to explain to Anna who the Crazy Gang were. But she seemed to love it — and was certainly very taken by him.

Afterwards we stocked up at a delicatessen on various sorts of pastas, ciabatas, olive oil and a variety of Italian delicacies we both enjoyed and set off for Eversfield. On Saturday night we gave a dinner party for Chris Tar — who used to command the King's Troop Royal Artillery and now had a business in Devon — and his wife, Jackie. Caroline and Peter were also invited but not invited was my lurcher, Tess, who, while we were having drinks, took the smoked salmon off everyone's plates, delicately leaving the slices of brown bread and lemon exactly in place.

Fortunately there was plenty of Italian food to

compensate. Chris later wrote saying how much they liked Anna and how well we had coped with the 'canine theft of the first course. You showed great steadiness under fire.'

On Monday it was back to work. In fact, you're always working if you are running a stable with horses to exercise and sheep and poultry to feed. Some clients came for riding lessons and I took them out on the moor. It was an arduous day but I looked forward to coming home, knowing that Anna would be there.

After we had fed the horses and finished in the stables, I went through the back door and into the kitchen. I half expected to see Anna there but she wasn't. I pulled off my boots in the cloakroom and went into the hall — no sign of her in the drawing room. So I called to her up the stairs.

'I am here.' Her voice came from the bedroom. I went eagerly up the stairs, two at a time. Maybe this was the special way Italian women traditionally welcomed their men home.

But she was on her knees by a bedside chest of drawers with neat piles of handkerchiefs and socks and underwear which she was tidying up and redistributing in separate drawers. Scattered on the bed were some blue airmail letters which she must have found and thrown there.

'What are you doing?' I asked.

'I'm tidying up.'

'What are these doing?' I pointed to the letters on the bed.

'What are they?' she said accusingly.

'Private letters,' I replied.

She looked at me and shook her head. 'You are obsessed with her, aren't you? All you English are obsessed with her.'

'I told you about her,' I said. 'I told you about her the first night we were together. '

I gathered the letters up and put them back in the top drawer. Then I went into the bathroom for a shower.

It was just the two of us for dinner and the subject was not mentioned again. Anna said she was keen to ride and since I had no clients the following day we made plans to go out in the morning. She was a little apprehensive, not having had much experience with horses, but I promised I would take good care of her.

I decided that we would take the horses and drive to Dartmoor. The riding was easier there. It was a misty damp morning, mild for January. I had put Anna on a small cob who was ideal for novices. I took her on the leading rein as we wended our way up the steep paths to the moor.

Once we reached the flat terrain I leant across and released the catch of the leading rein. I could see the flash of apprehension in her eyes. 'Don't be afraid,' I said. 'Arthur is very well behaved.'

'*Comme toi,*' she smiled.

We rode beside each other and, glancing out of the corner of my eye, I could see her slowly begin to relax and enjoy herself. It was a sight I had seen many times and each time it was equally gratifying. I trusted Arthur and he was repaying my trust by giving Anna confidence.

'*Contente?*' I asked.

'*Oui. Très contente.*'

We rode several miles across Dartmoor without encountering another soul. We could have been the only two people left in the world. There was a lone pub where I knew we could get a pint and a pie for lunch. I indicated it to her in the distance, inquiring if she was hungry.

She nodded. But something in her manner seemed to have changed. I asked her if anything was wrong.

'You came here with her, didn't you?' she said.

'Yes,' I replied. 'I did. But she's gone now.'

# 13

Anna left before the end of the month to go back to Italy. She told me that she was still in the process of winding up her late husband's estate, there being a lot of red tape to be got through. She also had business meetings there and in France and, later, in the States. Since neither of us had a desk job it made sense to keep in touch by mobile phone when she was in Europe. We hardly ever used a land line. She travelled a lot and sometimes when I called her I would ask what the weather was like in France and it would turn out she was in Italy.

I continued my work at Eversfield. On Saturday, February 14th 1998 — Valentine's Day — I was sent a single red rose. At first I thought it might be from Anna, but there was a note attached from someone who claimed to have met me at a party in London. It didn't give her name but it did give her phone number. I had indeed gone with some friends to a party after a dinner in London earlier in the month and I had spent part of the evening talking to an attractive girl there.

But I smelt a rat. The previous year I had been set up by a female journalist from the *Mirror* in this fashion and I was pretty sure that this was the same trick and, most probably, the same woman. If it was, I wanted the chance to meet her again and tell her just what I thought of her, face to face.

These traps are carefully planned. What had happened the previous time was this. Andrew Neil, the former editor of the *Sunday Times*, had invited me to a party at Daphne's restaurant in London for the launch of his book, *Full Disclosure* — an account of his years at the paper and the Wapping revolution. It was a celebrity-filled evening, a lot of television and media people turned out plus quite a few MPs. I was a free spirit at the time and certainly enjoyed the company and the champagne. I was introduced to a very attractive girl who told me she ran a business producing custom-made waistcoats and we spent part of the evening talking to each other and getting on rather well. I was very keen to see her again but somehow she disappeared into the throng before I had the chance to take her telephone number.

It had been on my mind to call Andrew and thank him for the party and see if he knew who the girl was. But I never got round to it. Some months later, however, she got in touch with me — or so it appeared.

On Valentine's Day 1997 a red rose arrived at Eversfield with a telephone number on it. I rang the number and a girl answered. I asked her if we knew each other and she said we did — we had met at Andrew Neil's party and spent some time talking together.

I was unable to come up to London so I asked her if she would like to come down to Devon. She sounded tempted but said she couldn't get away. We kept in touch by phone over the next few days and had some quite steamy conversations — not all of the steam coming from my end. She sounded extremely forward and I was rather excited by her.

Later in the month I had to come up to London to discuss a possible business deal. The meeting was at Claridges so I rang the Valentine's girl and asked her if she would like to have a drink with me there later in the evening. She eagerly agreed.

But when she turned up it wasn't the girl I had expected — the one who ran the waistcoat company. Far from it, she was short and plain and dumpy. But she had obviously gone to a lot of effort to dress for an evening out. My heart sank. After our telephone conversations I could hardly say 'hello — goodbye' so we had a drink at Claridges and then went on for a meal at Trader Vic's in the Park Lane Hilton. Not only wasn't she very attractive, she was pretty hard work when it came to conversation. It was with relief that I paid the bill, said goodnight and put her in a cab.

But I had been stitched up. Her name was Carole Aye Meung and she was a journalist on the *Mirror*. Some days later she wrote an account in the paper — complete with photographs that must have been secretly taken — of how hard I had tried to seduce her. Not true. I have rarely tried harder to end a meal and escape home. Parts of our previous telephone conversations might have been deemed seductive but I fear Miss Meung in the flesh would have a great deal of difficulty in being seduced by anybody.

So when I spoke to the rose-sender of 1998 I told her I suspected exactly who she was. However, she insisted this was not the case.

'Well,' I said, 'I'm pretty sure you're a journalist.'

She seemed deeply offended. 'No, I'm not. You've got the wrong idea,'

But I knew I hadn't. I agreed to meet her in London the next week to confirm my suspicions and to let her know just how low I thought she was. When I arrived in town I deliberately kept her on the hop by changing the location of our assignation. I was sure that if she was the girl from the party she would soon tell me to stop mucking her about and if she was a journalist she would agree to anything to get her story.

I eventually gave her half-an-hour's notice to meet me outside the Ebury Street Wine Bar. It gave me scant satisfaction when I turned up to encounter, once again, the unappealing features of Miss Meung.

'How could you have written that despicable stuff?' I asked her.

'Listen,' she pleaded, 'it was all in good heart. I don't think I was horrible to you. Let's go in and have a drink and make up.'

I told her I'd rather have a drink with the devil — 'in my opinion you're a ghastly, deceitful woman.'

I didn't want to be photographed with her again so I walked off. But not fast enough. There was a telephoto lens trained on us the whole time. Rather to my surprise neither the photograph nor any article by Miss Meung appeared in the *Mirror* in the succeeding days.

But I was certain that sooner or later some half-truth or untruth would come out of the undergrowth and ambush me. I had no real professional advice on how to deal with the media, nor could I afford any. Camilla Courage, although we were no longer going out together, kept in touch and was only too aware of my problem. She introduced me to a City friend, who said he knew the right man to help me.

It was a friend of his called Peter Trowell who, he assured me, was extremely reliable. He said Trowell was aware of my situation and could 'sort out my public relations'. He offered to get him to ring me. But I was loath to give my telephone number to a stranger so I said: 'No, I'll phone him.' Which I did.

I told Trowell that I believed he could help me with regard to the hostile treatment I got from some of the tabloids. He said he was sure he could do something. He thought I had been hard done by but he had excellent contacts and he was certain he could sort my future out in a positive way.

Something about him, however, didn't sound quite right. So although I said I would meet him when I was next in London, I never, in fact, told him when I was there and we never met — and never have. But I reasoned that to dismiss his offer of help out of hand might be to create a new enemy in the media and I needed that like a hole in the head.

Anna arrived to stay at Eversfield the following weekend and a female client came down for a couple of days' riding. We all ate together with Peter, Caroline and my mother. It was relaxed and uneventful. After the unpleasant 'Valentine' experience in London life seemed to have returned to normal.

On March 1st I joined my family and the rest of Devon and most of the rest of rural England in the Countryside March which swamped central London. More than 350,000 people turned out — one of the largest demonstrations the city had ever seen. We were urging the government — and the public — not to support the Foster Bill that sought to outlaw hunting wild animals with dogs. If it was passed that would be the end of hunts as we knew them, something that had been part of the fabric of the countryside for more than five hundred years.

I was completely committed to the cause. Not only would a ban on hunting upset the natural order of the countryside but it would create widespread unemployment among farriers, vets, livery yards, professional huntsmen and people with stables like my own and others with hunters for hire. People would no longer come down from London and many pubs and small hotels would undoubtedly close.

It was a really serious matter but it proved to be an agreeably social day. I met up with family and friends at Zianis for lunch — London was so completely swamped it would have been impossible to find anyone without a rendezvous. And the sheer force of numbers did the trick — the government subsequently backed off the Bill.

Later in the week I had to go to Denmark on business. Some Danish people who had enjoyed their course at Eversfield were investigating the possibility of setting up a similar equitation centre outside Copenhagen and had asked me over to provide advice and suggestions.

When I got back to Devon there was an urgent message to call Anna at home. I did so immediately. There was no answer at Beaulieu-sur-Mer but I caught her on her mobile. She sounded anxious, almost troubled.

'What's the matter?' I asked.

There was a pause at the other end. Then she said: 'James, I'm only going to ask you this once. Will you marry me?'

It came so fast I barely had time to take on board what she had just said. She was clearly distressed and I sensed that even to pause would upset her. It was impossible to think through the consequences of her suggestion. But I was certain of one thing — I didn't want to lose her. So I said: 'Yes. Sure. Let's get married.'

She seemed relieved and promised that she would come over as soon as she could. Although her proposal was completely out of the blue, I was optimistic. By saying 'yes' it meant we could be together and learn more about each other. Anna seemed to fit well into my life. She was kind and pretty and caring. She was worldly and mature and had a good sense of humour. I wasn't sure that I was in love with her — I wasn't sure that I could ever fall in love again with anybody properly — but I loved being with her.

In the subsequent days I told my closer friends and most of them seemed to think it was a good idea that I should settle down. After all, I was going to be 40 on April 30th. One army colleague suggested that I should get away from the tabloids and go to Las Vegas or somewhere similar to get married. That seemed rather a good idea. We could take a party of friends with us and perhaps make a sort of holiday of it.

But that was in the future. However agreeable marriage might be, it was important to expand my business both at home and abroad. It was spring and Eversfield was not up to capacity. The overheads were high and I was working all hours just to keep the place ticking over. Business deals, whether in Denmark or a major one that was pending in Spain to front up the international business for a string of riding schools, seemed forever in negotiation and always a few steps away from fruition.

Very early morning in mid-March I got a phone call out of the blue. The voice at the other end was male with a heavy French accent. He said that he was Jean-Marc Medecin, the boyfriend of Anna's sister Lucia, and he wanted to speak to 'Monsieur James'. I told him he'd got the right man.

He immediately went into what sounded like a rehearsed speech about how Anna had financial problems and she knew I had financial problems, and how Anna was unhappy and she knew I was unhappy. I listened in silence to see where all this was leading. He then said: 'Do not contact Anna for the next week. Then come out suddenly here to Monte Carlo — do not telephone her first — and surprise her. She will love you for that.'

I was somewhat puzzled by his line but I thanked him for his call and put the phone down. Something was wrong, I didn't know what. But it needed to be confronted, so I rang Anna straight away.

'What's all this about?' I asked her. 'What's the matter?'

She was clearly upset. 'You never come to see me here. I am always coming to see you in England. I think you do not love me any more.'

I replied. 'That's not true. I told you when you were here last that I would come to see you the first opportunity I had, but I've been very busy.'

'When can you come?' she demanded

I looked at my desk diary. 'I could get out next Tuesday. But where are we going to stay?'

'Stay with me,' she said.

When she had last been in England she had told me that she had rented out her house at Beaulieu-sur-Mer and I knew that Jean-Marc and Lucia occupied her one-bedroom apartment in Monte Carlo. Anna had become largely itinerant but occasionally slept on the sofa there.

'Are you sure you have enough room?'

'No problem, no problem.' She sounded relieved and much happier. 'Tell me your flight when you know it and I will meet you at Nice. I am so glad you are coming, James.'

As I sat on the British Midland morning flight to Nice on Tuesday, March 16th 1998 I was unable to pretend to myself that I had any great desire to go to Monte Carlo. There was a lot of work to be done at Eversfield and I had had to cancel some clients and that meant the loss of revenue. I was certainly looking forward to seeing Anna again, but Jean-Marc's phone call had hardly made me warm to him. Anna had told me that he was some sort of musician but he couldn't get any work so she had been obliged to support both him and her sister for the past six months.

The plane landed on time at Nice Airport. I looked for Anna at the point just past customs where people usually wait but she wasn't there. I went down into the baggage hall and after about fifteen minutes retrieved my suitcase. Still no sign of Anna. I tried to call her on my mobile — but the battery was flat. So I went to buy a *Herald Tribune* to get some French change and called her mobile from a pay phone. I got a recorded message. I tried her home number at Beaulieu-sur-Mer — another recorded message. I took my bags and went outside to where the taxis were. No sign of her. I tried her mobile once more. Again I got a message. I went outside again scanning each arriving vehicle but she didn't appear. I wondered what the hell was going on?

My dilemma was that I didn't know what her address was in Monte Carlo, nor in Beaulieu-sur-Mer come to that, although she was unlikely to be there. After what must have been an hour I resolved to take the next flight back to Britain. Something had gone wrong. She must have tried to contact me but found my phone out of order. I made one final call to her mobile from a pay phone and, at last, she answered.

'Where *are* you?' I asked.

My mother helping me at Longleat Horse Trials, 1995.

*Top:* Eversfield Manor at the end of autumn. A peaceful home!

*Bottom:* Me and Francis Showering in southern Algeria, 1993. This Tuareg and his camel came across us. We hadn't seen anybody or anything for 200 miles. He ate with us and then went on his way.

My father, John Alfred Hewitt, as a captain in the Royal Marines, and (right) my grandfather, Alfred James Hewitt in Naval uniform, circa 1923.

A picture Anna Ferretti gave me of herself,
and (right) me aged five.

*Top*: With my squadron officers in Germany 1992.

*Bottom*: Celebrating the end of the Gulf War with from left to right, the author, SCM Evans, Captain Robert Tarling (second in command), Captain Rupert Mackenzie-Hill, Corporal of Horse Roberts and Corporal of Horse Barry, 1991.

Dear ___, Well done! Well done! You must be mighty relieved to get the boys out in one piece, touch wood. You did a marvellous job from what we could gleam from the press. Your G-1 letter arrived and thank you for it. I had everything crossed from then on. Thank god no chemical or Biolog the oil fires are bad enough. I am glad to see 'owl' sat on watch and key tag will return. Of course I know its all not over yet. The aftermath can be awful if one lets it get to you, but the worst is over and do your best to get back and see us as soon as you can. Let me know what you want for ___ birthday (within reason). The Polo match should be a good show, don't get hit on the jaw! again. Caroline & Peter came down to the local pt-to-pt venue where 'Granville' was running and we had a picnic in the R-R (own). He ran green as expected but came out of it in one piece (p.u.). Needless to say it was bloody cold! Three of these friends came down over the weekend and went to the E.D.H. ball the night before — some pale faces on the Sat!. Julia is well as you well know and everyone this end waiting for warm weather but well. Lizzie has just been made a partner in her firm (more money!) but thrilled. Hope the parcel arrived in reasonable shape and you didn't find it too mundane. Glad you got the medicine! Syra is sending me some photos, the ones of the wedding arrived and are v. good. Aunt ___ well and always asking for news. Please give me a ring as soon as possible ___ the great care of everyone. Please convey my hearties congratulations to your 'Squadron' and tell them "marvellous". Anna

*Left and below*: A letter received from my father after the Allied victory in the Gulf, and a letter sent to my mother from Lance Corporal Bebbington, Trooper Stafford and Corporal of Horse Roberts. It was written on the now famous British forces airmail paper known as 'blueys'. My mother had sent them a card and present congratulating them on the Allied victory.

*Inset*: This was sent to me after an entry in the *London Gazette*.

Dear Mrs Hewitt                                  5.3.91

I wanted to take this opportunity to thank you for your card and the present. It was very kind.

I must apologise for not writing sooner. But now we've been through the war and popped out of the other side in good spirits.

Today we spoilt your Son something cronic. With coffee and breakfast in Bed. But it was well deserved. Your Son commanded the squadron with easy determination. But thanks to us his quite brilliant crew he had only to worry what the squadron was doing.

At times we were at more risk from 1 troop than we ever were by the Iraqi army.

Thanks again.

2nd Bebbs (gunner)  Lcpl Bebbington
3rd Staff (driver) tp Stafford
1st Robbo (ldr) CoH Robberts

---

By the QUEEN'S Order the name of
Captain James Lifford Hewitt,
The Life Guards,
was published in the London Gazette on
29 June 1991,
as mentioned in a Despatch for distinguished service.
I am charged to record
Her Majesty's high appreciation.

*Secretary of State for Defence*

*Above:* Skiing in the Zermatt 1985.

*Inset:* During a state visit at Windsor.

'Where are *you*?' she replied.

'Hanging around Nice Airport where you said you'd meet me.'

'Didn't you get my message?' she said.

'What message? Nobody gave me any message.'

'I told British Midland that I had made a reservation for you on the helicopter. I have been waiting at the heliport?'

I managed to calm down and made my peace with her and went across to the helicopter booking desks. No reservation had been made for me with any of the companies but there was room on the next flight and I took that.

I shared the twenty-minute trip with an English couple who were on their first visit to Monte Carlo and quizzed me where to go and what to eat. It transpired that they were on their honeymoon. They were very friendly — and very much in love.

Anna was at the heliport waiting for me. She looked radiant. After we hugged and kissed she introduced me to Lucia — whom I had only met fleetingly at the Casino — and my telephone agony aunt, Jean-Marc. He proved to be a dark-featured, square-jawed man in his early thirties. Lucia looked a little like her sister, but not nearly as pretty. I gave her a box of chocolates and Jean-Marc a bottle of port. For Anna I had had a little silver box engraved with the words 'Je t'aime.' She was delighted.

Jean-Marc announced: 'We will go to the apartment.' He then led the way to a block of flats which were adjacent to the heliport in the new part of Monte Carlo. He had the key to what turned out to be a small but well-appointed apartment facing towards the Royal Palace.

'Is this your apartment?' I asked Anna.

'No,' Jean-Marc answered for her, explaining that this belonged to a black German pop singer called Halloway who was renting Anna's house.

It all seemed a bit strange but I didn't give it much further thought. I bought them lunch in the Café de Paris. We sat outside in the warm sun. I had a glass of beer and some white wine with my fish and began to unwind. When we had finished we went for a stroll and sat on the harbour wall and watched the world go by.

Anna and I stayed for a couple of nights at the singer's apartment. The next day I arranged for us to play tennis at the house of a friend that overlooked the Eze, just above Monte Carlo. At least, I played with Jean-Marc and the girls watched.

But on Thursday morning Jean-Marc arrived before breakfast and announced that we had to move out as Halloway had phoned to say he was coming back that day.

Jean-Marc got hold of a taxi and took us to a decrepit sort of boarding house just outside Monte Carlo close to the railway line. It looked grotty from the outside and was pretty tawdry on the inside. After we had checked into our closet-sized room, I took a bath in the hope of making myself cleaner than my surroundings.

'You're not happy,' Anna's voice came from the bedroom. 'What's the matter?

'When you asked me to come down here you said there was plenty of room,' I said. 'Now we're shacked up in this cockroach-ridden place.'

I could hear her lifting the phone. 'Don't worry. I know the manager at Loew's Hotel. He owes me a lot of favours. I will get us a room there. We can stay there free of charge.'

It was with relief that I paid the bill at the hotel by the railway without having to spend the night there and we moved back into town with a clean and comfortable room at Loew's. Our mood improved appreciably.

Jean-Marc and Lucia came to the hotel the next morning and suggested we should have a picnic. The girls went off and bought baguettes and cheese. Then Jean-Marc drove us to a beach he knew a little further down the coast.

The day was bright and the March sun unusually warm. We sat on the rocks eating our baguettes and throwing pieces of bread to the fish.

Without any warning Anna suddenly stood up and

announced: 'I am going to swim.'

She pulled off her shirt and waded into the sea in her underwear.

'You must be mad,' I yelled, 'it's freezing in there.'

'You join me, James,' she called back. 'Don't be pathetic.'

I had no particular desire to go in but I didn't want to be a kill-joy. Besides, Jean-Marc was already in the water as well. So I stripped down to my boxers and took up the challenge. Within seconds I was in the Mediterranean beside her. I must say I admired her pluck — it was extremely cold although I had encountered lower temperatures in army training exercises off the coast of Norway. Anna and I jumped around in the water and hugged and clung on to each other for warmth.

We didn't last long in the sea and gratefully spread ourselves out on the wall to let the sun unfreeze our bones. Anna was laughing and smiling and after the nonsense of the past couple of days I was reminded of exactly what it was that I had found so attractive and endearing in her.

I was due to go back to London the next day but we wouldn't be apart for long as she was coming to stay the following weekend and I had arranged a house party for some of my friends who had come to know and like her. It was nearly four months since we had first met.

We said goodbye at the hotel. I had a morning flight. Anna said she was going back to Sorrento later in the day to see her father. We had arranged that she would make her way to the home of Rupert MacKenzie-Hill in Chelsea by lunchtime the following Friday so that he and his girlfriend Juby could drive her down to Devon. I reminded her of this and she said: 'No, that won't be necessary. I will come my own way.'

I asked: 'Are you sure?'

'Yes,' she replied. 'I thought it would be nice if Lucia and Jean-Marc came as well. That will be okay, won't it?'

My heart sank. 'No problem,' I heard myself say. 'The more the merrier.'

When I got back to Eversfield I began to regret having

to prepare for guests let alone the additional pleasure of entertaining Jean-Marc and Lucia. The sheep were about to lamb, two of the horses needed attention from the vet, the manager had fallen ill and a party of three had booked for two days of lessons. There was little time for sleep.

I was about to go out riding on the morning of Wednesday, March 25th when my telephone rang. It was Anna.

'Where are you?' I asked.

'I'm in Italy,' she said, 'and I have a surprise for you.'

'What is the surprise?' I hated surprises.

'It wouldn't be a surprise if I told you,' she teased.

'Very well,' I agreed, 'at least give me a clue.'

'Will you be at home at 10.30 p.m. tonight?'

'Yes,' I said. 'My mother's coming over for dinner. I'll be here.'

'You will have your surprise before then. Au revoir.'

It didn't take an enormous leap of the imagination to work out what the surprise was going to be. In fact, I was genuinely glad that I was going to have Anna to myself for a couple of days before the others arrived. I just prayed that the surprise didn't include the early arrival of Jean-Marc and Lucia.

It was past six o'clock by the time we had stabled the horses for the night. I took a quick shower and then went down to the study to interview a local man called Anthony Pitcher to replace one of the staff who had had to move to North Devon. He came highly recommended by a nearby farmer friend. Anthony had, in fact, worked at Eversfield under the previous owner. We talked for about an hour, at the end of which I was pretty sure he was right for the job, so I offered him the post then and there. I told him it would be useful if he could help at the weekend as we had people coming and he was happy to do this.

Mother and I ate dinner in the kitchen. We decided not to wait for Anna — who knows what time she would arrive. In fact, I had given up hope of being 'surprised' that day and gone to bed and was reading myself to sleep when I heard a vehicle coming up the drive. I looked out of the window to see a black cab and Anna emerging from it.

She was at her most affectionate and I had planned a little surprise for her. I suggested she opened my bedside drawer. She looked at me, an expression almost of shock on her face.

'Go ahead,' I said. She gently eased it open and inside she found a sapphire and diamond engagement ring. Once it had belonged to my mother but she had given it to me many years ago in the expectation that one day it might seal a relationship. Anna seemed a little taken aback but she expressed her delight and slipped it on her finger where it remained for the rest of the weekend.

The following day — the Thursday — I had to go into Exeter, a drive of about an hour, to pick up a new pair of spectacles. There comes a time when you have to acknowledge that your difficulty in reading documents is not just because of poor light but because your short vision is beginning to atrophy. I was about to be forty and was forced to face up to that sad fact. My mother and Anna came with me in the Range Rover.

When we had parked the car, Anna said she wanted to do some shopping and went off on her own. We agreed to meet back at the car park at three. But three-thirty came and went and there was still no sign of her. We thought she must be lost and set out to look for her but she found her way back about twenty minutes later saying she had lost track of the time.

That evening a family dinner was hastily convened at Caroline and Peter's for us formally to announce our engagement. It was just them and my mother and Anna and myself. Anna had said that Lucia and Jean-Marc might be coming but shortly before we left Eversfield she said they had been delayed. I asked her how she knew and she showed me a new mobile phone she had bought on her way through London.

Nor did they turn up the next day. I went back into Exeter to collect Harry Sutherland — an old army mate. We went back to Eversfield to get ready for the local Point-to-Point. Anna had put on an outfit with a mini skirt for the races and when she asked me, 'What should I wear?'

Rather wickedly I said that she looked just right. When we got to the Point-to-Point and all the other women were in tweeds or trousers she was understandably a bit miffed — it was also quite cold — and stayed in the car making calls on her new mobile phone. She seemed impatient and said she wanted to go home. Despite her protestation we stayed for the last race. It had been a really good day's racing and I remember Harry and I both came away fairly even.

Rupert and Juby and Mark MacCauley and his girlfriend arrived on Saturday morning. Another friend, Simon Newnes, came over from his farm in Somerset. It was an action-packed weekend. Harry Sutherland, who is fluent in French, gave Anna a riding lesson in the outdoor school behind my house. Some people rode, others went for walks. After lunch there was a furious game of darts in the pub. In the evening we ate well and afterwards sat by the fire and played cards and Monopoly and generally enjoyed each other's company.

On Sunday morning Anna suddenly announced that she thought it would be a good idea if we had a clay pigeon shoot. This came as something of a surprise — the weather was cold and drizzly and on the two occasions we had shot when she had stayed before, she had steadfastly refused to fire a gun.

But the others were agreeable. Rupert and Mark set up the trap, which was on the flat roof above my bedroom window, while I went to prepare my shotguns. By law they have to be kept under lock and key and mine were in the safe in my study. I took the key out of its hiding place in the lantern in the hall and removed them from the safe with a quantity of cartridges.

Since it had been Anna's idea I suggested that she go first. She was a bit nervous but I supported her shoulder and arm while Rupert prepared the first clay. I shouted 'Pull', Anna aimed and fired and very nearly hit the clay, meanwhile stumbling backwards from the recoil of the gun.

'No more,' she pronounced holding a sore shoulder. I

took a look. It was a little red but no real damage done and the rest of us finished the competition. Anna retired inside to use the phone. She was getting poor reception on her new mobile one and said she needed to keep in touch with her business.

Despite the wintry weather it was the lambing season and it's important to be on hand at this time of year in case there are any problems. If need be you can teach a new-born lamb how to suckle on your little finger and introduce it to the mother's teat. Rupert and Simon helped me catch the ewes and we managed to save most of the lambs.

It was one of the best weekends at Eversfield any of us could remember and nobody wanted to leave on Sunday night — especially with the heavy traffic back into London — so we agreed we would all drive up on Monday morning.

I rose early and put on a suit as I had a meeting in London that afternoon. But two of the new-born lambs had obviously had a bad night. They were lying in the cold, wet grass and didn't look as if they would survive. I collected them up, took them into the kitchen and tried to revive them on the Aga. Rupert then wrapped them in towels to try and rub some life into them.

I went to the neighbouring farm to get some milk powder. When I got back and mixed it and gave it to the lambs, the weaker of the two responded and survived. The other took a little drink but it was too late. It was sad. Living in the countryside you are used to life and death twenty-four hours a day, but the death of this lamb who so nearly made it was just very emotional.

All of this meant that Anna and I were late leaving for London. Mark had kindly asked us to come and stay with him but about halfway there Anna had a change of heart.

'I don't want to stay with anyone, there is no freedom,' she said.

'Well, what do you want to do?' I asked.

'We will stay at the Hyde Park Hotel. I will pay,' she announced. 'Lucia and Jean-Marc are in London and we can meet them for dinner.'

# 14

I duly dropped Anna at the Hyde Park Hotel in Knightsbridge and went off to my meeting. I was due to fly to Spain the following day at the request of a leading businessman who was the owner of a string of stables and much else besides. He was one of Spain's leading and most controversial entrepreneurs and rejoiced in the splendid name of Jose Maria Ruiz Mateos y Jiminez de Tejada, Marques de Olivara de Montemayor y de Camp Nuble. But he answered to Jose Maria. After attending the meeting in connection with the trip, I had an appointment with my doctor in Chelsea before driving back to the hotel.

When I entered the reception area I found Anna waiting with Lucia and Jean-Marc. I greeted them both and said I was sorry they had been unable to make it down to Devon. They had missed a good weekend. Jean-Marc said they had been delayed in Monte Carlo and he hoped they might be able to come on another occasion. I asked him where they were staying and he said they were at the Sheraton Hotel which was directly opposite the Hyde Park. I assumed that Anna must be paying for them. I told them I would take them to a restaurant they would enjoy — Zianis in Radnor Walk — for dinner. They both appeared pleased.

But Anna was displeased with our room. She said she wanted to change it. I found a duty manager who took me up to take a look at it. He told me the hotel was virtually full because of a large Chinese delegation. The room seemed perfectly acceptable to me but the manager showed me another, slightly more spacious one. Anna came up to see it and we agreed to take it. She said she had made an appointment with the hotel hairdresser to come to the room and do her and Lucia's hair. I agreed to take Jean-Marc for a drink in the bar. He was very friendly. He apologised for the mix-up with the apartment the previous week in Monte Carlo and invited me to come back in May for the Grand Prix. He said he had 'influential friends' and we could watch the race from a 'privileged position' on a yacht. We had quite a wait and quite a few drinks and what I best remember of the meal at Zianis was that we had quite a lot more red wine.

Anna was in an amorous mood when we returned to our hotel room. Afterwards she started taking pictures of us with a disposable camera which was on top of the mini-bar. But I was mindful of the fact that I had to get up at six the next morning and was anxious to snatch a few hours' sleep.

The following day I was unable to wake her to say goodbye. She was in the deepest of sleeps. I retrieved my car from the hotel garage and drove to Heathrow. There I handed it over to valet parking. But as I lined up in Terminal Two for check-in it dawned on me I had made a foolish mistake that I had never in all my years of travelling made before — I had forgotten my passport. The drama with the lambs in the kitchen must have thrown my last-minute preparations.

I telephoned Becky who was house-sitting at

Eversfield and working in the stables and asked her to look for it. I was certain I had left it either in a coat pocket in the cloak-room or in the drawer of my desk in the study. The minutes ticked by as I waited for her to call back. The gate closed on my flight — not that I could have boarded it anyway. My mobile rang — Becky reported that she was unable to find the passport.

There was nothing for it but to return to Devon and look for it myself.

I telephoned Madrid from the car and said I might have to take the 8.00 p.m. flight which would get in at 11.00 p.m. That would mean missing an important dinner. Did they still want me to come?

'No problem, James,' came a warm Spanish voice. 'We will make reservations for you on the 8.00 p.m. flight and also the 4.00 p.m. one — maybe you will make that.'

Speeding down the M4 I called Anna on her new mobile phone. She seemed surprised to hear from me. I told her what had happened and that I was hoping to make the 4.00 p.m. flight. She asked me if Becky was at the house. I told her that she was but she had been unable to locate the passport. I asked her what she was doing.

'Shopping,' she replied.

'And after that?' I inquired.

'More shopping.'

The passport *was* in my desk drawer — if Becky had moved some papers she would have found it. But she probably hadn't liked to pry too much. On the way back to Heathrow I rang Anna again. I told her I thought I might make the four o'clock flight.

She replied: 'There is no four o'clock flight.'

This seemed a strange thing to say. How would she know this, I thought, and why would she mention it? But I didn't dwell on the matter. I was in a hurry and I didn't feel like having an argument. In fact, it turned out she was right — there was no 4.00 p.m. flight. But I caught the later plane. I was met at Madrid's Aeropuerto de Barajas by Senior Carlos Roma, a cheerful and charming man whom Jose Maria had assigned to look after me while I was in

Spain. After checking into the hotel, we made it to the meal which seemed to go okay as for the first time in my rather fraught day I was able to relax.

The following day — Wednesday, April 1st — I had a packed schedule of meetings starting at breakfast. At lunchtime I met up with Jose Maria at Naturbier, Madrid's famous beer parlour. He was most welcoming and seemed most of all concerned that I should have an enjoyable time in Spain, leaving the nitty-gritty details of business to others. The idea was that I should advise him on the best ways of setting up, marketing and promoting international riding holidays in various *estancia* and stables owned not just by him but by associated companies. Jose Maria told me that it was his idea that Carlos should stay at my hotel, the Melia-Castilla, to deal with any problems and ensure that my trip went smoothly.

This he did, most efficiently. But some matters, unfortunately, were to prove beyond his control. That night I was taken to the spectacular flamenco at the Café de Chinitas. Everyone was extremely friendly and at the end of the evening it was exhilarating to dance with the professionals. Afterwards they brought me a special guest book, eagerly showing me a page with the signatures of King Juan Carlos and Queen Sophia of Spain and, beside them, those of Prince Charles and Princess Diana. They were not unaware of my part in her life.

I went to bed late that night — it must have been nearly three in the morning — but awoke just before 8.00 a.m. and, as I always do in European hotels, switched on the television to watch Sky News. It was Friday, April 2nd — not a day I will easily forget. For a moment I thought I was still dreaming — there in the first item of the news, were shots of my house, of Anna Ferretti, of me and of the headline in that morning's *Mirror*: DIANA LOVE LETTERS SCANDAL.

I could hardly believe my eyes or ears. The front page of the *Mirror* contained the following:

*Sensational love letters from Princess Diana to*
*James Hewitt were rescued by the* Mirror *last night.*

*The 62 hand-written letters had been taken from a*
*safe at 39-year-old Hewitt's Devon home yesterday*
*while he was abroad on business. They were snatched*
*by his fiancée, Italian beauty Anna Ferretti, who*
*then tried to sell them to the* Mirror *for £150,000.*
*We immediately handed them to Kensington Palace*
*officials who thanked the* Mirror *for their safe*
*return. In the poignant notes Diana pours out her*
*heart to ex-army Major Hewitt. Many were written*
*at the height of her affair with the man she adored.*

I had been prepared to face Scud missiles and Iraqi
artillery but nothing had prepared me for the devastation
of a moment like this. To begin with I was hopelessly
disorientated and at a loss what to do. In the army you are
taught that if you are not in a position to retaliate
immediately, it is essential to evaluate your options. I tried
to order my thoughts as best I could. It seemed my first
duty was to inform my hosts.

I went down the corridor and knocked on the door of
Carlos's room. I asked him if he'd seen the television. He
hadn't. So I explained what had happened, as best I could
in my stunned state. I warned him that there were sure to
be journalists on their way right now looking for me.

He was very sympathetic. He suggested I stay in Spain
and maybe the whole thing would blow over. 'Some hope,'
I thought. But I was grateful to him. In principle, however,
he was right. I could see that I could deal with the situation
better — at least initially — in my hotel room where I could
use my mobile in privacy and I had access to a phone and a
fax, rather than try to sort things out while I was in transit.

Back in my room I rang my solicitor, Rod Dadak, and
asked him if he'd heard what had happened. This was at
9.00 a.m.

'Everybody in England has heard what's happened,'
he said. 'It's the main story — it's all over the place.'

I told him we had to get the police on to it. He
suggested I take a look at the *Mirror*'s allegations first. He
would fax them through to me.

As I waited I tried to convince myself in my mind that it just wasn't true. I could not believe that Anna could have betrayed me in this manner. But when I went back over her behaviour from her premature arrival on Wednesday night — my surprise, the new mobile phone, the way she went missing in Exeter, all her phone calls at the Point-to-Point, the unexplained failure of Jean-Marc and Lucia to arrive for the weekend and their surprise presence in an expensive hotel in London — my fears deepened.

And yes — she had initiated the idea of a clay pigeon shoot on Sunday. She must have thought the letters — only about a dozen of them, not 62 — would still be in my drawer. And when she didn't find them there she assumed — correctly — I had put them with the rest in the safe. So she needed to discover where I kept the key. In fact, there were many more from Diana in the safe but I had put most of the Gulf War 'blueys' together in a brown envelope.

But why on earth would she do this for the *Mirror*'s 'alleged' £150,000? She was in the process of negotiating the sale of her fabric company to the Japanese for more than £10 million — or so she said. And she knew the value that some people had put on those letters. I had had offers of several million dollars from American collectors and university libraries for them. Anna was aware of that. I had told her. And I had also told her that I had never replied to them as I had no wish to enter negotiations with anybody about them.

The whole enterprise reeked of insanity. I was sure Jean-Marc was behind it. If Anna were to leave the South of France and come to live in England, he and Lucia would lose their sole means of support. My initial thought was that this must have been some crazed last ditch effort by him to make some money.

But the *Mirror*, when it came through on the fax machine, told a different story. There was a picture of Anna at the *Mirror*'s London office with *Mirror* executives. I think I could make out the pinched features of Piers Morgan, the paper's editor, who had pursued me down the years, never losing a chance to muddy my name.

The *Mirror* story was risible. Anna had, apparently, decided to sell these letters before I did. 'I knew there was a lot of interest and there was no time to lose,' they reported her as saying.

No time to lose? I had had the letters for seven years — why the sudden urgency?

As I read on my suspicions moved from Jean-Marc towards the *Mirror* itself. They claimed that I had asked Anna to marry her — not quite the way I remembered it. The story said that she suspected me of seeing other women and so she travelled to the *Mirror*'s Canary Wharf headquarters with her accomplice, Jean-Marc Medecin, and 'unveiled her audacious plan'.

According to the paper she had taken two of Diana's letters from her Prada handbag, told them she could easily take more from a drawer in my bedroom and agreed to hand them over for £80,000.

'To expose her ruse,' the story went on, 'the *Mirror* strung her along for the next eight days. That night our representatives drove Anna and Jean-Marc to Devon. On the journey Anna phoned Hewitt at home pretending to be in the South of France where she has a house. She said she had a "surprise" for him. The surprise would be herself.' Jean-Marc apparently stayed with the *Mirror* minders at an Exeter hotel and Anna took a taxi to my house.

My stomach turned to ice as I read on. Anna, they said, had contacted the *Mirror* representatives the next day — that must have been when she disappeared in Exeter — to tell them the letters had been moved from the bedroom.

The paper tried to dignify the planned robbery as if it were an adventure story. 'The ice-cool beauty then played the role of Mata Hari and stayed with Hewitt at his home watching and waiting.'

I was right. She guessed the letters must have been in the safe and she suggested the clay pigeon shoot to see where I kept the key. The *Mirror* reported it was in a desk drawer; in fact, it was in a lantern in the hall. But how much of their report was fact and how much was fiction was impossible to tell at this stage.

They were certainly right about the name of our hotel in London — but by then I was pretty sure they were paying for it. They reported that Lucia had flown from Monaco 'to join the operation'.

Again I'm pretty sure the *Mirror* must have paid. If they did, they flew in the woman who actually committed the burglary. The paper admitted that it now took the initiative in the crime. 'The next day Hewitt flew to Spain. Anna joined *Mirror* journalists in a hotel to plan the next stage of the operation. We then drove her, Lucia and Jean-Marc back to Devon.' The following morning Lucia opened the safe while Anna distracted my 'housekeeper' (presumably Becky, my groom).

The minders then drove them back to the *Mirror* in London. The *Mirror* reported Anna as saying when she met with the people there: 'James would be very angry with me. I am only doing this because he cost me so much. I want more money than I first asked for. I want £150,000.'

Her reported motivation seemed to have changed from preventing my imminent sale of the letters and the allegation I was seeing other women to the amount of money I had cost her. According to the *Mirror* she had calculated the sum at £30,000 in hotel and air bills — with £5,000 for our hotel in Monte Carlo the previous week. She had, indeed, paid her own travel costs but I had paid everything else save for the Hyde Park in London and the Loew's Hotel when I went down to Monte Carlo following Jean-Marc's telephone call.

The *Mirror*, having admitted aiding and abetting the burglary, then admitted double-crossing Anna. 'We had no intention of meeting her demands.' They claimed she asked them to copy the letters so that she could take them back to Devon. Instead they gave her £1,000 to go shopping — and to enable them, presumably, to buy time.

They must have told her that they would meet her at 6.30 p.m. and give her back the letters. 'We did not keep the meeting,' the article concluded. 'Instead we delivered the letters to Kensington Palace.'

And underneath this account of the role played by *Mirror* employees in stealing my property and double-crossing Anna Ferretti was a prominent box with the headline: WHAT THE PALACE SAID LAST NIGHT. 'We appreciate the decision of the *Mirror* to respect the dignity and privacy of the Princess by not publishing her private correspondence and also thereby avoiding further distress to her family. Kensington Palace spokesman Michael Gibbins.'

If sensational headlines such as DIANA LOVE LETTERS SCANDAL with samples from the letters in Diana's writing such as 'Darling James' and one of Diana's pseudonym signatures 'Julia' — put between two kisses — plus summaries of what was in some of the letters was Kensington Palace's idea of 'avoiding further distress to her family' then they must have lost touch with reality.

I felt outraged and betrayed. In the history of dirty tricks they didn't come much dirtier than this one. And for the *Mirror* to confess their involvement in an organised crime seemed madness. People were going to go to jail for this.

I had to know how Anna had got caught up in all of this. I kept trying her mobile phone. It was perpetually engaged or switched to the answering machine. After numerous attempts I eventually got through. I was steaming with anger when I heard her voice.

'What have you done?' I yelled at her.

'You lied to me,' she said, sounding very nervous and unsure.

'What lies?' I demanded.

'On 14th March you were with a woman in London. You sent her a rose and a card and you left a house with that woman in London?'

'What woman?

'They took a photo of you and listened to your conversation with this woman and you were talking about sex ...'

The penny dropped. The Valentine's Day set-up with Carole Aye Meung. They must have shown Anna a picture from this year and probably played a tape from last year.

Anna then started on a stream of incoherent accusations. 'You did not tell me where you were going. You told me you were leaving on a flight at eight o'clock the next day but you were not leaving and you did not tell me where you were going. You lied to me, someone you knew, and you knew that I was happy to wait for you. You didn't catch the flight until the evening.'

'You are absolutely, unbelievably stupid,' I burst out.

Anna repeated that she had seen the photo and heard the conversation. I tried to tell her it was a journalistic wind-up. I found it impossible to control my rage.

'I trusted you and you let me trust you. Jean-Marc and everything was just a complete and utter travesty. I can't understand what you have done to me. I don't want to see you ever again.'

I asked her where she was — knowing wherever it was she was with *Mirror* minders. She refused to tell me and asked me where I was. I told her I was in Spain. She said she had tried to ring me on the number I had given her but she couldn't get me.

'Why do you want to know?' I asked.

'To be able to speak to you.'

'So that you can tell the journalists,' I shouted. 'You stupid woman.' I couldn't stop myself repeating: 'You stupid, stupid woman.'

Anna became more upset. 'James, I am completely destroyed. My life is worth nothing.'

I felt no sympathy for her. 'Give the ring back,' I demanded. 'Send me the ring. Give me that back, okay?'

'Yes, of course I will do that.' She began to sound very distressed. 'The journalists are looking and called me and want to know everything about what you are doing. They told me what you were doing. It was normal, my reaction. It's normal I should think that. I am completely destroyed psychologically.'

'Just shut up and give me the ring back, okay?' I bellowed. 'Just send it to the house.'

Anna went on the offensive. 'You are naughty, very

naughty. You tried to play fast and loose with me.'

'I don't understand. You believe other people — that's fine. You believe the journalists are your friends — that's fine.'

'I saw the picture,' she insisted.

'That was set up. It was set up by the journalists. You hear what they want you to hear. I thought you loved me.'

'Yes,' Anna replied.

'I thought you loved me. Now that is very difficult to believe. Now everything is finished. Right? Everything.'

I punched the button to cut off the call. I felt drained and bewildered and no nearer the real truth of what had actually taken place. I then rang my solicitor for an update on what was happening. He advised me to stay out of the country for the time being. Already some presenters had implied on television that I was somehow involved in this plan to make money from the letters. If I came back there would be a media circus. I told him I had spoken to Anna. He said he would have advised me not to do that. I explained that I knew that but I just had to find out if she had really done this to me.

'And did you?' he asked.

'The *Mirror* did it to me,' I replied.

I had requested the switchboard to hold all calls on the phone in my room. I rang down to them to see if there were any. There were five calls from British newspapers and television companies wanting to talk to me. The circus had begun. It was time to leave town.

I called Carlos and told him that the British press were looking for me and some of their local correspondents and stringers might well be on their way. He said that one was already in the lobby, but he had put a plan into action. If I took the freight elevator in ten minutes time there would be a car waiting at the service entrance to the hotel.

I called my brother-in-law, Peter Bayley. He knew nothing of what had happened but turned on Sky News as we were talking and was soon in the picture. He said he would look after things in Devon as best he could. I told him to reassure Becky that it was not in any way her fault and we agreed to speak later in the day.

A large grey Mercedes with a driver and Carlos in the back was waiting at the rear of the hotel. There were people in the street and I glanced around nervously as I went to get in. I didn't want to face the press. I had no desire to answer any questions about the robbery or Anna until I knew the true facts and I very much doubted if they were contained in the *Mirror* story.

Carlos had already purchased our tickets to Cordoba. We made our way through Madrid's densely crowded AVE Station. At any moment I expected a hand on my shoulder from a journalist or to be confronted by a photographer. This wasn't paranoia — I knew the British press were going to track me down sooner or later.

There were two of Carlos's colleagues waiting for us on the train. They were aware of my situation and tactfully considerate. The AVE is a hyper-modern fast train, built to take people from Madrid to Seville during Expo, and we would reach Cordoba in less than two hours. The battery on my mobile phone went flat. I tried to use the one on the train but it was impossible to get a signal, certanly to England. However, as we were approaching Cordoba, Carlos got a call on his mobile from Scotland Yard. They wanted to interview me. I said that I was detained in Spain for the next few days and the officer said they would arrange to interview me in Madrid. Carlos was surprised that Scotland Yard had managed to get his number since the mobile was neither his personal one nor did it belong to his company.

At Cordoba we found a shop where I bought a new battery for my mobile and an attachment so that I could charge it in a car. We were then driven to El Guijarrillo, a beautiful ranch just outside the town which had stables with eighty classic Andalucian grey horses. They had arranged for me to ride round the vast estate with one of the chaps from the stable, Javier — a fine horseman. He spoke very little English and was not acquainted with my current problems so it was an escape of sorts. We rode far out into the olive groves. The terrain was hot and dusty with the ground irrigated to retain what little rain fell in the area.

After two peaceful hours which did much to restore my equilibrium, we returned to the Estancia. I wanted to get back on the phone but Javier indicated to me that I should try the indoor riding arena. As we entered he signalled to a stable hand and quite suddenly, out of nowhere, came the sound of classical guitar music. Javier started to manoeuvre his mount in a series of dressage movements. He gestured to me to follow. I had enjoyed dressage to music in my days at Saumur. Although there was a language barrier, horses and all things equestrian were international. Javier and I managed to piece together a small repris as I mirrored his movements around the arena, progressing from shoulders-in to half-passes and even piaffes and passages. My stallion was highly schooled and responded superbly. A crowd of workers gathered to watch us. It was a surreal situation. I desperately needed to get in touch with England but I didn't want to disappoint our audience.

The owners of the Estancia insisted I visit the tack room before I left. It was magnificent, with many elegant carriages and a succession of enormous glass cabinets containing elegant saddles, harness wear, head kit, stirrups and spurs — everything polished to perfection.

Suddenly my mobile phone rang. It was Camilla Courage. She had heard the news. Although my hosts in Spain had been sympathetic to a fault, it was just wonderful to hear a loving voice from home, and especially Camilla. She asked if I was all right and if there was anything she could do. I said that I had had better days but that I thought it would be some time before the real truth emerged. She pledged her total support and I thanked her deeply for that.

Her call brought me right back to reality. As soon as I reached the small hotel I had been booked into in the middle of Cordoba, I hit the phone and remained on it for the next two hours, trying to piece together what had been happening in England. Peter reported that my mother had telephoned Okehampton police station to find out what they were doing about the burglary. Obviously they knew about the story from the media but, to my mother's surprise, they said they had not done anything because there had been 'no formal complaint'. My mother was furious. 'Well I'm making one now,' she told them rather curtly. So they had been to Eversfield Manor to interview Rebecca Mills — Becky.

I called Becky for a first-hand account. She was only 21 and greatly shaken by the whole business. Usually she helped me out as a groom, but she would sometimes house-sit for me while I was away. On Tuesday she had felt badly because she had failed to locate my passport in the drawer. But I had assured her when I finally got down there that I understood that she didn't want to go through all the private papers in the desk. Becky told me — as she had told the police — that after I had left she had locked up the house and had gone back into the yard to work with the horses in the stables.

The next morning, Wednesday, April 1st, she was again working with the horses when she heard a car coming up the drive. She went out to see who it was. There were two women and a man in it. Anna Ferretti got out and said hello and told her she needed to get into the house. Becky had only seen Anna on a couple of occasions and was certainly not expecting anybody. So she asked her the reason.

Anna then told Becky that she and I were about to get married and she wanted to surprise me by doing up some rooms in the house. So Becky let her in. Anna said she needed a tape measure and Becky went to look for one in the laundry room. She came back with it and Anna asked her to come upstairs to help her measure my bedroom and the guest bedroom at the back of the house for new curtains. In all Becky reckoned they were together for 20 to 25 minutes and during that time Lucia must have found the key and stolen the letters, locking the safe and putting the key back in the lantern in the hall to make it look as if nothing had happened. Anna asked Becky to say nothing to me about her visit as the redecoration was going to be a surprise.

Becky sounded very upset on the phone. I told her not to worry — she had done nothing wrong. But I was wretchedly worried myself. I desperately needed to get at the truth and find out what had really motivated Anna to do this. I called her mobile number and an unfamiliar woman's voice answered the phone.

'Who is that?' I asked.

'It's a friend of Anna's,' she said, speaking French with an English accent.

I said: 'Your French is fucking awful — even for a journalist — now pass me over to Anna.'

It was obviously a *Mirror* person. 'You can't speak to her,' she said. 'She's not well. She's at the doctor's.'

I persisted with the number and managed eventually to speak to Anna later in the evening. When she came on the line she sounded deeply distressed. I asked her where she was. She said she didn't know, she was being moved around. She was barely coherent.

I said: 'Go to the police, hand yourself in.'

She pleaded that it wasn't possible. I genuinely believe she would have if she hadn't been prevented by those who were 'looking after her'.

There was little more that I could do that day. Carlos had arranged a meal at a popular Cordoba tapas bar that evening. He suggested that Andalucian red wine was a good way to wash away my worries but I was mindful of the fact that I need to keep a clear brain for the days ahead.

Not least the following morning. I was awoken by a call from someone called Peter. For a moment I thought it was Peter Bayley, my brother-in-law but it wasn't. It was Peter Trowell. He asked how I was and what was I doing about the situation and could he help. I wanted to get him off the line so I thanked him but said everything was now in hands of my lawyer.

'Lawyer' in fact had turned into 'lawyers'. Rod Dadak's firm was acting for a division of the *Mirror* on other matters and Rod felt there could be a conflict of interests if I were to instruct him to proceed against the *Mirror* with anything which might involve a conflict with the *Mirror*. So I engaged the services of another firm who had served me in the past.

My next call, thankfully, was from the real Peter — Peter Bayley. 'You certainly gave Anna a piece of your mind, didn't you?' he said

'How did you know?' I replied. 'On second thoughts, don't tell me.'

But he did. The *Mirror* had bugged our conversation and under the headline YOU STUPID, STUPID WOMAN, GIVE ME MY RING BACK printed a transcription of it. The journalists who wrote the story were Tanith Carey and Nic North. I wondered if their duties extended to driving Anna down to Devon.

But that was only the second page story. On the front page they printed an extract from one of Diana's letters 'Please can you burn my letters after reading them now in case they get into the wrong hands.' The paper said I had betrayed her trust by not destroying them. But the significant word was 'now'. Diana had been writing to me for nearly five years. That letter was written when I was about to go into battle. There was a fair chance I would end up an Iraqi prisoner or a corpse and the 'now' referred to that eventuality. Ironically the Iraqis didn't turn out to be the danger — but a 'patriotic' British newspaper did. It often turns out that you don't know who your real enemies are — until they strike.

I was later faxed the relevant pages from the paper. There was a picture of police officers outside the stables of my house and a report which contained the amazing statement: 'Police have begun an investigation into the alleged theft of the letters. A top cop said last night: "Following a formal complaint made earlier today in connection with allegations of theft, the Metropolitan Police and Devon and Cornwall Police have been asked to look into these allegations." The spokesman would not say who had made the complaint. But earlier police had said there would be no investigation unless Hewitt complained.'

First the Palace, now the police. It seemed amazing. A newspaper prints a detailed account of a burglary in which it admits its own involvement up to the hilt and the police see no need for an investigation. Was I living in a world gone mad?

The paper had an 'interview' with Anna Ferretti whose minimal, fractured English had miraculously matured into the most exact prose.

'People may see what I did was wrong' — well, not the Metropolitan Police, I thought — 'I now see how stupid I have been but I am also very relieved they are back with their rightful owners. They are beautiful letters written by a caring woman who was deeply in love. Now that she is gone it is only right that these mementos should be with her sons.'

Whoever was the author of Anna's words went on to attack me for being a 'sponger' after Anna had spent this invisible £30,000 on me and repeated the allegation that I was seeing other women.

Peter told me that the Metropolitan Police were due to come and inspect the safe later in the morning. As best I could I described to him its exact contents in the exact positions I had left them. The one thing I did remember for certain was that the 'blueys' from Diana were in a brown envelope on the second shelf from the bottom.

As soon as Peter's call finished my mobile phone rang again. It was an old friend, Henry Cole. He had been in Moscow when the story broke but now he was back in Britain. He had often advised me on my dealings with the media before and acted as an agent. He said that I was mad not to have come out with a statement putting my side of the story. He had a deal on the table with the *Sun* who had long wanted to talk to me and he would arrange an interview with Stuart Higgins the editor.

It made sense. The *Sun* were obviously going to publish something on the story and I may as well have my say. I made some notes on a hotel pad. My lawyers had warned me to be careful about what I said at this stage. The phone rang again within minutes. It was Higgins. He was very friendly but probably not delighted that his rival tabloid had had two days of exclusives on a story that was developing in every news bulletin.

I was duly guarded in what I said. In answer to his questions, I gave brief answers some of which surfaced in the *Sun* the next day: 'I just feel numb and raw. This was a woman I was engaged to, a woman I loved and planned to marry. Now I don't know what to think. Have I been taken in and conned? I just don't know. I'm certainly not prepared to believe the *Mirror*'s account of what happened. Mrs Ferretti approached me first and instigated the relationship. Looking back there are certain oddities. I don't even know if Mrs Ferretti is who she says she is now. I find it difficult to believe anybody. I find it very difficult to come to terms with the whole situation. I feel extremely sad for her. I have spoken to her and advised her to talk to the police. I am very sad about the whole thing. I never intended that these letters should be published.'

Higgins seemed eager for more sensation but I had answered his questions as frankly as I could in the circumstances. I repeatedly asked him if the conversation was being taped and he repeatedly said that it wasn't.

But I needed legal assurances. I rang Mark Stevens, a solicitor now acting for me. He told me that he knew Higgins and would speak to him. He did this straight away and came back to me saying Higgins wanted another conversation. I told him I had nothing more to say.

In the following day's *Sun* the story occupied five pages under the headline I'VE BEEN CAD, and there was a telephone number to call to 'Hear the Hewitt Interview in Full.'

I had indeed been had.

My phone rang again — again it was Peter Bayley. His voice was a whisper. 'There are four policemen in your study — two local and two Metropolitan. One's a sergeant from the Organised Crime Squad — I think they're taking over the investigation. Only one problem.'

'What's that?' I asked.

'We can't find the key to the safe. It's not in the desk

drawer.'

'Why did you look there?'

'That's where they said it was in the *Mirror*,' he replied

'It never was in the desk drawer,' I said. 'I left it in the brass lantern in the hall, directly opposite the study door. Anna saw me take it out — she knew where to find it.'

'Hold on while I look,' he replied. There was a pause lasting only a few seconds. 'Got it,' he said, 'call you back when they've gone.'

I lay back on my bed and tried to sort out my thoughts. Strange as it may seem I was now less angry with Anna. The *Mirror* had double-crossed her, they were putting words into her mouth and they had set her up. What I wanted to find out was how they did it? The only way — since the police had condescended to investigate the theft — was for her to be arrested. I still believed that in an English court of law there was a chance that some truth might come out.

So I telephoned her again. This time it was she who answered, not a minder. I asked her where she was. She wouldn't say. But I could tell from her voice that she was frightened.

'Tell me where you are,' I demanded.

'Waterloo, at the station,' she said. 'I am ...'

But she never finished. I could hear the phone being snatched from her, presumably by one of the *Mirror* people.

I realised she must be about to get on the Eurostar to go home. I feared that the moment she left the country that was it. The police were hardly going to issue an extradition warrant for a crime that they didn't consider worth investigating. So I immediately rang Rod Dadak.

'Anna's at Waterloo,' I told him. 'They have police there on duty all the time. They've got to stop her leaving the country.'

There was a knock on the door of my room. Any knock might mean that a journalist had tracked me down but I listened carefully. It was the code knock that Carlos had thought up, a little cadenza that let me know it was him.

'Everything okay?' he inquired.

'Could be worse,' I replied.

'You can't leave Cordoba without seeing the Mosque,' he said.

He was right. The Great Mosque of Cordoba built by Abu Amir al-Mansur during the Islamic occupation of Spain more than a thousand years ago is quite magnificent. When the Spaniards obtained their freedom, instead of knocking down something so splendid they cleverly built a Catholic church within it. As the guide itemised the various armies that had occupied Cordoba, from the Romans in the sixth century to the French in the nineteenth, I tried to put my own problems into context but it didn't do much good.

On the journey back to Madrid I heard from Scotland Yard. Two British police were at the British Embassy in order to interview me. I said I would be there by 2.00 p.m. Peter Bayley called to say the police had left Eversfield Manor. He said they had dusted the safe and its handles for finger prints (it later turned out there were only mine — Lucia must have worn gloves). And a detective with gloves on had taken everything out of the safe — which must have included a shoe box containing a lot of personal letters, many of them from Diana — but put it all back again without comment.

'You only committed one crime and I think you got away with it,' my brother-in-law observed.

'What was that?'

'You left a shotgun in the alcove. I sort of tried to put my body between it and the police and since they weren't really looking for it they didn't seem to notice it.'

I enjoyed his sense of humour. It helped to keep my morale up. And, in my forgetfulness, I had indeed committed a crime — it is against the law to keep such a weapon other than securely under lock and key.

The Mercedes was waiting for us at Madrid station. As we made our way through the traffic I fiddled with the car radio and managed to find an English language station. Within minutes I heard the news that Anna Ferretti had been arrested. I felt dreadful — sick. But also relieved. I was certain this was the only way there was any chance of getting to the bottom of this nightmare.

Rod Dadak kept me a copy of that night's West End Final Edition of the *Evening Standard*. Across the front page were the words: DIANA LETTERS WOMAN HELD. 'Drama as police swoop at Waterloo as she tries to board train to France.'

It went on to say she was held at Waterloo International Station after being approached by plain-clothes officers from the Metropolitan Police. 'Detectives had been keen to question Mr Hewitt's spurned fiancée over allegations that she stole intimate correspondence from the ex-cavalry officer's safe at his home in Devon.'

# 15

I thought it was somewhat strange for the police to use the British Embassy for what was an inquiry into a robbery in a private house. It seemed to me that a room at a hotel or maybe a local police station would have done. The choice of location caused me to wonder if powers other than the police were already involved in this case.

I asked Carlos to come with me. I felt it was a good idea to have an independent witness. Shortly before two o'clock I pressed the buzzer at the main entrance to the British Embassy, an austere, well-fortified, concrete structure in the centre of the city. A voice answered and I gave my name. They were expecting me. After a short wait a security guard let us in. Inside the front door there was another time-locked door that wouldn't open until the outside door was locked.

We were ushered down the hall and into a small

conference room, simply furnished with a table and some chairs and blast curtains on the windows. Two men were waiting for me. One introduced himself as Detective Inspector Richard Taber of the Metropolitan Police. I cannot recall the name of his colleague but Taber did most of the talking. They wanted to know who Carlos was — a secret policeman, a private policeman or a security guard? He replied that he was a businessman and a friend.

They offered us a cup of tea. Taber then took out two dossiers and began to question me. From the tenor of his initial approach I got the feeling that they were investigating the possibility that I was part of a conspiracy and maybe not just the victim of a crime. He wanted to know every single detail about my relationship with Anna Ferretti from the moment I met her. I told him all the relevant facts right up to the previous day's phone call in which she explained to me she had stolen the letters because I had lied to her and was seeing other women.

This took quite some time. Taber then turned to the second dossier on the table and said that since this contained sensitive information he thought it might be a matter for my ears alone. I told Carlos this was fine by me and he said he would go and change cars as the driver had earlier informed him that some journalists had begun to recognise the grey Mercedes.

Taber then moved on to my relationship with Princess Diana and the content of the letters. He asked me what was in them and I pointed out that it was hard for me to say as I didn't know which letters had been stolen. He said they were nearly all blue air-mail letters addressed to me in the Gulf. I told him that these were letters the Princess had written in early 1991.

'Love letters?' he asked.

'Yes,' I replied.

Taber asked me if it had ever been my intention to sell the letters. I told him that this had never been the case. People had offered me substantial sums for them but I hadn't even replied to their letters for fear that such correspondence could be misconstrued. He wanted to know what 'substantial sums' meant in this context and I told him that it meant millions of dollars.

I certainly felt when I was given my statement to sign that they no longer thought I was implicated in a conspiracy. They must have seen that it would be very irrational behaviour on my part to ignore offers in the millions for the letters, only to join together with two Italian women and a Frenchman to try and sell them to a newspaper for £80,000.

I told Taber that I had heard Ferretti had been arrested. He seemed surprised I knew this but, of course, he knew as well. I asked him what the course of events was likely to be. If the *Mirror* was to be believed — and that was always a very big 'if' — both she and possibly the people from the paper might have indulged in criminal behaviour. He wouldn't be drawn on this and was not really prepared to give anything away. It was understandable. He conducted himself professionally and by the book.

He asked me about my future movements. I said I had business obligations that would keep me in Spain until Monday but would then return to England. He told me to remain in touch. If there was a problem with the press at Heathrow the police would do what they could. I thanked him and we said goodbye.

As I left the embassy and stepped back into Spain, I reviewed the situation with very mixed feelings: I may have defused the idea of a conspiracy involving me but without a doubt I sensed the hand of the Palace already hovering over the case.

A lawyer friend had warned me that the *Mirror*, having been wrong-footed by Anna's arrest, would now do everything to stop the case going to court. He was right. The first fax the next morning was a *Mirror* story headlined JURY COULD READ THEM. Underneath it said: 'The Diana letters to Hewitt could be read in open court if his fiancée Anna Staiano Ferretti is charged with theft, legal experts warned yesterday. And if she was found guilty, the court could order Kensington Palace — which now holds the 62 letters — to hand them back to Hewitt. Legal expert Robert Roscoe, of Victor, Lissack and Roscoe, said if the issue went to court, the letters "would become an exhibit" available for scrutiny. He added: "I would be surprised if James Hewitt maintained a formal complaint."'

How well he doesn't know me, I thought. If the *Mirror* believed I would not pursue the case and tell everything I knew about the theft, they were wrong. I wanted the case to go to court and I could see no reason why the contents of the letters — once it was established they were from Diana to me — needed to be disclosed.

Throughout my time in Spain my lawyers and my brother-in-law, Peter, and two former army colleagues kept me abreast of the stories in the British press, whether by phone or by fax. I have since verified them from a cuttings file that a lawyer kept.

Fortunately not everyone in England was appraised of the situation via *Mirror* propaganda. The *Daily Telegraph* reported that while the copyright in the letters belonged to Diana's estate, the letters themselves were legally owned by me. The paper pointed out: 'The Princess's private office now faces a legal and moral dilemma over the ownership of the letters.' They accompanied this with a picture of Diana and me the day she brought Prince William and Prince Harry to Combermere Barracks. She loved that photograph.

The law of England was not something, however, that appeared to be too familiar to the *Mirror*'s editor, Piers Morgan, whom the *Telegraph* interviewed. 'The question is whether or not Mr Hewitt is going to ask for them back,' Morgan stated. 'If he does, we will lead the stampede to stop him. We will campaign vigorously to stop James Hewitt ever having these letters in his possession again.'

The paper went on to report that Morgan's decision not to publish the letters had not stemmed from legal advice that it would infringe copyright to do so. He was reported as saying: 'I felt it was a step too far to publish, particularly when the letters talk of her love for a man who is not the father of her two children.'

I wondered just how concerned Morgan had been about these children when he instructed his journalists to drive Anna, Lucia and Jean-Marc down to Devon and then put the whole subject into the headlines.

His propaganda remained relentless. The headline in that Saturday's *Mirror* was THEY STAY. In a story labelled EXCLUSIVE, the *Mirror* reported the following as fact. 'Kensington Palace officials yesterday told why Diana's family would never hand back the sensational love letters the Princess wrote to James Hewitt. Diana's family are determined to keep the 62 notes and thwart any attempt by Hewitt to get them returned. Trustees of the Princess's estate, including Diana's mother Frances Shand Kydd and her sister Sarah McCorquodale, have been consulted by the Palace over what to do with the letters. And officials at the Palace have told detectives investigating the alleged theft of the notes that they will not be returned.'

An (unnamed) Palace source told the *Mirror* that the Spencer family were very grateful that the *Mirror* did not publish the letters. The source went on: 'The police behaved entirely properly when they came to the Palace yesterday but they were politely told that the letters were going nowhere. If Hewitt wants them back he will have to come to the Palace himself and get them — and his chances of succeeding via that route are less than nil ... Hewitt may have a legal right to the letters but morally he has the rights of a sewer rat.'

Did one of Her Majesty's officials really say all of the above with phrases like the letters were 'going nowhere' and 'he has the rights of a sewer rat'? The lawyer who kept the press cuttings for me always called this 'Exhibit X'. If you believed this was a faithful transcription of a Palace statement, he said, then you would believe everything the *Mirror* wrote. If, on the other hand, these looked more likely to be the words of a *Mirror* journalist, could you believe anything the paper attributed to anyone in this case? I leave it to you, the reader, to make up your own mind.

All the papers carried news of Anna's arrest and the *Sun* had a report from Nick Parker in Monaco saying Anna Ferretti was not Anna Ferretti. He had shown a photograph of her to a barman and a British cleaner at the Hotel de Paris. The cleaner said: 'That is definitely not the real Anna Ferretti. I have worked here for 18 years and know her and her husband.' Parker added: 'Mystery also surrounds the fashion "tycoon" Alberto to whom Anna claims she was married. A Milan-based label called Ferretti exists but it is run by a woman called Alberta who has never stayed at the hotel.'

When Peter read that story to me over the phone and asked me what I thought, I could only give one reply: 'I just don't know.'

'Well, whoever she is,' he said, 'she's been released on police bail. The news said she spent eighteen hours in custody.'

I feared that she might have jumped out of the frying pan into the fire. The *Mirror* had promised readers her 'world exclusive' story on Monday and I was pretty certain the minders would be making sure no other paper got to her.

The press knew I was staying at the Hotel Melia-Castilla. Journalists lingered in the lobby and there were always photographers outside. I used the service entrance route to go to a dinner organised by Jose Maria for some of his fellow businessmen and their wives. It was a curious double life trying to cope with the problems in England while attempting to put on a reasonably carefree face for the sake of the Spanish. Inside I felt far from comfortable but they did everything to put me at my ease.

On Sunday we travelled three hours north-east of Madrid to Soria where I was scheduled to visit Sr Rioja's property. It was a well-established riding school that was in complete contrast to Andalucia. No graceful grey stallions here, but solid horses — the kind that are used for herding cattle. There were pens with baby bulls on the estate with an established bull-ring nearby. One of my mounts was actually a picador's horse. On the day of a bull-fight it would have its flanks thickly padded and protected from penetration from the bull's horns and be blind-folded before it was ridden into the ring. But these horses have learnt to lean in to the path of the approaching bull so that they won't be knocked over by the impact.

This was a well-run equestrian centre. There was a certain 'wild-west' appeal to the place and the surrounding terrain — barren, dry and dusty — was very much like cowboy country. It occurred to me that this 'John Wayne' approach might be the best way of marketing the experience.

I managed to get a telephone signal and talk to Peter on the way home. He had been desperately trying to get in touch with me all day. He told me that both the *Sunday Mirror* and the *News of the World* had headlines saying I was about to sell the letters.

The *Mirror* we had expected. They were in a difficult position. Their primary justification for taking part in the robbery was that it would prevent me from selling the letters. They had told their readers that they were participating in a crime to prevent a greater crime. But this was completely untrue for the simple reason that if I were to sell the letters I would not be committing a crime. They were my property. I was free to dispose of them as I wished. But, as I have said, the letters had been in my possession for more than seven years and I had never had any intention of selling them.

Peter said they had got to Terrence Rowland and used him as a source for saying that I wanted £5 million for the letters. Terrence had worked for me for four years but had left some months previously because of personal problems, largely brought on by the stress he experienced in looking after the security of Eversfield. Journalists and photographers so frequently staked out the place by day that he found it hard to sleep at night, fearing a break-in. So he had gone to live near one of his sons in Somerset.

Some months after I got back to England, towards the end of the summer, he turned up at my house, crestfallen about the *Sunday Mirror* story. I asked him how it came about. He said his daughter had a friend whose father worked for the *Mirror*. The paper was aware that he was down on his luck — he had been sleeping rough at some stage. A journalist had made contact with him in February 1998. He was put up in a guest house and offered £17,000 if he would give them some stories about me.

According to Terrence for five nights in succession two journalists, one of them David Rowe the writer of the *Sunday Mirror* piece, had taken him to a pub, plied him with drinks and got him to talk. Terrence was adamant that he never said that I was likely to sell the letters. He promised me he had told the journalists: 'If *I* were him, I'd sell the letters.' But whatever he said, the story was always going to end up like it did. It was an essential part of the Ferretti/Valentine's Day sting.

The *News of the World* story, however, came like a bolt from the blue.

The paper's 'chief crime reporter', Neville Thurlbeck, reported that I had met a 'middleman' called Peter Trowell, whom the paper described as 'a broker for many major Fleet Street stories' and asked him to sell some of Diana's letters for £2 million.

The meeting, Thurlbeck wrote, had taken place on Wednesday, March 25th at the Hollington House Hotel in Newbury in Berkshire. Trowell described how 'at 7.30 p.m. Hewitt breezed in clutching a buff-coloured folder and ordered a lager. Then he bragged: "I got held up because I was having a liaison with a particularly demanding lady."' Apparently I then asked Trowell to find a buyer for the letters.

The story was a complete fabrication. Not only have I never met Peter Trowell in my life, he had certainly chosen the wrong day to invent our meeting. On that night I interviewed Anthony Pitcher until past 7 p.m., had dinner with my mother and waited for Anna Ferretti who was due to 'surprise' me at 10.30 p.m. It would have been physically impossible to fit in a 400-mile round trip to Newbury which would have taken about seven hours on the road.

Thurlbeck's article said that Trowell had met an 'army pal' of mine in the Coopers Arms pub in Chelsea on Friday, March 20th. The friend, Thurlbeck wrote, told him the letters were for sale. Such a friend does not exist.

Trowell must have been looking for a story on me that he could sell from the moment we first spoke on the phone, perhaps before then. Unfortunately for him the *Mirror* got there first. He would have known that rival tabloids would have been in the market for a Hewitt/letters story. Perhaps he hoped that his phone call to me on the previous Friday would have given him something worth selling. Or maybe he had already concocted the story of this fictitious meeting. I wondered exactly who this man was who could sink so low and do me such potential harm.

A few weeks later I got my answer. An edition of the magazine *Private Eye* provided some facts about Peter Trowell. They described him as 'a sometime con man and jailbird with a long history of dodgy antics'. He had set up the entrapment of William Straw, the son of the Home Secretary. While he was in prison he had befriended Darius Guppy (Earl Spencer's best man) and had later secretly tape-recorded a conversation with Guppy. *Private Eye* reported that the conversation 'duly turned up in a Sunday tabloid'. With heavy irony the magazine totally undermined this 'impeccable source' who claimed I had asked him to sell the letters.

My solicitor complained to the Press Complaints Commission about the *News of the World* article with affidavits from my mother and Anthony Pitcher. An acquaintance who knew what was going on subsequently told two army friends of mine, Tim Dobson and Rupert Mackenzie-Hill, that Trowell had admitted to him he had never met me. They urged the acquaintance to provide an affidavit confirming this. He agreed to do so but a few days later changed his mind. Here was a man who knew the truth but was not prepared to tell it. Apparently he didn't want any press coverage that might harm his position in the City.

But these were problems yet to come. Back at my hotel in Madrid I took stock of the situation. Ever since the police interview I knew I had a fight on my hands. I wasn't just up against the *Mirror*. Diana often used to refer to 'the men in grey suits' within the Palace who were out to discredit her. These Sunday stories, however false, were certainly out to discredit me and — whatever my legal rights — I feared that Kensington Palace might make use of them to justify holding on to my property.

I called Rod Dadak. He had seen the stories in the papers. I told him I thought there was a real danger the establishment was going to close ranks on this affair and I would never see the letters again. I asked him who exactly was in charge of the letters now they were at Kensington Palace. He said that the responsibility lay with Princess Diana's executors — her mother Frances Shand-Kydd, her sister Sarah McCorquodale and the Bishop of London, the Right Reverend Richard Chartres.

I said that we had to act fast. Rod agreed but pointed out that the police would need the letters as evidence in their investigation. 'Then why haven't they taken them into police custody?' I asked. It was one of the many grey areas in the case. Rod said he would write to Lawrence Graham, the executors' solicitors, on Monday to establish that the letters were quite clearly mine and to ask for their immediate return.

By Monday the hotel was almost under siege from the press. Even the service entrance route was now monitored. Reporters fired questions at me as I went past. 'Did you try to sell Diana's letters?' 'What are you going to do about Anna Ferretti?' 'Were you involved?' Regardless of the question, I replied with the same answer — a polite silence.

I had a final meeting in town with Jose Maria's business affairs and marketing people in which I was due to be debriefed on my fact-finding tour. But my mind was so preoccupied with the problems at home that I was unable to do justice to it. Carlos understood this only too well and suggested that we could go into greater details at a later date.

I hoped that I could get a flight back that afternoon. But Carlos, who had contacts everywhere, warned me that Madrid Airport was heavily staked out by television crews and photographers. He thought that it might be an idea to drive to Toledo — about an hour from Madrid — and fly from there, maybe to an airport other than Heathrow.

We looked into the logistics of this but it involved changing planes and, at the end of the day, I had to go back to Heathrow at some stage to retrieve my car. I might as well face the music in Madrid. After the *Mirror*'s vilification of the past few days, how much harm could some cameras and some questions do? They weren't bullets. So I made a reservation in economy on Tuesday's British Airways flight to London.

Since her release by the police I had tried again and again to contact Anna Ferretti. Only once had I got through to her and she had managed to mumble something about 'they are taking me in a helicopter'. But since then her phone had not been working. I was genuinely worried about her. She was caught up in something she could never have foreseen and she was not in the company of people who had her well-being at heart.

When I got back to the hotel there was an envelope full of faxes waiting for me. I tore it open. The front page headline of that Monday's *Mirror* consisted of just two words: THE LOVERS. Beneath it was a full-page photograph of me and Anna embracing in the sea at Monte Carlo. Inside, page three was filled with four more photographs taken of us at the same time. I scanned the story — it occupied numerous pages — then closed my eyes and lay back on the bed.

This put a completely new complexion on events. When the *Mirror* 'exposed the scandal' the previous Thursday they claimed that Anna had taken letters from my house and then tried to 'hawk them to the *Mirror* for £150,000'. Her reason, they claimed initially, was to sell them before I could. That was on April 2nd. Now they were publishing photographs of us taken on Thursday, March 19th — two weeks before her 'spontaneous' act.

It was immediately apparent that I had been set up. Jean-Marc had telephoned me and suggested I come down to Monte Carlo. He had done much of the organising on that trip, including guiding us to the rejected railway hotel. It was he who took us to the beach where we went into the sea. Now I came to think of it Jean-Marc had gone into the water immediately after Anna to encourage me to come in. And, out of sight, a photographer with a long lens was lying in wait for us.

Was Anna part of it? Who took the pictures? A paparazzi friend? A *Mirror* photographer? Was this the first step in the paper's overall plan? At this stage I had no way of knowing.

Along with the photographs was Anna's 'exclusive story' as told to the same pair of *Mirror* reporters who had covered the robbery. This time they covered our sex life in a manner that managed to be both intimate and crude. Quotations were ascribed to Anna saying on the one hand how much she loved me and on the other how bad a lover I was — what both had in common was the fact that, even in translation, none of the expressions or phrasing sounded remotely like the Anna I knew.

Why had she let her name be attached to something like this? There was only one person who could explain that and it was Anna herself. When I got back to London my first priority was to establish my right to the letters and my second was to get the truth out of Anna Ferretti.

But getting back to London was not a comfortable process. It's a myth that an individual can book himself on to an international flight under an assumed name.

Maybe those with contacts can, but I had none. The name on the ticket has to correlate with the name on the passport. It's also a myth that the list of passengers on any flight is kept strictly secret. The media seem to have no difficulty in getting hold of the names, whether by hacking into the computer or offering bribes I don't know.

So not only did I have to run the gamut of television crews and photographers and press at Madrid Airport on Tuesday but about twenty journalists had booked themselves into the economy cabin of the BA flight I was taking. Carlos was a trooper. He shepherded me through the wall of cameras waiting at check-in and, although he had no boarding card or passport, managed to accompany me right on to the plane. There was a rabble of cameras and outstretched tape recorders already on board which we had to push our way through.

There we said goodbye. I have an enduring debt of gratitude to Carlos Roma which I hope I have partially repaid in these pages. One week previously he had been a stranger to me. But he had given me friendship and support and committed loyalty far beyond the call of duty.

The only British people I had encountered in the past seven days had been journalists and their questions had usually been abrasive and sniping. I had a real fear that maybe everybody in the country had been polluted against me. But on that British Airways flight I learnt differently. The head of the cabin crew came down to where I was sitting in economy and said they had kept me a seat in Club Class where I might be more comfortable.

Without exception the stewards and stewardesses went out of their way to look after me. They prevented the press with economy tickets from coming into the front section of the plane. One or two journalists had cleverly got Club tickets as well but a reporter who sat beside me was asked to resume his rightful seat. At one stage in the flight there was another concerted effort to get to me and the cabin staff formed a phalanx to prevent them.

In this atmosphere it was not easy to concentrate. I was offered some newspapers and turned tentatively to the *Mirror*. For the first time in six days the front page was not filled with another story about me. GRANT: WHY I'VE DUMPED ANTHEA — it read. The paper had found some other people to publicise. But inside there were a further four photographs taken in Monte Carlo and more 'revelations' from Anna under the headline I FLUSHED HEWITT'S RING DOWN THE LOO WHERE IT BELONGED. I doubted if that was any more true than the words that were attributed to her.

I busied myself with some paperwork, making a list of things to be done and a log of my trip in Spain. There was a fax among my papers on which my brother-in-law had scribbled 'save this for the journey home'.

It was an article from the *Sunday Telegraph* with the headline WHY I'M BACKING HEWITT by Auberon Waugh. 'If I had received love letters from the Princess of Wales I would certainly want to keep them,' he wrote. 'After a five-year love affair a man would be very odd who did not wish to keep his lover's letters and even the unsupported claim that Major James Hewitt wishes to make money from them does not alter the legal fact that letters belong to their recipients just as the copyright in them stays with the writer.'

He went on to suggest that if Diana's trustees tried to keep them they might be guilty of condoning theft and receiving stolen property. I have never met Mr Waugh but I wish him to know how much his words meant to me. They fortified my resolve to fight this case to the bitter end.

I had boarded the flight feeling beleaguered, but it is amazing how powerful the support of strangers can be. The cabin crew seemed to relish protecting me during the journey. I thanked each one of them as I left the plane. At Heathrow, true to their word, the Metropolitan Police had asked their colleagues from the Hounslow force, who police the airport, to look after me and stop me being hassled by the press on either side of customs. Reporters kept shouting questions at me but as well as a freedom of speech in Britain there is also a freedom of silence and I truly had nothing to say.

The Hounslow Police had thoughtfully arranged that valet parking should bring my Range Rover round to a side entrance of the airport terminal. That did not deter a *Mirror* photographer from stalking me there and taking my picture. 'Cash on Delivery: Hewitt tips the man who retrieved his car £20' was the caption under the picture the next morning. *Mirror* reporting was as accurate as ever — in fact, I was handing him £10.

# 16

The look on Rod Dadak's face said it all. He had had a fax from Lawrence Graham, the executors' lawyers. They were going to make a fight of it. More than that, it looked as if they were going to do their damnedest to make sure I did not get my property back. They said they didn't accept that the letters were sent to me with the intention I should retain them, quoting Diana's line: 'Please can you burn my letters after reading them now in case they get into the wrong hands.'

I told Rod that the wrong hands meant Iraqi ones. Diana had written this fearing I might be captured — or worse.

For a moment I wondered what had happened to the letters I had written to Diana. She had told me that she had kept most of them. Perhaps they were in the possession of the executors as well.

'They must know what the law is,' I said to Rod.

'I don't think this case is just going to be about the law,' he replied and pointed to the second page of the Lawrence Graham fax. It said that I had 'manifested an intention to disclose the confidential contents of the letters by disposing of them to or for the benefit of the press world-wide'.

How on earth did Lawrence Graham come by such information? The only reason they gave was that they had read in the press that I had offered certain letters written to me by the Princess to a Sunday newspaper. So the words of Mr Peter Trowell were the reason the executors thought they should receive stolen goods and hold on to them after the rightful owner asked for them back.

It seemed outrageous to me. Rod told me not to get too excited — the early exchanges in matters of this sort were always fairly extreme. I asked him how many matters of this sort he had been involved in and he acknowledged this was a fairly unprecedented situation with the Palace, the press and public opinion all playing their part. He guided me through the various legal options but — as I have said earlier — the fact that his firm acted for a division Mirror Group meant that he could no longer handle my case as it inevitably involved the *Mirror*.

Despite the fact that they no longer appeared to suspect me of conspiring to rob myself, I was still unable to understand the behaviour of the police with regard to the robbery. The letters were stolen goods — nobody seemed to dispute that — yet the Metropolitan Police were content to leave them at Kensington Palace. One would have thought they should have been taken to a safe in a strong room at Scotland Yard. Were the police fearful of an internal leak if the letters were in their custody or were they fearful of the executors? I just didn't know.

What I did know was that the police had no great desire for me to see the letters. When a householder has been robbed it must be the natural progression of justice that he should identify his stolen property. But it seemed not to be necessary in this case. However, I was determined to see the letters. When Peter Bayley and I went to Stephens Innocent, the firm which was now looking after my affairs, I had asked the lawyers if they could arrange this. Nicola Namdjou, the solicitor assigned to the case, said she thought there would be no problem. She quickly came back with the news that the police had agreed that I could go to Kensington Palace to identify the letters.

Mark Stephens, the senior partner, introduced me to John Critchley, a barrister, who had reviewed the correspondence between Rod Dadak and Lawrence Graham and had drafted a long and fiery reply. We spent the morning going through the various details. Before lunch we were joined by Geoffrey Robertson, the QC who had sheltered me during the *Princess in Love* storm and who had actually introduced me to Mark Stephens. He advocated a more terse and direct approach and the letter was redrafted accordingly. Nobody expected that the executors were immediately going to change their minds, but it was essential to let them know how relentlessly I intended to pursue the return of the letters.

It was agreed that Peter would drive Nicola and me to the meeting at Kensington Palace. As I sat in the passenger seat of his Volvo Estate and looked out at the damp, grey London streets I was aware how the speed and pressure of the events of the past days had kept my adrenalin pumping. Now it was time to order my thoughts and control my emotions. It wasn't easy. We went through Knightsbridge, past Hyde Park Barracks and drove parallel to Rotten Row on to Kensington Gore. To say this brought back memories would be an understatement.

We slowed down at the southern end of Kensington Gardens — an area which eight months previously had been carpeted with flowers — and turned up the avenue to the Palace. It had been more than five years since I had last come here to see Diana.

Peter pulled up at the barrier and I rolled down my window. I didn't recognise either of the policeman on duty — I hadn't expected to — but it was apparent they had been expecting me.

'Major Hewitt?' the sergeant asked.

'Yes.'

He gave me a warm smile. I was surprised. I don't know why — maybe I had expected a degree of hostility. He pointed towards the Palace. 'You know where to go, sir.'

'Yes,' I said. 'Thank you.'

Nicola had been told that we could see the letters in the Kensington Palace offices. I knew them — they were underneath and slightly to the west of Diana's private apartment. I directed Peter further up the drive to an area adjacent to the courtyard where we could park.

I led the way into the offices which were really converted store rooms with low curved ceilings similar to cellars. One of the secretaries had been deputed to meet us. She let us in and showed us where we should proceed through another door and on to the room where she said Michael Gibbins was waiting.

First we had to pass through another office. As we did so, a man rose from his desk and came across to me.

'James,' he said.

'Hello, Paul,' I replied.

It was Paul Burrell, Diana's butler. I held out my hand and he took hold of it.

'I'm sorry about this,' I said. 'It's none of my making.'

'I know that,' he said. And then, unexpectedly, he grabbed my other hand and held it tightly. I could see tears welling up in his eyes.

'It's so good to see you,' he said.

'It's good to see you, Paul,' I replied. There was so much more I wanted to say but I couldn't at that moment find any words. Besides, people were waiting.

I had never met Michael Gibbins before. His office was at the far end of the hall. He introduced himself, indicated that we should sit at the round table in the centre of the room and offered us some coffee. As he was helping serve it he explained that he looked after the day-to-day winding up of Diana's estate. He told us that it was his birthday but he didn't appear to be enjoying it very much. He was extremely ill at ease. I suspect he had not been looking forward to this occasion. I wanted to know how he had come by the letters. He said that the *Mirror* had contacted him asking him if he would accept them and if he would write a letter on Kensington Palace notepaper thanking the *Mirror* for not publishing them. He said he had written a letter but he had refused to do so on Kensington Palace notepaper. He seemed proud of his stance on this.

It would have been useful to learn a lot more of Mr Gibbins' dealings with the *Mirror* but other people began to arrive and there was no time.

Wendy Batchelor was the solicitor who was handling the matter for Lawrence Graham. She clearly knew Gibbins quite well. And then there were two officers from the Metropolitan Police.

One of them introduced himself as Inspector Sharpe and we, in turn, introduced ourselves. There was no room for small talk, you could have cut the atmosphere with a sword. Sharpe turned to Gibbins. 'Would you be kind enough to get the letters?'

Gibbins went to an adjoining room where there was a safe and opened it. He came back with a brown envelope and gave it to Sharpe.

'This is how proceedings will be conducted.' Sharpe looked at me. 'You will be shown the letters. You will identify them, but you will not touch them.'

He had clearly taken instructions as to the bounds of this procedure and repeated them in a cold, automatic voice. I didn't warm to him at all — but we weren't there to like each other.

However, his approach riled me. I felt insulted and angry. The *Mirror* had ridden rough-shod over me in print for the past week and now the police seemed intent on doing the same.

'I want to be able to handle them,' I demanded. 'I don't know how many there are for a start. They're my property and I'd like to read them.'

'You will not be allowed to read them,' Sharpe replied in a dispassionate voice.

'I don't see how I can identify them without looking at them properly,' I countered. 'Why can't I read them?'

'It is not necessary for you to do so,' he said.

I said nothing more for the time being. I didn't know what the rules were if something was meant to be in police custody. Sharpe opened the police bag and methodically placed the letters in front of me.

I lifted one up, waiting for Sharpe to order me not to touch it. But he said nothing. It was obvious to everyone round the table that I would have to touch the letters in order to identify them. But I only looked at each one long enough to check the handwriting.

'I confirm that this is a letter written to me by Diana, Princess of Wales, and that it is my property,' I said pointedly. I did this with each letter. It took quite a long time. There were sixty-four of them — Nicola made a note of the number. Michael Gibbins seemed to get more and more agitated, chain-smoking throughout.

When I had finished Sharpe put the letters back in the envelope and signed it in our presence. His assistant had taken down a statement with regard to the conduct of the proceedings.

Sharpe then asked me to sign a document confirming that these were the sixty-four letters taken from my safe. I told him I couldn't. He asked why not and I pointed out that I had no idea of the exact number of letters that were actually taken nor the number of letters from Princess Diana that were originally in the safe. I had never counted or filed them. He seemed very interested to learn that these were not the only letters I had received from her. But I was not prepared to elaborate on the others.

Sharpe then looked round the room. 'Right, that seems to be it. Are there any questions?'

'Yes,' I said. 'Those letters are my property and I want them back.'

The inspector seemed surprised by this. 'Well — you can't have them. They're in police custody.'

'Fine,' I said. 'If they're in police custody, take them to a police station.'

Sharpe became even more defensive. 'No. We want them here. We think they're safer here.'

I looked at him. 'Safer here than in a police station?'

'We think they'll be safe here,' he insisted. 'I'm telling you: you can't have them back.'

'Very well,' I said. 'But how do I know that other people won't look at them?'

'They are in a sealed police bag,' Sharpe replied. 'Nobody can open it without it being signed by myself or another officer as a witness.

'If it is opened again,' I said, 'I would like either me or my representative to be there.'

'Very well,' he replied. 'In that case a representative of the executors is entitled to be there as well.'

The position of the executors seemed to be at the forefront of police thinking. Nicola had been taking notes throughout all of this. She now looked up and said to Sharpe: 'I would like to ask a question.'

Sharpe nodded his assent.

Nicola turned to Michael Gibbins. 'Mr Gibbins, can you tell me how and when the letters came into your possession?'

He replied that they had been given to him for identification the previous week.

We had discussed this issue in the solicitors' office. What was crucial to the question of whether it was Anna Ferretti or the *Mirror* itself who initiated the idea to steal the letters was whether Anna really had — as the paper claimed — gone to their office with two letters and said she could get more.

So Nicola asked Gibbins, 'Before you received the bulk of the letters, did the *Mirror* earlier send you two specimen letters to authenticate?'

Gibbins, chain-smoking hard and looking more uncomfortable than ever, glanced nervously across to Wendy Batchelor for help. She seemed to indicate that there was no need for him to answer this question so he merely repeated that all he had done was to authenticate the letters.

---

I was dying for Nicola to nail him down on this matter. It was vital to me. If Geoffrey Robertson had been there I was sure he would not have let Gibbins off the hook. But this was not a court of law and probably not the place for a cross-examination. I had to content myself with the knowledge that when the case eventually came to trial, people would be under oath and we might get nearer the truth.

Sharpe stood up and said that the process of identification had been completed to his satisfaction and we were now free to leave. We did so with the minimum of ceremony. In the outer office I again encountered Paul Burrell. He had been waiting for me.

'Is everything okay?' he asked.

'Nearly okay,' I replied. 'How are things with you?'

'Not bad,' he said, 'in the circumstances.'

'Of course ...' I began.

There were too many people around to say anything more personal. When Diana and I had been together Paul had been a friend and protector. This was the man who had stood resolutely by her in her final years and beyond.

'You did so much,' was all I could say.

'I did my duty,' he said. 'Goodbye, James. I hope everything goes well with you.'

'You, too. Goodbye, Paul.'

I stepped out into the courtyard. We were right outside Diana's front door where I had come that first evening more than twelve years ago. Paul had not joined her staff then but when he did he immediately made his mark. He did more than his duty. He was instrumental in helping Diana regain her well-being and self-esteem. He was discreet about our relationship but managed to indicate he was in favour of it. The sight of him brought back memories of days that were extraordinarily happy and full of love. When I returned from the Gulf, Paul was the first person to welcome me back on English soil. He greeted me so effusively and positively bubbled with enthusiasm as he drove me to see Diana at Highgrove.

And now all that had been reduced to sitting round a

table with hostile strangers, not even being allowed to read the letters that were a record of our love. I looked at her door and remembered days gone by.

I subsequently had a further meeting with Detective Inspector Taber from the Metropolitan Police Organised Crime Group to go over some points on the statement I had given in Madrid. Again I asked him about the progress of the case but he was non-committal. I said surely he had spoken to Piers Morgan and the staff at the *Mirror* who had publicly acknowledged their role in the crime. He refused to be drawn. I urged him to do so if he was going to get at the truth. I inquired if he knew where Anna Ferretti was. He said he didn't but he did volunteer that she had surrendered her passport and had been released on bail so she was presumably in the country.

Anna's last 'article' about her and me in the *Mirror* had been headlined: I FLUSHED HEWITT'S RING DOWN THE LOO WHERE IT BELONGED. But this was yet another piece of fiction printed under her name. It was simply untrue. She had handed the diamond and sapphire ring over to the police when she was taken into custody. In fact, at a time when the police knew I was back in London two officers had flown down to Exeter and then driven to see my mother to ask her to identify the ring, which she did. The ring, in fact, had been mine — my mother had given it to me. I would have thought it would have been easier — and cheaper — for the police to have asked me to identify it.

During my days in town I continually tried to contact Anna on her mobile phone but to no avail. I phoned the Hyde Park and one or two hotels which I knew she had used but there was no one registered under her name. There was little more I could do in London for the time being. It was Easter and time to return home to Devon.

The lambs that had survived had matured while I was away. They no longer clung to their mothers for suckling but had turned their meadow into a playpen as they skipped about. It seemed more like twelve months than twelve days since Rupert and I had mounted our life-saving operation in the kitchen. I checked and double-checked the contents of the safe but — as Peter had reported — the only thing that had been taken was the envelope with the letters. Everything else in the house seemed to be in order.

It was good to get back on my own horse, Pearl Button. I rode out each morning for hours far into the depths of the Devon countryside, hoping to put some distance between myself and the madness of the past ten days. But it stayed with me, every waking moment and far into the night. There were too many questions that needed to be answered.

My mother and my sisters and their families came over for lunch on Easter Monday. To begin with everyone tried to avoid talking about Anna and the *Mirror*. I told them about the various stables I had visited in Spain and listened to the others discussing the prices certain horses had gone for at the pre-Easter market and how well my nieces and nephews had fared at local pony club events.

But none of us was under any illusion as to what was at the top of all our thoughts. It hung over us like a doom-laden cloud. As soon as the children got down from the table to go out and hunt for the Easter eggs that I had planted in the grounds, the conversation turned to the robbery and its consequences. Peter and I tried to bring everyone up to date to the extent that we could.

We were still at the table — it must have been nearly four o'clock — when the telephone rang. I got up to answer it. There wasn't a voice at the other end, just the sound of somebody sobbing uncontrollably.

'Anna?' I said.

It was her. I tried to get her to tell me where she was but between the sobs and tears all I could make out was her saying how unhappy she was and how sorry she was. She sounded almost hysterical.

I beckoned Caroline over — she had formed a good relationship with Anna over Christmas. At one stage Anna had confided to her that she thought she might be pregnant, although it turned out to be a false alarm. Caroline took the phone and spoke gently to her in French.

Eventually Anna calmed down and began to speak more coherently. I took back the receiver and asked her to tell me where she was and how I could see her. She said she had been told by her lawyer not to see me but she promised to call back later in the evening when I was alone.

Amazingly, she did — at about ten o'clock that night. But she wasn't forthcoming with very much information, just that she had been having the most terrible time with some thoughtless and cruel people. I said we had to meet. I needed to know everything from the beginning. She replied that that would not be possible at the moment but, if I liked, she was prepared to meet Caroline. I told her that Caroline was no longer at my house, she and Peter had gone to have dinner with some friends in Gidleigh. Anna asked if I had the telephone number and I gave it to her. She promised that she would speak to Caroline and make arrangements to see her. Then she began to become upset again and said she had to ring off.

I sat alone in the study for a long time, looking at the clear night sky and just thinking about Anna. How on earth had it all turned so rotten? I knew from bitter experience the moment you become a plaything of the tabloids they will employ every trick in the book to use you for stories, true or false, and ultimately make your life a misery. The phone rang again. It was Caroline. She was going to see Anna in London the next day. The news filled me with hope. At last we might be getting somewhere.

Peter and I decided that it would be prudent for them to go to my solicitors, Stephens Innocent, first before seeing Anna. Despite her distress, there was always the possibility that this was another set-up by the *Mirror*. Anna had told Caroline that she was staying at a hotel called Eleven Cadogan Gardens. She was in Room 10 under the assumed name of Jones. Nicola Namdjou advised Caroline that Anna's room might be bugged by the paper so she should telephone her and arrange to meet in the hotel's lounge.

Both Caroline and Peter were later required to give witness statements to the police about their meeting with Anna. I have drawn on them to recount what happened.

---

Peter dropped Caroline at Eleven Cadogan Gardens and lingered for a while outside to see if there were any reporters or photographers. When it appeared there were none, he went off to park the car.

Caroline entered the hotel and was shown to the lounge. 'I saw Anna Ferretti bent down and looking at the fire,' she told the police. 'I walked towards her and she turned round and stood up. We embraced as friends. We sat on a sofa. I asked her: "Is anyone else listening to this?" and she said: "No, no." She said that she was very stressed and that she was taking tablets. She showed me blotches on her legs and arms.

'She asked: "How is James?" I said: "Devastated. We all are. We want to know the truth." She explained that Jean-Marc had the photographs taken of James and herself. I asked: "Did the *Mirror* take them?" She said: "I don't know." She said: "James has been with other women, the woman with the rose." I said: "Yes, but that was twelve months ago."

'She then explained that when she went to the *Mirror* with Jean-Marc she had been shown a table covered with photographs of James with other women. She told me that it was Piers Morgan who showed her the photographs. She implied that she could cope with that but they had tapes of James talking. She had heard them talking "sexy talk". I could see that she was very upset about this. She said: "I was jealous and I wanted to hurt him."'

Caroline asked her if Lucia took the letters but Anna insisted: 'I am responsible.' Caroline got the impression she was covering up for her sister. Caroline went on: 'I said: "The newspaper said you had two letters." She said: "I never had any letters." She told me that she had received no money from the *Mirror* but had told them that they must pay for furniture for James. She said that her life was ruined, that no one was talking to her and that her family weren't speaking to her. She said that she wanted to help James and that she would sell her house in order to do so.

'She also wanted to get back at the *Mirror*. She didn't

want any other woman to go through what she had gone through because of the *Mirror*. She was venomous about the *Mirror*. They had taken her filofax and photocopied everything in it including her photographs. They had taken her mobile phone away from her. After she had been released from the police station, *Mirror* journalists had taken her in a helicopter. Over a period of three days she had been taken to various places and did not know where she was. She told me that she had taken notepads from the hotels so that she would know where she had been. She showed me one notepad from a hotel in Buckinghamshire. She also said that the *Mirror* had taken her to Newquay. The impression I got was that she was a prisoner of the *Mirror*.'

At this point Peter came into the hotel and joined them. Caroline and Anna had been conversing in English — which Anna spoke slowly and with difficulty. After greeting Peter, Anna started to talk to him in French. The following is taken from his police witness statement.

'It had been her intention only to photocopy the letters for the *Mirror* before returning them to the safe. She had wanted to do that in the village but she had been taken directly to London by the *Mirror* journalists having been told that it would be necessary to use a specialist photocopier that could only be found in London.

'Two *Mirror* reporters had gone down to Devon with her — in fact, she may have actually said three, Nic North, Tina and Lucy. She said that Nic North was hanging around in the garden while she was inside. I took that to mean that when the letters were taken, she was in the house and he was outside.'

So I believe Nic North — described by the *Mirror* as their Chief Reporter and the man who described every detail of the robbery and Anna's subsequent story — played a slightly larger part in the incident than actually reporting it. And 'Tina', as I was later to find out, was Tanith Carey, his partner.

Peter and Caroline went back to see Anna at the hotel at 11.00 a.m. the following day. She was less upset. She offered them some coffee and then calmly, in French, told Peter her version of events which was subsequently formally recorded in his witness statement. This was Anna's version of what happened.

Jean-Marc Medecin had approached the *Mirror* to see if they would buy photographs of James Hewitt and Anna. They were interested and Jean-Marc arranged for the photographs to be taken. He needed the money. Neither he nor Lucia had any and Anna had been keeping them for the past five months. As Jean-Marc was her sister's fiancée Anna was 'prepared to go along with it'.

Jean-Marc persuaded her to come with him to the *Mirror* and meet Piers Morgan, the editor. Morgan sought to turn her against James, showing her the photographs and playing the tape. She was asked if she had seen Princess Diana's letters at James's house. She said she had seen a bundle of them but had never read any of them. She repeatedly made the point that she did not have any letters when she went to the *Mirror* but she was persuaded by people at the meeting to go and get the letters, having been assured by 'Tina' that there was nothing wrong with taking them as they did not belong to James. 'Tina' told her that she wanted to photocopy them and return them to James's house.

In the week before the crime the *Mirror* journalists, Jean-Marc and Lucia stayed at two different hotels near Bratton Clovelly. Anna stayed with James and said the journalists 'were ringing her every five minutes' and telling her what to do.

After James had gone to Spain. Anna spent the night before the robbery at the 'Fishing Hotel'. The booking was made under an assumed name but Nic North paid the bill. After gaining entry to the house, Anna got the key to the safe from the wall lamp. She repeated that she took the letters with the intention of photocopying them and returning them. But after she had taken them, Nic North said they couldn't be photocopied locally, they needed to be photocopied on a special photocopier and he then drove her all the way to London.

Peter had told me on the phone the gist of what Anna had said and later sent me copies of the police witness statements. What was I to make of them? In a way they were a relief, at least I was now hearing the story from Anna rather than reading about it in the *Mirror*. But to what extent was she telling the truth? One lawyer suggested to me the notion of letters being taken for the purpose of 'photocopying' with the intent to return them smelt like legal advice on how to bypass the 'intent permanently to deprive' requirement in burglary. How much money did Jean-Marc get for the photographs — or for his part in the robbery? How much, if anything, did Anna get paid for her part — or her two 'world exclusives' about me? I still wanted to find out.

But the thing that puzzled me most was this: If Jean-Marc wanted to make some money out of photos of Anna and me, the natural thing for him to do would be to take them to one of the French magazines. They quite often ran picture stories on me. But he didn't. Instead, out of all the magazines and newspapers in the world, he just happened to choose the *Mirror*. Why?

# 17

At a legal level, Stephens Innocent had been in contact by letter and by telephone with Lawrence Graham about the return of the letters. Things didn't look good. The executors suggested that the 'preferred solution' for the benefit of the Princess, her sons and me was that the letters should be burnt. This seemed more than a little insensitive — they were a remarkable record of a remarkable woman writing in time of war.

It also seemed pretty strong stuff, coming from people who were in possession of my property, stolen from me. I had no wish to harm Prince William and Prince Harry. I had been a friend to them when they were younger and I had no intention of publishing Diana's letters. But didn't the executors realise that the *Mirror* had copies of the letters so their destruction would be meaningless in preventing the paper printing the contents?

I said I did not wish the letters to be destroyed. The executors asked me to reconsider my position. I again asked them for my letters back. They said they would return them to me provided, among other things, I promised to keep not only these airmail letters but all letters written by Diana to me in a bank safe deposit box with access only upon the executors' prior written consent. They also wanted me to promise to make a will ensuring my executors should destroy all the correspondence.

Again it seemed more than a little offensive that the holders of stolen goods should seek to impose conditions not only on the stolen items but also on other letters still in my possession. Did they want to come down to Eversfield Manor and go through the safe looking for Diana's letters?

I couldn't believe they could take this position and when I contacted my solicitors they agreed, saying it was inconsistent with my rights as the owner of the letters. To make quite sure, they discussed the case with Counsel and he advised that if I were to initiate civil proceedings against the executors in a conversion[1], a court would be likely to rule that I was indeed the owner.

I was relieved to read this. I was beginning to have doubts about whether there was any justice in this matter. We robustly declined the executors' offer. They then suggested that we should leave matters for a while until media interest in the case died down and we agreed to that.

What I didn't want to die down was my quest for the truth from Anna. She had told Peter that, despite her solicitor's advice, she would be prepared to meet me. I was in the same situation. My lawyers advised that if I was seen talking to Anna it could be disadvantageous when it came to a police prosecution and might cause speculation that I was in some way influencing her evidence.

But I knew Anna was in a distressed state. I also knew

---

[1] A legal term meaning 'the appropriation of and dealing with the property of another as if it were one's own without right'.

that whatever she had done for whatever reason, she had been used and hung out to dry by the *Mirror*. Alienating her would do my cause no good. So I spoke to her on the phone at her hotel. She seemed totally shattered by what she had been through. Jean-Marc and Lucia had left the country the day she was arrested at Waterloo. She felt friendless and alone. She said she had been through hell at the hands of the *Mirror*. Whenever I asked her any questions she just dissolved in tears.

The following week I learned that the police had returned her passport to her. To me this indicated that they had no immediate plans to charge her with anything. This seemed very strange. I tried to find out to what extent the police had investigated the *Mirror*'s role in the robbery. This was stranger still. As far as I could gather nobody on the paper had been questioned by the police about it, despite the fact that Piers Morgan had conceded in the *Guardian* that his staff were conspirators in what he described as a crime to prevent the greater crime of me selling the letters. As I have already written, this was a brazen lie — solicitors on all sides knew that my selling the letters would not be a crime. And besides, as I have said repeatedly, I had no intention to do so.

Did the police — or the Palace — want Anna to go away and thus the whole matter to go away? It certainly looked that way. Anna had moved to a friend's flat in Battersea. I arranged to pick her up there and take her to an army colleague's house in Chelsea so that we could talk in private. She was in really bad shape. Her nails — which were usually long and well-manicured — had been bitten to the quick and she had let herself go quite a bit. She told me she felt she had been the captive of the *Mirror* as they moved her around the south of England.

Sometimes it was three journalists — Nic North, Tanith Carey and another woman — and sometimes it was two men and two women 'looking after her'. She said she bitterly hated her minders

I asked her if she knew that Jean-Marc had arranged to have us photographed in Monte Carlo. She shook her head, saying she knew nothing about it. Then she said that Jean-Marc had poisoned her against me. He had persuaded her that I was not a nice person. He had told her that while I was in Monte Carlo I had talked to him about other women I was seeing and that I was relentless in questioning him about her finances. I told her neither of these things was true: I had hardly had any individual conversations at all with Jean-Marc when I was there.

The rest of her story was very much the one she told to Caroline and Peter. Anna said she had broken down in tears when she heard the tape of my 'sexy talk' with another woman. At that point Piers Morgan had said to her: 'We'll get him.' They then suggested to her the plan to take the letters. Anna said the 'Tina' in Peter's statement was Tanith Carey, North's collaborator.

She went along with them and only smelt a rat when she got in Nic North's car which was waiting for her after the burglary and found she was being driven not to the photocopier in the local village but to London. At Canary Wharf North ran into the *Mirror* building with his bounty, leaving her, Jean-Marc and Lucia in the car. Later they came to get her and, inside the *Mirror* offices, a female interpreter read the content of some of the letters to her in French. They offered her £1,000 in expenses which she accepted. She wished she hadn't.

I was candid with her. I said that the only way we could get any form of redress against the *Mirror* was for a prosecution involving her to come to court. There was a danger she could go to prison. Anna said her solicitor had warned her of this but he thought any sentence would be no more than 80 days. I don't know how that length of time was arrived at but she promised she was prepared to serve it if it meant that Piers Morgan and the *Mirror* were also brought to justice.

I asked her how they had compiled her 'world exclusive' stories on the Monday and Tuesday about us. Anna said the journalists kept trying to turn her more against me. She reported them as saying: 'If he loved you, why did he send the police to arrest you at Waterloo? He hates you. He's attacking you. He's got these lawyers against you. He wants you to go to jail.' Despite this sort of pressure, she had not given an interview to the reporters. Most of the material in the articles, she said, came from Jean-Marc and Lucia, with whom she was now at odds. Some of it was gleaned in conversation with her but completely warped.

She was worried about her family. Her father was ill in Italy. Mimmo was greatly upset about the publicity. As the main trustee of Alberto Ferretti's estate, he was trying to prevent her from getting any more money from her trust fund. However, she desperately needed more money to pay her legal fees. She broke down in tears. It seemed unfair to press her on the other questions I needed answers to.

I had called a taxi and it had been waiting outside. I offered to accompany her back to Battersea but she said she was all right on her own.

As she left she said: 'Please forgive me, forgive me, forgive me, I love you, forgive me.'

I said: 'I forgive you.'

I didn't see her again in London. We talked from time to time on the telephone when she was back in Monte Carlo. She told me everybody there seemed to have read about the robbery and she found herself cold-shouldered in some restaurants and hotels. She asked me if one day I would come down and be seen with her. I said that I would but first I had to try and get some justice in Britain. She assured me again she would help me with that.

It was near impossible to get any information out of the police about what they were doing to investigate the crime. On June 25th my solicitors wrote to the Crown Prosecution Service who are responsible for deciding whether a prosecution should take place. The CPS reply contained the following paragraph:

*On 18th May the Metropolitan Police submitted a file relating to the allegations of theft, burglary and copyright infringement against Ms*

> *Ferretti. The totality of the evidence which had been*
> *obtained by the police was carefully reviewed. It was*
> *concluded that there was insufficient evidence*
> *disclosed on the file to provide a realistic prospect of*
> *a conviction of Ms Ferretti. I'm sure you will*
> *understand that matters which are printed in*
> *newspapers do not constitute evidence which can be*
> *used in criminal proceedings.*

Nicola Namdjou vigorously contested this. What had been printed in the *Mirror* was an admission by Anna that she had robbed a house and an admission by the *Mirror* that they had helped her. Nicola wrote to Detective Inspector Taber with a copy to the CPS: 'Such admissions are clearly capable of being used as evidence in a criminal prosecution since, contrary to the position stated in the CPS letter to my client, admissions are an exception to the rule against hearsay.'

We intended to continue to fight the CPS decision but, for the time being, since they stated they did not intend to bring a prosecution, this liberated the letters from being in police custody. We contacted Lawrence Graham and asked for them back. They continued to insist on unacceptable conditions. My solicitors indicated we might be open to some agreement but suggested that the greater danger lay with the *Mirror* who had copies of the letters. Any conditions must include a promise from the *Mirror* — enforceable by injunction — that they would never publish the contents of the letters.

Lawrence Graham wrote back saying that the issue was 'dead'. The executors didn't want to be involved in a 'James Hewitt v the *Mirror* High Court battle'. They did not want the *Mirror* to publish the letters but they didn't believe they would do so. (Such faith must have taken a severe knock on January 1999 when the *Mirror* in successive days published letters written by Princess Diana, Prince Charles, Princess Margaret and the Queen. The reporter was Nic North.)

But in July 1998 the advice to me from the executors

was that they considered 'all parties would do best to let sleeping dogs lie.' By coincidence this was exactly the attitude of the police. Detective Inspector Taber wrote to my lawyers that since the executors had not expressed any intent in pursuing a prosecution for breach of copyright, he did not believe it would be right to engage in any investigation without their co-operation.

What about the small matter of the theft? Taber felt that for such an investigation to proceed it would require the co-operation of Ms Ferretti. She was now not in the United Kingdom and there was no indication, he said, of when she was likely, if at all, to return. This must have been obvious to him from the very outset so why, we wondered, did the police return her passport to her?

Taber also told my solicitors that he had spoken to 'those representing her' and had asked if Anna was prepared to give a witness statement regarding these matters. He had been informed that she was not.

As far as I knew Anna had no one representing her. She told me she had not been happy with her solicitors and had paid them off before she left the country. And what about the witness statement she had given the police when she was in their custody?

Clearly the police needed to hear her story again. Taber wrote: 'It is difficult to understand how a successful investigation could be undertaken without her co-operation.'

A good place to begin might be with the people from the *Mirror* who drove her to and from the robbery, covered the operation from extremely close quarters and then received the stolen goods. But the police did not disclose to me or my lawyers whether at any stage they had interviewed anyone from the *Mirror*.

Taber, in a later letter to my lawyers, gave as his main reason for not pursuing the *Mirror* the fact that the executors of the estate had no wish to be associated with an investigation and prosecution. The theft, as I've said before, had nothing to do with the copyright owners. They were not the victim. I was.

And I remained the victim. The case of the robbery that everybody had read about but that had, apparently, never happened was closed.

And what about the letters that had been in police custody? We requested their return from Taber. 'As these were never taken into police possession, this is a matter which I suggest be taken up with Kensington Palace,' he wrote back.

I was not alone in thinking that I had not been well served by the police. The *Guardian* wrote: 'By its own admission the *Mirror* was guilty of inciting and abetting a theft, handling stolen goods and profiting from the crime. The Princess's trustees were also guilty of receiving stolen property which they have steadfastly refused to return. And yet, bizarrely, neither the editor of the *Mirror* nor the Princess's solicitor has been arrested and the police have made no attempt to recover Hewitt's documents. Would Jack "Zero Tolerance" Straw (the Home Secretary) care to explain why?'

I knew that the only chance I had of reopening this case was to persuade Anna to come back to England. For this reason I had tried to keep in regular telephone contact with her. But in the last few weeks all I had heard when I called her was an answering machine with an automated French voice. I had heard rumours from friends in the South of France that she had resumed her relationship with Frederick Depoux, a French jet-ski instructor with whom she had been involved before she had met me.

He was not a man we had ever discussed. I felt that just as I had had relationships before I met her, so she must have had relationships. I had taken her declaration on our first night together that she had not been with a man for three years with a pinch of salt. It had all been fun then. But now it was desperately serious and as I pondered deep into the night I realised that if she were back with Depoux, there was next to no chance that she would come over and help me.

So I tried the various numbers I had for her. The last was for a beach house she said she sometimes used. It must have been about four in the morning my time, five in France. On this occasion she actually answered.

'Where are you?' I asked.

'I can't speak now. Ring me in the morning,' she replied sleepily.

'You're with him, aren't you?' I demanded.

'No, no,' she said. 'Ring me in the morning.' And she cut off the call.

I rang back immediately and this time a man's voice answered the phone.

'Please, do not disturb us,' he said.

'Fine,' I said to him. 'I just wish somebody had told me.'

I drove down to Devon later in the morning feeling very low. I called Anna again, and again a man — presumably Frederick Depoux — answered. I apologised for waking him so early but explained that I needed Anna's help.

'You have caused a lot of problems.' he replied. 'You have taken my wife. You stole my wife from me.'

'I've what? Your wife?' I was incredulous. I couldn't believe it. My whole system almost seized up. 'I didn't know you were married.'

'I didn't mean wife,' he hastily corrected himself. 'I mean my girlfriend.'

'Whoever she is,' I told him, 'I need her help.'

'You ruined her life,' he said.

'What about mine?' I countered. 'I just want to speak to Anna.'

'This is my house,' he said. 'You must not ring my phone again.'

'Very well,' I said. 'Would you just tell Anna that I would like to hear from her?'

But it was to be a very long time before I did.

# 18

Life at Eversfield Manor was pretty much stalled that summer. Any plans for the future were put on hold while I worked at the task of getting my letters back and tried to get to the bottom of what really happened and how I could persuade the police to investigate the case thoroughly.

Some previous clients came back to ride but I did nothing to encourage new business. I was wary of people, fearful that if they weren't actually journalists themselves they were perhaps looking to get a story out of me that they could sell.

One Saturday evening in June I had seen a car above the back drive with some people milling about. I assumed they were just more press and decided to do nothing provided they kept their distance.

But on Sunday morning the same car came up the main drive and a man and a woman got out. I knew them.

They were Colonel and Mrs Bury who lived across the valley. I asked them to come in and Mrs Bury explained they had heard I was selling up.

I said: 'No, absolutely not.'

They said they had read in the papers that I was going to live in Spain and they were looking for a place locally on behalf of their son, Mark. I told them it wasn't so — they shouldn't believe anything in the papers about me. They laughed. I made them a cup of coffee and suggested that since they were here they might as well take a look at the house, which they did.

Towards the end of the summer I realised that I was spending so much of my time in London, occupied with the letters, that running 40 acres in Devon was no longer economic. I also needed to release some capital to pay for future litigation. And I just wasn't really enjoying life there any more — the place was too big for me on my own.

So I contacted the Burys and asked if Mark was still interested. It transpired that he was and we very quickly came to terms for the sale of the house.

It's never easy to leave a home. I loved Eversfield — there had been some very good times there when it was full of friends and warm memories of when I was just on my own, fishing in the evenings or walking the dogs. Parting with the animals was the saddest task. I sold my hunter, Arthur, with the house and Mark Bury promised I could come back and ride him. There was some consolation in that. I knew various dealers in the neighbourhood and over a period of weeks I sold all the other horses through them. I gave the sheep to my sister, Caroline, for her farm. Aida, my black labrador, who had given birth to a fine litter earlier in the summer, went off to work on an estate in the north of Wales. I couldn't bare to part with my lurcher, Tess. She was always by my side when I was at home, getting up and moving from room to room when I did, never letting me out of her sight. She went to stay with my sister, Syra, in her farmhouse but one day I hope to have a home where she can be with me again.

In the last week of September the removal vans came to take my furniture and belongings away, much of it to storage as I was moving to a small flat in South Kensington. I could see a press photographer lingering at the end of the top drive. Since the number of the local removal firm was on the side of the lorries, I went across to the boss, a local man whom I knew, and warned him that someone from the press might ring up and pretend to be associated with me and ask for the address I was moving to. He said: 'Actually your mother took rather a strange call just now.'

Alarm bells immediately began to go off in my mind. What had happened was this. The telephone had rung in the kitchen. The place was noisy with men packing things up and my mother, who is slightly hard of hearing, could only make out a female voice asking to speak to the removal people. My mother handed the phone to the boss. The woman on the line said she was Mrs Smith — which is the surname of my sister, Syra — and started asking him strange questions like 'where are you taking the stuff?' But as she didn't make a great deal of sense, he handed the phone back to my mother who assumed, in the confusion of the kitchen, that it was someone from the removal office. The woman asked her when and to where the stuff was being moved and my mother in all innocence gave her the destination and told her when I was moving in.

All this was information I had been trying to keep secret. When my mother realised what had happened, she was terribly upset about it and felt she had let me down. I was burning with anger, not at my mother, but that a journalist could stoop so low to cheat information out of *her*.

Already the *Mirror* had published details of my car and its number plate on the front of their newspaper, so it was time to change that, too. I sold the Range Rover and bought a four-year-old Jaguar, a good town car. It was well-alarmed and had a secure boot which I reckoned would be the safest place for my papers and personal belongings. I also had to move some cash from my safe in Devon to a friend's safe in London and I hid that in the boot of the car.

On Thursday, October 1st 1998 I drove from Devon to London. It was already dark when I parked the Jaguar outside my South Kensington flat. I wouldn't be able to occupy my new home until the following week but I was going to Majorca for the weekend to attend a friend's wedding. I had a business meeting in a local pub which must have lasted over an hour and then drove to the east side of the City to pick up a friend who was working late and had kindly offered to give me a bed for the night. We drove back to her house in Wandsworth in South West London.

I parked the car, then went round to the boot, unlocked it and opened it. It was empty. Nothing there. It had been completely cleaned out. My briefcase with my passport and air tickets had gone. The money had gone. So had some traveller's cheques for Majorca and other cheques I was going to pay into the bank in the morning. Worse than any of that many of my most treasured belongings had gone, too. There was a stud box with my grandfather's cufflinks which meant a lot to me, the sapphire and diamond ring my mother had given to me and which Anna Ferretti had returned, other studs and cufflinks including a pair given to me by Diana with an owl on them and the little cross on which Diana had had engraved 'I will love you forever.'

I was devastated. I immediately dialled 999. The police arrived very quickly, within minutes. I told them what had happened and agreed they could take the car away to have it forensically vetted. I then went with them to the local police station to give a statement. I was beginning to get used to giving statements to the police. It wasn't easy to be certain of every item that had been in the boot, especially which documents were in my briefcase.

The next morning a uniformed policewoman came round to see me at Rupert's house in Chelsea and took a further statement. She said the station had been inundated with calls from the press about the break-in and the best thing to do would be to issue a short press statement. I contacted my solicitor and we gave out the barest details.

I wondered how the papers had got wind of the robbery. Doubtless some people listen in to the police radio for just this sort of information. Maybe there are leaks when the information goes out to other stations detailing the stolen goods. Maybe there was a mole in a police station. It was impossible to tell.

The front page of the *Daily Mail* the next day had an inappropriately cheerful picture of me and the headline: HEWITT 'ROBBED OF DIANA PAPERS'. Both the *Mail* and the *Mirror* wrote that a manuscript containing details of my relationship with Princess Diana had been stolen from my car — although I had made no mention of this in my press statement. The assertion (which was not true) was attributed to an anonymous detective. The *Mirror* said I had lost £60,000 in cash and the *Mail* £50,000. It was, in fact, a great deal less than that — although still enough to hurt pretty badly.

I picked up the car at Putney Police Station on the Saturday. I was told they had found no fingerprints on it so the chances of tracking down the culprit seemed next to nil. A *Sun* reporter and photographer were waiting for me at the station and some other paparazzi followed me as I drove to Petty France to get a replacement passport. Perhaps I should have asked them to take a photograph for me — the one taken in the booth by the Passport Office, which still remains in my passport, shows an understandably drawn and drained face. But I was determined to go to the wedding in Majorca anyway. There seems to me little point in curling up in a ball and wallowing in self-pity when adversity strikes.

About a month later a friend telephoned me and said he had read in a paper that a man had been arrested and charged with breaking into my car. I rang Detective Inspector Whitehouse, with whom I had been dealing on the case, and asked him if this was true. He confirmed that it was. It did seem a bit strange for me to have to learn about these things from the papers. Whitehouse said that the man was a sometime thief and they had tracked him from a thumb print on the car's boot. None of my belongings had been found in his place.

There was no point in saying I had been told at Putney Police Station that there were no prints but mine on the car. Maybe that was deliberate disinformation. Some weeks later a journalist rang me and asked for my reaction to the fact that the man was not going to trial. I said I had none. The police rang with the same news later the same day. The Crown Prosecution Service had found that there was insufficient evidence to proceed. That had a familiar refrain to it.

I never for a moment believed that my boot had been robbed by an off-the-road chance man. I'm certain it was a deliberate crime done to order by professionals. No attempt was made to break into the car itself. I had been more than a little remiss in leaving the car for that hour outside my flat and I had paid a high price for it. Was it connected with the phone call to the kitchen in Devon? Possibly. Was I followed to London? Possibly. Could someone have seen me transfer cash to the car? I actually don't think so.

Who would want to get their hands on my papers? Well, they contained 'intelligence' — valuable information in the correspondence between my lawyers and myself with regard to the robbery of my safe and how we intended to proceed and also with regard to the return of my letters and how we intended to proceed on that. I am not making any allegations against anyone. Sometimes security agents, seeing the opportunity in a situation, act independently in order to steal something they can sell. Equally, if certain people thought that I had diaries or a manuscript in there with details of Princess Diana or the Palace or both, they might want to find out what they contained.

I truly don't know who was behind it and I doubt if I will until some private document unexpectedly turns up in someone else's possession. What I do know is that criminals do not silence an alarm system and unlock the boot of a car unless they are extremely well prepared and have a targeted motivation.

As the year drew on, the attempt to get my letters back seemed to have reached stalemate with neither side agreeing to the other's conditions. In the army, when you have explored all avenues and negotiations have reached an impasse, that is the time for action. In this case that meant going to court. I knew the fees would be enormous. Stephens Innocent helped me investigate the feasibility of my receiving legal aid but this proved not to be possible and the firm was unable to work for me on a 'no-win, no-fee' basis.

This was a serious set-back. But 1998 had been such a rotten year that I was damned if I was going to let it end without a fight. I knew the man who could help me. Michael Coleman was senior partner of a firm of solicitors called Harkavys and he had been most impressive in getting a large sum of damages from a tabloid paper for Sarah Millford Haven when it had incorrectly accused her of having an affair with me. I had always remained in contact with him, not least because the parents of his girlfriend, Emma, lived near me in Devon.

I called Michael and outlined my predicament. In fact, he had kept abreast of things and was already well-informed about most of what had been happening. He was due to come down to Devon that weekend and suggested we have lunch. Michael is a straight-talking man who cuts to the heart of the matter. He listened sympathetically to my situation and said that he saw no problem, he could get the letters back. More than that, he was passionate about righting the wrong that had been done to me.

I said I couldn't embark on another round of expensive legal fees. He said that he would not charge me anything. He would issue a writ and would act on a 'no-win, no-fee' basis.

It seemed too good to be true. And it was. Michael warned me that if we lost, although I wouldn't have to pay him I would probably be liable for the other side's fees which could run into hundreds of thousands of pounds. Was I prepared to risk that?

'Yes,' I replied without hesitation. 'I'll risk everything to see justice is done.'

'Don't worry,' he assured me. 'We won't lose.'

On December 7th Michael wrote to Lawrence Graham giving them due warning that if they didn't return the letters within 24 hours Harkavys were instructed to issue proceedings against them.

It hardly came as a surprise that this did not bring about the immediate return of the letters. So at 10.00 a.m. the next morning Felicity Rowan, a Harkavys solicitor, went along to the High Courts of Justice in the Strand to obtain a writ. Normally an outdoor clerk would perform this task but Michael wanted a more senior figure to make sure that things went smoothly and there were no press leaks.

When the girl clerk at the courts read the details of the application and saw that the writ was for the return of 64 letters written by Diana, Princess of Wales she was completely taken aback.

'I'm not sure if I should issue this,' she said to Felicity. 'It's going to cause a lot of trouble.'

Felicity informed her that she had no choice. The girl nevertheless went to get the chief clerk of the law courts. He confirmed that they had no option but to issue the writ. Felicity then took it across the Strand to the offices of Lawrence Graham which were directly opposite the Law Courts. Michael had wanted the writ to be served immediately so that Lawrence Graham would not learn about it from the press. But word travelled faster than Felicity and a newspaper telephoned Michael Coleman asking him if it was true I had issued a writ before she had even crossed the road.

Lawrence Graham's response was one of surprise that I was suing them. They pointed out they were only acting for the Estate of Diana, Princess of Wales and as such were not appropriate defendants.

Michael had anticipated this. He wrote back: 'You take the view that you should not be a defendant because you are holding property on the instructions of some other person. It might be useful to apply that reasoning to different facts such as a fence in possession of stolen jewellery being held on behalf of an unidentified burglar. Is it truly your suggestion that in those circumstances the owner of the jewellery couldn't sue the fence who holds the jewellery but will have to instead sue his principal, the burglar?'

He pointed out that it was they who were in possession of my property and were refusing to return it. If they were making no proprietary claims to the property, then he failed to see any possible defence they could put forward. If they were aware of conflicting proprietary claims to title to the property, then their well-established remedy in law was to interplead.

He pointed out to them: 'Your clients, using you as a vehicle of communication, have been making unwarranted demands of our client with menaces, the menace being that unless he capitulates to your clients' demands, his property will not be returned to him.'

The decision whether a defendant is going to contest a writ has to be taken within fourteen days but since that was running close to the Christmas holiday period Lawrence Graham asked for more time to prepare their defence which Harkavys agreed to.

It wasn't the most festive season for me with the prospect of a litigation that could be ruinously expensive. But there was no turning back. I went down to Devon to spend a quiet Christmas with my family.

It was something of a relief on my return to learn that the executors did not seem keen on a court case. They were prepared to relax some of the conditions they had imposed the previous year but they still wanted my assurance that the letters would be destroyed on my death.

In most other respects they did no more than ask that I abide by the law with regard to the letters. In exchange for their return I would give the executors a letter saying that I would not infringe their legal and equitable rights with regards to copyright, that I did not intend to publish the letters and that I agreed I would keep the letters in a safe place.

Should I agree to have the letters destroyed on my death? It would avoid a court case. And what if the jury were all influenced by media stories about me and returned a verdict that was not in my favour? It would clean me out, no doubt about that.

But this was one of these occasions where a matter of principle was at stake. It seemed to me completely unjust that the executors felt they could tell me what to do with my property just because they had it in their possession. And their absolute refusal to do anything to prevent the *Mirror* publishing the letters made me even more outraged.

So I told them I couldn't agree to the posthumous burning of the letters and the court would have to decide who was the rightful owner.

Days passed. I didn't sleep well. Had I made an enormous mistake? My solicitors phoned me. I expected it to be with news of the date set down for the court case to be heard, but it was with better news than that. It was with excellent news. The executors did not wish to go to court. They had dropped the demand that the letters should be posthumously destroyed. The letters would be returned to me on the other terms we had agreed.

A time for the handover was set at 12 noon on Wednesday, February 3rd 1999. Michael Coleman's girlfriend, Emma, drove him, Felicity Rowan and me from Harkavys offices in Harley Street to the Strand. The traffic was light and we arrived at Lawrence Graham's offices twenty minutes early. We were asked to wait in reception. Michael thumbed his way through some documents, Felicity made notes and I just sat, glancing at my watch, thinking. It had been almost exactly ten months since the letters were stolen. If the robbery had never happened I would have continued with my life at Eversfield, maybe with Anna, maybe not. I had intended to lead as low-key an existence as I could. But at that moment I hardened my resolve to write this book so people could learn what I had been through and decide for themselves on the fairness of my treatment at the hands of the press, the police and the Palace.

Just before noon Wendy Batchelor, the Lawrence Graham solicitor who had been at the Kensington Palace identification, came into reception and ushered us up to a conference room. We sat down at a large table. She had the letters with her in a thick lawyer's folder with a ribbon round it.

Michael handed her the release documents that confirmed we were no longer proceeding with the writ and my letter containing the agreed conditions. Miss Batchelor gave him a cheque for his costs[2] and handed over the envelope with the letters. Michael carefully opened it and described what he was doing. Felicity took copious notes. Inside the envelope was a police plastic evidence bag with not only the 'blueys' inside but another four empty police evidence bags. The date on which they had been used, who had opened them and who had sealed them was recorded on each.

Michael counted the letters and handed them to me. I noticed there was a yellow sticker among them which had not previously been there. Michael asked Miss Batchelor whose writing was on it. She said that it was that of a senior police officer who had examined a letter in relation to *Mirror* copyright. It seemed the assurance Sharpe had given to me at Kensington Palace that my representative would be present should the letters ever be looked at again had been overlooked.

It had been a very cold meeting — acrimony was in the air — and I was thankful when it came to an end. Miss Batchelor offered no apology nor, when we left, did anyone shake hands or express relief that the matter was over.

Michael and I went back to his house in Upper Wimpole Street. I thanked him for his success in the case and we celebrated with a cup of coffee. He suggested I might like to look at some of the letters on my own before they were taken to the safe where we agreed they would be kept until we moved them to a secure vault out of the country.

---

[2] Only Harkavys' costs — in law the only costs recoverable are those incurred after the writ has been issued.

I sat down and began to read a few of Diana's letters. No longer were they mere pawns in a legal game. They were real. They brought her to life so vividly. She wrote as she spoke, full of vitality, sometimes teasing, very self-aware of the effect she had on people at official occasions, sometimes surprised by their nervousness, unconfident herself in much of her private life, devoted to her sons, upset by her husband. She had found a new role in the Gulf War, she was absorbed by it, she did everything she could to visit the families of the troops. She said she was known at Kensington Palace as the 'War Correspondent'.

And every letter ended with some encouragement or praise to raise my morale and expressions of more love and devotion than any man has a right to deserve. She was some goddess who had passed through my life and the lives of the world. What was she really like? Here, in her own hand, was probably the only true record that future historians could rely on.

The next day the newspapers prominently reported that Princess Diana's executors had handed back my letters. A lot of papers had contacted Michael asking for an interview with me. But my past experience of print interviews was that, however open and receptive the reporter seemed, the resulting article was usually top-heavy with hostile and untrue stories from past interviews. When I took the matter up with individual reporters afterwards they would usually say their piece had been changed or abridged at the editor's behest.

It seemed the only way to get a brief message across was to go on live television so I accepted an interview from GMTV, the ITV breakfast show. The interviewer, Fiona Phillips, was more than fair and I was able to denounce the Peter Trowell story and say that although I was anxious to draw a line under things and move on, I was still looking at the possibility of a private prosecution against those who robbed me and profited by it.

After that Michael was inundated by requests from nearly every other talk programme on British radio and television for me to give further interviews. Several foreign stations offered absurd sums of money. But I declined them all. There was nothing more that I wanted to add at that stage.

Some weeks later Terrence Rowland came to see me again. He had been contacted by David Rowe, the Plymouth-based correspondent who had written the story for the *Sunday Mirror*, and been offered more money for news about any girls I was seeing at present. Some way into their conversation Terrence asked him how it was that the *Mirror* had persuaded Anna Ferretti to rob the house. Rowe told him that the newspaper had found out I was seeing her and representatives had gone down to visit her in Monte Carlo. They brought with them photographs of me with other women and the tape-recording of me and their Valentine's Day plant. They said: 'Listen to this — this is your boyfriend.' Anna apparently 'went berserk' and fell in with a *Mirror* plan to revenge herself on me.

I asked Terrence if he was sure that this was what David Rowe had said. He assured me that it was. He then offered to contact Rowe again. The two of them agreed to meet in Exeter. This time Terrence tape-recorded the conversation. He asked David Rowe if the *Mirror* really had taken the photos and recordings to Monte Carlo. Rowe promised him this was the case.

These facts would make it appear the whole sting was set up by the paper and, as opposed to Jean-Marc randomly choosing the *Mirror* from all the newspapers in the world, the *Mirror*, in fact, chose Anna and him.

A senior Fleet Street figure outlined to a lawyer friend of mine a possible scenario for what really happened. The editor of the *Mirror*, he suspected, ran the whole operation. The paper persuaded a vengeful Anna — most probably with money — that all she had to do was temporarily to remove the letters from my safe so that they could be photocopied. It was then the editor's intention to publish them and have several weeks of scoops.

But before that could happen Piers Morgan's bosses discovered how deeply implicated his reporters were in this robbery. The *Mirror* is a Public Limited Company and its shareholders would hardly approve of its employees being involved in a criminal act. So the plan was changed. Why not get Kensington Palace on side by handing them the letters? First, it would make the *Mirror* look good in the eyes of its readers. Second, and more important, it implicated the Palace in receiving stolen goods. And, third, when the police began to investigate the case, they would find themselves in the uncomfortable position of adding Princess Diana's executors to the list of defendants. Or not — as the case turned out to be.

He thought the *Mirror* bosses realised that any gain in circulation by publishing the letters would be temporary. They were more likely to alienate their readers in the long term by printing Diana's private correspondence. But Morgan was still able to get nearly a week's worth of headlines by giving details of this laudable crime to prevent a greater (non-existent and not possible) crime, publishing pictures and extracts from the letters, and then for good measure trashing me for a couple of days, illustrated with his Monte Carlo photographs.

This appeared to me to be the most likely chain of events. It would require Anna going back on her story that she knew nothing of the photographs being taken in Monte Carlo. If she didn't know, it always seemed strange that she then willingly went with Jean-Marc to the *Mirror* to sell them — before she heard any tape-recordings of me and the Valentine girl.

So it seems there are now three possible permutations regarding the robbery.

1 — as above, the *Mirror* planned it all.

2 — Anna went to the *Mirror* with Jean-Marc's photographs and was persuaded to take the letters.

3 — Anna went to the *Mirror*, as the paper said, with two letters and asked for money to provide them with the rest.

I was completely unable to contact Anna for much of the winter. But one afternoon at the end of February I was with a friend in a pharmacy in the Fulham Road when my mobile rang. I stepped into a corner of the shop so as not to annoy the other customers.

A familiar voice said: 'Hello James. I heard that you got your letters back. I am so glad.'

It was Anna. She said she was speaking from the Canary Islands where she was spending the winter. I told her that I would love to talk to her as there was a lot I wanted to know. I was a little wary of her — until we actually met and I could confront her face-to-face, I had no way of evaluating whether or not she was in the pay of some newspaper and looking for a story.

I told her I needed to see her. She said that she would be back in France for the summer, maybe we could meet then. I wondered if we would or if I would ever see this elusive butterfly that had brought such chaos into my life again.

On April 29th — the day before our birthdays — my twin sister Caroline gave birth to a baby boy. I used it as a pretext to call Anna and tell her. She and Caroline had an understanding of each other. All I got was a French answering service but soon afterwards Caroline received a fax from Anna saying how happy she was to hear about the baby.

I took it as a cue to contact Anna once more. This time she did return my call and agreed that we should meet the next time she was in Paris.

Thus on Wednesday, May 26th 1999 I took the 8.23 a.m. Eurostar to Paris. Annoyingly I had forgotten my mobile phone so I was unable to confirm our rendezvous at the Hotel Crillon. But when I got off the train at the Gare du Nord Anna was there waiting. She wore her habitual dark glasses and looked suntanned and healthy and happy.

We took a taxi to the Café de Theatre where she suggested we have lunch. But it was a sunny day and the place had no tables outside. So we walked a few hundred yards down the Champs Elysées and found a restaurant that had tables on the pavement.

She told me she was in Paris because she was now working for a construction company and was having a meeting that night. She said that she hadn't spoken to her sister, Lucia, or Jean-Marc since they left her at Waterloo.

She had been having troubles with her house at Beaulieu-sur-Mer.

I got the feeling that she was now living with Frederic. I asked her how their relationship was. She maintained he was just a good friend.

I said I needed her help. She asked what she could do. I told her I needed the statement she had made to the police after she had been arrested. She said she didn't have a copy. She would have to come to London and get it off the solicitors she had used.

She asked me what was so important about the statement. I explained that if we were going to proceed against the *Mirror* we needed to know exactly what their role was in the robbery.

As we left the restaurant she asked me if I would like to stay with her in Paris that night. I said I didn't think that would be a very good idea.

I turned to her.

'Anna, there's one thing I absolutely need to know. Did Jean-Marc go to the *Mirror* or did the *Mirror* come to Jean-Marc?'

'Their reporters came to Monte Carlo,' she said. 'They brought with them the pictures of you with other women and the recording. That's where it began.'

'When we were photographed in the sea, did they organise that?' I asked.

'Yes,' she shrugged. 'It is all in my police statement.'

I had heard enough for the time being. I walked her to the friend's apartment where she was staying and gave her a farewell kiss on the cheek. I said I wanted to catch an earlier train home. I hoped she would soon come to London for her statement.

As the train drew out of the Gare du Nord I analysed the implications of what Anna had said. If the police believed her statement — and it was corroborated by David Rowe's admission to Terrence Rowland — then they must have known that Piers Morgan and the *Mirror* masterminded the whole thing from start to finish. But, as far as I was aware, the police had not even interviewed anybody on the paper about the crime.

I took stock of my relationship with Anna. I had been swept away by her when she first came into my life. She was a tonic — full of passion and affection and fun. She was exotic but she fitted very naturally into my life during that Christmas and those winter weeks in Devon. She had been a wife and she was a mother and she certainly knew, as she said, how to look after her man. My friends and family took to her instantly and liked her a lot.

When she had suggested marriage it had come as a surprise but I felt at the time I was just being tested as to the strength of my affections. No date was fixed, no cermony planned. But I certainly didn't want to say anything negative that would disrupt a relationship that was working well and brightening both our lives.

But had she already been turned against me by the *Mirror*'s photographs and tape-recording by the time she made that call? It was not a question that I had been able to bring myself to ask her, perhaps because I knew the answer would have been too painful.

I can only presume that she had. And I can only presume that from that moment on all her behaviour was motivated by a desire to take revenge on me or make money out of me or both. Yet we continued to be lovers as before. Either Anna was an exceptional actress or maybe jealousy and passion were mixed up in her in such a way that she found the very situation itself a form of dangerous excitement.

I don't know. I don't think that I really know her, nor ever will. I do know that she hurt me deeply. She is not without guile, but she found herself being manipulated by some very unprincipled and unpleasant people and was ultimately hurt herself. I hope she finds contentment in the future.

With regard to the robbery of my house, I have written to my MP[1] asking him to find out why there has been a cover-up, my solicitor has persisted in asking the police to

---

[1]  Since the writing of this book, Alan Clark has sadly died. He was a friend and a fair man.

investigate the matter and I have sought ways of funding a private prosecution of all those who instigated and took part in this crime.

A criminal trial is clearly the last thing that the executors or the Palace want. But the duty of the police is to carry out the law of the land regardless of any pressure group, however powerful or influential. The fact that DI Taber admitted that because the executors had no wish to proceed against the *Mirror* neither would he and the fact that, when a decision was taken not to prosecute, my stolen property was returned not to me but to the executors might well give rise to the thought that the police were not always acting in the interests of the private citizen.

As far as I am concerned, this particular story has not yet come to an end.

# POSTSCRIPT

I t was not my wish to end this book with the *Mirror*'s
grubby conspiracy to steal Diana's letters. But I
wanted to try to fathom why they did it? Earl Spencer,
in his funeral oration to his sister, noted: 'It is a point to
remember that of all the ironies about Diana, perhaps the
greatest was this: a girl given the name of the ancient
goddess of hunting was, in the end, the most hunted
person of the modern age.'

In the last months of her life, Piers Morgan was
tirelessly to the fore of those hunting her down. What was
his motivation? Why persecute somebody who was doing
no wrong, committing no crime? Earl Spencer had an
answer: 'My own and only explanation is that genuine
goodness is threatening to those at the opposite end of the
moral spectrum.'

For a few short weeks after her death, the *Mirror* and
other tabloids agreed to a code of better conduct and kept

their distance — but not for long. Like a serial stalker who cannot stop himself, Morgan had to start hunting her again, this time from beyond the grave.

He and his paper now have copies of Diana's letters. But as they read them, they will, to their dismay, find little in them with which to condemn her. On the contrary, as I have said, they are a record of a woman of outstanding patriotism and endless concern for those fighting for their country and the fearful plight of their families. They will learn of a mother whose commitment to duty was as fierce as her devotion to her sons. Despite the frequent agony of her own isolated existence, she always had time for the troubles of others — visiting the handicapped, the sick and the dying in hospitals and hospices. Yet all is related with a tremendous sense of humour — it is typical of Diana to say she was thinking of putting on a leather mini-skirt after the nun who had organised her visit to those sleeping on the streets had warned her they would be lying on their mattresses.

In nearly every aspect of her behaviour, she was more royal than the Royals. Even in 1991 she saw the war had changed people's attitudes in a greater way than she believed possible and they now wanted to know what was going on. To survive, the Royal Family needed to become more open and in touch with public emotion. Little did she know that it would be her own death, six years later, that would bring about the most radical change in the behaviour of royalty that this country has ever witnessed.

And in every one of her letters — both those that were stolen and those that have never been seen by others — she gave me hope and support and undying love and devotion.

She had grown enormously in character and in confidence from the 24-year-old girl I had first met, who had unburdened her heart to me. Diana was physically ill and mentally distressed when we started to ride together. Anyone who had thought at the time that a diversion in the shape of a riding companion might alleviate her grief was more right than they could ever have anticipated. As

the months and years passed, the closed community of the
Court was aware of the change in the Princess and
probably much more besides. At any time, our relationship
could have been terminated by the Palace. No attempt was
ever made to do this.

Diana was a skilful actress. She had to be. Sometimes
when she was at a low ebb, as we rode at Windsor, she
would confess to me that she felt utterly isolated within the
Royal Family. Yet she could then visit the Mess for lunch
and hold twenty officers in the palm of her hand. It wasn't
her status that made her so commanding, it was her pure,
open, contagious charisma.

I have never met anyone with such direct and
undiluted charm. It was a gift from the gods. Whether it
was a gathering as small as a meal in my mother's kitchen
or a huge banquet, she was simply unable to prevent
herself from being the centre of attention. I would watch
her at functions on television and see the power of her
presence. She even knew when the cameras were on her —
well, I suppose they were on her all the time — and she
would tell me in advance that a touch of her nose or an
adjustment to an earring was her private signal to me.

Diana became increasingly aware of the effect she had
on people. She was slightly surprised when powerful men
would become reduced to nervous schoolboys in her
presence. The Palace did not like this increasing adulation,
as it put the Prince of Wales in her shadow. She told me
that this was the reason she was not permitted to visit the
troops in the Gulf, although the effect on morale would
have been overwhelming.

It was said that Diana manipulated people. She did,
and there was good reason for this. Nobody in royal circles
was more a victim of manipulation than she was. Once she
had given birth to the two princes and it was clear that her
husband had now wholly reverted to Camilla, Diana was
treated like a loose cannon. She endured years of turmoil
with no one in royal circles prepared to help or counsel her.
The press was told she was close to the Queen Mother. This
wasn't true — she told me she found it impossible to

communicate with her. The person she respected most was the Queen. She attempted to seek guidance from her and received a sympathetic response. However the Queen's hands were tied — it was her duty to preserve the smooth running of the royal succession.

But Diana never gave in. She fought back fiercely. I admired that in her enormously. She wasn't going to drown beneath the 'off-the-record' briefings that were given to the press about her. She knew only too well that there was an atmosphere of jealousy and mischief. She learnt how to use the press and manipulated them so that, when the day came, that she wanted to get her own way, not even the Queen would be able to prevent her.

All the time I was with her, she knew she would never be Queen herself. But she was equally determined that the Royal Family must adapt and continue to govern so that William could one day assume his rightful role as monarch. Her devotion to her sons knew no bounds. I watched her with them as we played together over the years. No mother could have been more full of love and joy and happiness. This infected their lives. They were young then and maybe they thought that all mothers were like that, but they should know that their childhoods were charmed, not because of their position, but because they had a mother who was more than a mother — she was the best friend they will ever have.

She loved her own father very dearly. I spoke to her after he'd died and her distress was deep and inconsolable. She had a more ambiguous relationship with her mother. They would argue a lot but she was always asking me if I didn't agree 'what a beautiful woman she was'.

Diana loved to tease. I remember when I first read *Winnie the Pooh* to the boys, for some reason I had grown up with the impression that the bear was merely called Winnie Pooh. So she embroidered a special cushion for me with a bear on it wearing blue trousers, a red waistcoat with yellow buttons and a blue bow-tie and underneath the words 'WINNIE POOH'. He was often referred to teasingly and lovingly in her letters.

Ours was a charged relationship. Diana needed more from me than just a lover. She needed a total support system and this I was grateful to give. When I was posted to Germany I was unable to provide it. I think she always felt I could have sacrificed myself a little bit more but I knew that, by then, she was much stronger and able to cope. But it caused a temporary cooling off in our relationship only for it to return stronger than ever before. The letters are testimony to that.

We often speculated what would have happened if we had met when she was a single girl living in South Kensington and working in a kindergarten, and when I was a subaltern living up the road in Knightsbridge. Diana visited various women who dealt in the occult and one told her that everyone has a unique 'mate' somewhere in the world who is waiting to be found — or may never be found. Diana believed that we were those mates and we would have had a life together that was solid and happy. I just don't know. I do know she would have made a superb army wife. I also know that I loved her.

But that was not to be. The newspapers put an end to our romance, just as they contributed — as Lord Spencer suggested — to the end of her life.

The strange thing about the tabloid hunt in the last months of Diana's life was that the papers misjudged the true feelings of their readers. Diana was portrayed as the playgirl of the western world, having an affair with a playboy who was, worse than that, Egyptian and the son of an allegedly shady father.

But when she died and the world stopped in its tracks, numb with grief they suddenly realised they had been playing with the life of someone whom millions looked upon as a form of living saint, someone who had brought light into their lives without them even having met her. The tabloids needed to look no further than the vast flood of flowers and their attendant messages in Kensington Gardens to learn that. It didn't take long for them to change their attitude to Diana completely. Death has a power to reveal truth that nothing in life can achieve.

It was my privilege to have known the true Diana. She changed my life. As I sit back now against her Winnie Pooh cushion, I miss her laughter.